Where Soldiers Fear to Tread

Where Soldiers Fear to Tread

by

RANULPH FIENNES

THE TRAVEL BOOK CLUB
LONDON : 1976

The Travel Book Club
125 Charing Cross Road
London, WC2H oEB

© 1975 Ranulph Fiennes
First published in Great Britain 1975

This edition by arrangement with
Hodder and Stoughton Limited

Printed and bound in Great Britain by
REDWOOD BURN LIMITED
Trowbridge & Esher

To my father Ranulph,
who died of wounds in Italy in 1943

Acknowledgments

To those Arab and British soldiers and to those Dhofari ex-communists mentioned in this book who spent many patient hours helping to provide the material, I am most grateful.

Venetia Pollock, Margaret Body, my wife and my mother were honest and therefore helpful in their many criticisms. So too were Malcolm Dennison, Mike Butler – whose Dhofar map I have followed – Peter Gordon-Smith and others.

All names mentioned in the book are real, save those of Tom Greening, Mike Muldoon, Fred Wahid and Kamees. These I have changed at their request, since they are at the time of writing, in the summer of 1974, still working in Dhofar and wish to remain anonymous. The Commanding Officer of the Muscat Regiment, Colonel Peter Thwaites, commanded and was, of course, present at all operations above company level described in the book.

The following brief selection of books and articles offers a helpful background to the region: P. S. Allfree, *Warlords of Oman*, Robert Hale, 1967; T. Altsungan, *The Land of Mahra*, 1947; Rev. G. Anier, *Kathir estrado males in Arabia*, 1956; Theodore Bent, 'Exploration of the Frankincense Country of South Arabia', *Geographical Journal*, Vol. VI, 1895; 'Muscat', *Contemporary Review*, Vol. 68, 1895; 'Oman', Department of Information, Muscat, 1972; David Holden, *Farewell to Arabia*, Faber, 1967; Harold Ingrams, *From Cana to Sabbatha*; George Martin Lees, 'The Geology and Tectonics of Oman and Parts of S.E. Arabia', *Quarterly Journal Geological Survey 84*, 1928; S. B. Miles, *The Countries and Tribes of the Persian Gulf*, 1919; Wendell Phillips, *Unknown Oman*, Longman, Green, 1966; Marco Polo, *The Book of Marco Polo, the Venetian*, Penguin 1965; Arthur W. Stiffe, 'Maskat', *Geographical Journal*, 1898; Wilfred Thesiger, *Arabian Sands*, Longman, Green, 1959; Bertram Thomas, 'The S.E. Borderlands of Rhubh al Khali', *Geographical Journal*, 1929; G. K. N. Trevaskis, *Conflict in Arabia Felix*, Corona, 1957; Barbara Wace, 'Master Plan for Muscat and Oman', *Geographical Magazine*, Vol. 41, 1969; Sir Arnold Wilson, *The Persian Gulf*, Allen & Unwin, 1928.

R.F.

Illustrations

Acknowledgments
[1] Peter Thwaite
[2] Ginnie Fiennes

1

IN the south of Arabia lies the Sultanate of Oman whose most southerly province, bordering on the Indian Ocean, is called Dhofar. Here in 1974, as for the past nine years, British officers die fighting in a bitter unsung war about which those at home know little or nothing; and yet upon the outcome of this war hangs the lifeblood of the West, enmeshed as it is with the growing energy crisis.

Over two-thirds of the oil requirements of the free world derive from the Persian Gulf countries. All of the giant tankers wallowing south from the shallow waters of the Gulf must pass through the narrow bottleneck of the Straits of Hormuz; one every ten minutes every day of the year.

These stormbound straits are twenty-five miles wide and are guarded to the east by the Iranian navy: to the west the coast is commanded by the Union of Arab Emirates and the Sultanate of Oman, and it is here that Russia is conducting a carefully planned war on two fronts. From within the Union and the Sultanate creeping subversion spreads insidiously side by side with perennial terrorist plots, and from without the attack is direct; for Oman's southern province of Dhofar, a mountain-girt wonderland no bigger than Wales, abuts onto Aden.

In June 1967, under Harold Wilson's expedient guidance, the British imperialists withdrew from Aden, and within three months the Russian and Chinese imperialists moved into the resulting power vacuum. Marxism had now achieved a firm basis in the Arabian peninsula from which to spread its wings. The land so long called Aden now became the People's Democratic

Republic of South Yemen; an official Marxist state that soon attracted revolutionaries from the far corners of Arabia, ablaze with desire to spread abroad the blessings of revolution. Dhofar was naturally their nearest target; only Dhofar and Oman blocked the way to the narrow Straits of Hormuz and the oil of the Persian Gulf.

Dhofar was ruled by the ageing Sultan of Oman whose reactionary rule and longstanding friendship with Britain were tailor-made for propaganda purposes. The people were oppressed and poverty-stricken, the army was poorly armed and consisted of under a thousand fighting men, half of whom were Baluchi mercenaries with a handful of British volunteers in command. Since the Sultan had no friends but the British, the Marxists feared no outside intervention and rightly gauged that the British, still smarting from memories of Suez, would not wish any major involvement in Dhofar. If pushed they would withdraw smartly, abandoning the Sultan rather than risk a furore in the British Parliament and press.

Readily available to help the Marxists with their initial moves was Musallim bin Nuffl, leader of the local rebels inside Dhofar, who had become fed up with the Sultan's repressive measures as far back as 1964. When foreign oil prospectors had arrived in Dhofar, bin Nuffl had been lucky enough to obtain one of the few new jobs available, as a lorry mechanic. He soon learnt of the prosperity in other oil-rich Arab lands and he noted that the Sultan used Indian and African labourers to help the American oilmen in Dhofar, not Dhofaris. No bicycles, no transistor radios; not even dark glasses might be bought by Dhofari towns-folk and none were allowed to hold any position of influence. Frustrated and enraged, bin Nuffl stirred up others of his tribe and after killing a few oil workers and destroying some lorries, he had taken his fledgling force off to Saudi Arabia and Iraq to train, calling them the Dhofar Liberation Front.

Once trained, they returned to harass the Sultan's forces in the mountains and to stir up trouble among the tribes. Bin Nuffl and his faction were not initially Marxists but non-revolutionary Muslims who wanted Dhofar for the Dhofaris, nothing more. They were simple-minded nationalists who would ultimately have to be purged from the rebel leadership once Russian and Chinese trained Dhofaris were ready to take the helm.

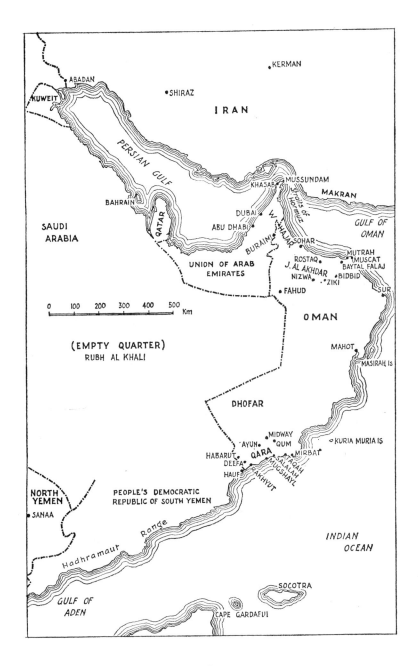

II

The Sultan had taken himself a wife from the Qara mountain folk and withdrawn into the fortified seclusion of his palace in Salalah, capital of Dhofar. Far from Omani plotters, he ruled through a few trusted Britons, mostly ex-colonial administrators from the Indian Empire. The increasing dangers of his position seemed to pass unobserved by the old Sultan in his comfortable seclusion. When nagged by his British advisers, he would point out that another regiment, his third, had been formed and, once active, it would soon put paid to troublesome rebels.

He did however admit that there was a serious shortage of officers. He relied largely on professional mercenaries from wherever he could get them; usually British, Pakistani, Indian and white African, but these were scarce. However, he had a longstanding agreement with the British Government that any British Army officer who wished to volunteer for a two-year attachment to the Sultan's army could do so and would continue to receive his pay from Her Britannic Majesty. In return for this agreement, the British used the Omani-owned island of Masirah as a vital Middle East transit base and a small airfield on the Salalah Plain as a transit camp.

This happy arrangement was in no way affected by the British Government's decision to withdraw all British forces from the Persian Gulf by 1972, since only individual volunteer officers – not whole British Army units – were involved. So, when in 1967 the Sultan made his request for more seconded officers, he got them.

At the time I was serving as a tank troop leader in the Royal Scots Greys. The regiment were engaged in the dreary Cold War task of holding NATO's front along the muddy Prussian plain of Westphalia. In practice this involved endlessly repeated withdrawals through gloomy pine forests. After five years in tanks I was keen for a change when a letter came from Oman. I had heard of the place vaguely and checked up on a map to locate its whereabouts in relation to the rest of Arabia. The letter was from a Major in my regiment who had spent the last year on a posting to the Oman Army.

His life there sounded colourful; a far cry from the mud and greasy tank engines of which I was heartily sick. His letter told of desert patrols in unexplored regions and terrorist arms caches found buried in the sand. More officers were needed he said. Why didn't I apply for a posting?

Without further thought I went to the Orderly Room and filled in the relevant application form. The Colonel signed it with an eagerness that I found slightly disconcerting and soon afterwards, in early 1968, I joined eight other officers from various regiments to learn Arabic at an Army school in Beaconsfield.

I failed the passing-out exam as convincingly as the other eight passed it, but no one seemed to mind and in June 1968 we flew to Oman via Rome and Bahrein in an RAF VC10.

White ensigns drooped in the clammy heat of Bahrein's Jufair harbour where a gaggle of Her Majesty's minesweepers relaxed between routine strolls around the Indian Ocean. The sea was scummed and lacklustre, drying fish smells clung to one's clothes, and the Arab taxi drivers muttered if cheated of the extra rupees they tried to claim.

Oman, we assured each other, would not be like this. Some of the others seemed very self-confident, treating the Arabs with raj-like disdain, and I wondered how Omani soldiers would react to their attitude. I felt unsure of myself, oppressed by the wet heat, and, in the back of my mind, worried that I would prove inadequate with the Arabs.

My tongue seemed to swell and make all the wrong sounds as soon as I tried to speak Arabic. The thought of giving articulate orders to soldiers made me shiver despite the heat. But my main worry was a total lack of knowledge of my prospective job. The majority of the other officers were from infantry units or the Royal Marines and knew how to command troops on the ground. In Oman there would be no tanks and my five years' military experience would not therefore be much help.

A BOAC strike kept us waiting in Bahrein for eight days and on the third day an event occurred that increased my uneasiness. One of the others, visiting a friend in the military hospital, watched an ambulance arrive from the airfield. It disgorged a stretcher case with a blood drip attachment; an officer from Dhofar it transpired, whose upper chest and shoulder had been ripped apart by a bullet. His evacuation from the mountains, they said, had been by mule, taking ten hours for the Sultan had no helicopters; the medical orderly had had sufficient morphine for three hours. The unfortunate fellow's name, my informant told

13

me, was Richard John – the major whose tales of adventure had enticed me to the Middle East and the only man I knew in the Sultan's Army.

We left Bahrein in an antiquated Fokker plane. Flying high, where the air was cool, its fan worked well, shooting an icy gust into my ear. But whenever the plane stopped en route – which it did at every opportunity – the cooling system gave up the ghost just at that moment when the plane began to sizzle in the baking heat of the concrete strip.

At Sharjah, a mercenary with a pencil moustache and sharp blue eyes sat next to me. He smoked an evil smelling cheroot that made my stomach stir. I checked the position of the Gulf Airlines brown paper bag. He shook my hand. "I'm David Bayley; it's good to be back in Arabia." He seemed a friendly type and told me that he'd spent three years with the Royalist guerrillas in the Yemen. He spoke a fluent but strange brand of Arabic to the Lebanese air hostess who came and sat next to him – but across the aisle so that she must needs lean over revealingly to speak above the vibrating of the plane. Being magnificently built and clad in the scantiest of orange miniskirts, as inadequate above as below, she managed to distract David from his cigar and the rest of us from our queasiness as we bumped through the thermals high above the gaunt Mussundam mountains.

Below us the azure rim of the Gulf of Oman fringed the baking land mass, so clear – as we began to descend – that the outlines of great fish were plainly visible beyond the shadow of the cliffs. Long-tailed whip rays, wedge-shaped sharks and schools of leaping dolphins.

"This must be it." David fastened his belt with the aid of the hostess. We entered a rock-bound valley so narrow that each wing tip seemed to scrape the crumbling cliffs and thudded down suddenly on a narrow concrete strip.

Bayt al Falaj – Oman's main airport and the nerve centre of the Sultan's Forces. It was mid-afternoon and hotter than I would have believed possible. The tarmac lines between the concrete blocks of the runway bubbled and hissed; the glare made it impossible to open both eyes. Stunned by this entirely new physical experience I shuffled lead-like to the bustle of the customs shed and thought of home, the rich green and red of Sussex fields, stretching south to the Downs.

A corpulent British major stood in the shade wearing khaki drill with medal tabs and little round glasses over little round eyes. I wondered how a man of over seventeen stone — a conservative guess — could stand such heat. He ignored us all as though we were rabble, staring right through us with a splendidly regal air.

David nudged me and muttered, rather too loudly I thought, "Evidently the pillars of the Indian Raj never crumbled: they were just transplanted elsewhere like Abu Simbel."

Somehow our baggage made it past the chaotic administration of the white-robed customs men and their pieces of chalk. A khaki Land Rover threw dust over us that mixed with the sweat. From it another face from the Imperial past hailed our forlorn huddle.

"You must be the new chaps. Sling your kit in the back and jump in. Bit of a squash but the Mess is just down the road. It's beginning to get hot here but not too bad yet. Just wait till July."

Thus comforted we were driven off to the nearby camp, the headquarters of the Sultan's Army.

A brace of Baluchi sentries, ramrod stiff and black as their beards, slapped ·303 bolt-action rifles as we passed a swing-bar gate into the camp. Our driver ignored them.

"Splendid place this, but a little antique for an operational H.Q." He waved at a whitewashed fort flying the red flag of the Sultan from one of four crenellated keeps: "All the operations of the Sultan's three regiments in northern Oman and down in Dhofar are master-minded from here. At present we've got the Northern Frontier Regiment in Dhofar whilst the Muscat and Desert Regiments are scattered around Oman." We stopped beside a dozen other Land Rovers in front of a low building. Two ancient howitzers, well polished, stared at us.

"You'll be kitted up with your Army gear this evening and allotted to your respective regiments as soon as possible. Well, here's the Mess. Ask the steward where your rooms are, then have a drink. Any problems, just give a shout for me."

Without telling us his name, he departed.

The first day passed as a bad dream very reminiscent of my first six months with the Royal Scots Greys . . . new officers should be seen but not heard. Also they should do the correct things in the right manner but never bother less recently arrived officers by asking them exactly what *is* correct.

My temporary bedroom was air-conditioned. It was like moving from a furnace straight into a fridge. The rattle of the conditioner was low and steady; I lay back on the bed and was soon asleep.

A barefoot Arab boy came in with hot sweet tea. It was evening; still breathless and sticky but the painful glare had eased. I reported at the correct time to the fort, up echoing stone stairs to an inner gallery off which were the offices of the higher ranking officers.

The Commander-in-Chief of the Sultan's Armed Forces was a Brigadier from the British Army. Every three years a new one took over, lent by Whitehall. This one was kindly. I felt immediately at ease. A small fit-looking man. Well-ironed sleeves rolled up on bulging biceps. After greeting me he briefed me quickly and clearly.

I was to join one of the Sultan's three regiments – the Muscat Regiment. To begin with at a garrison in northern Oman called Bidbid: later in the southern province of Dhofar.

"Have you had any experience of action?"

"No." I felt apologetic. "None."

"Nor have most people when they arrive here. Oman is quiet at present but that doesn't mean one can relax. Remember that. In Dhofar things are not so quiet as you will see." He indicated a vast wall map. "We are now here in the north near Muscat. In the centre of Oman is a great gravel desert which separates us from the southern province of Dhofar. After a spell of garrison duty here in the north when you can get to know your men, you will be sent to Dhofar where your job will be to help stop the further infiltration of communist-led rebels. It's tough country and the Dhofaris are born mountain fighters who know every inch of their land so you'll have to teach your men mountain guerrilla warfare tactics before you go. We hold the coastal strip down in Dhofar and we have, at the moment, free run of the great desert sands to the north but the mountains and valleys in between are no-man's land.

"Your men will consist of Omanis and Baluchis. Sultans of Oman and Muscat were titular owners of Baluchistan for many years until the present Sultan sold the port of Gwadar to Pakistan for one million pounds. Baluchi emigrants have settled here over the years and for want of any work at home many still come to join the Army as mercenaries. They are Muslims like the Omanis but they speak a dialect of Urdu, not Arabic. They care little who the enemy is or who officers them for they are simply professional soldiers saving as much money as possible to take home to their families.

"Many of our Omani soldiers are from settled oases: they are all volunteers but few are natural fighters. However they too have joined the Army because they can make better money than in the rare alternative jobs open to them. Very few have any education other than reading from the village Koran. They do not take easily to the rough warfare of Dhofar. You have to treat them, and the Baluchis, with care. Use a firm fair hand always. That way you'll get the best from them."

He then explained that each of the three regiments spent a nine months' period fighting in Dhofar, then eighteen more peaceful months in the north. This was worked on a rotary system. There were seven main garrisons all over northern Oman manned by whichever two regiments were not in Dhofar. It was known that troublemakers had long been infiltrating into the north but as yet there was open rebellion only in Dhofar.

In the Muscat Regiment, the Brigadier said, I was to command the Reconnaissance Platoon. This I would be pleased to hear was no longer camel-borne but used Land Rovers. Since I was a tank officer I would presumably feel more at home with vehicles even if tank tactics proved difficult to apply in my new command.

My Colonel, he explained, would also be a seconded British Army officer—as were the other two regiments' Colonels. This arrangement was important since, by having new commanding officers arriving every so often, the latest and the best in military tactics were continually being updated within the Sultan's Army. In theory anyway. To advise the Colonels on problems specific to Oman and Dhofar each regiment had a Second-in-Command with many years of local experience.

The rest of the officers were a mixed bunch: half were 'contract' officers. I must never refer to them as mercenaries for that was not a popular term. Most of them were men who had served in Oman whilst in the British Army and later, on becoming civilians, had joined up with the Sultan again. Despite the considerable difference in salary between these two types there was no bitterness since the higher paid 'contract' officers, without the protective insurance of the British Army, came off very badly in the event of their being wounded or sick from one of the many serious diseases prevalent in Oman.

Dusk was orange-tinted as I left the fort. Mosquitoes hummed in the bushes, a frenetic whine that mingled with the mounting cry of prayer for it was the hour of evening worship. A whiff of Persian ointment, unguent hair oils, came from the nearby billets; also the smell of excrement. The men used the bushes in and about the camp but this did not cause disease for the heat quickly desiccated the filth.

I put on a white shirt and slacks and went into the Mess. Attempting to enter unobtrusively, for the bar was open and the room full, I was frustrated by the double entrance doors. One set, of wire fly mesh, opened outwards, whilst the inner wooden ones opened inwards. The former, which I squeezed through, were heavily sprung and smashed back onto my hand as I entered the others. I yelped and swore. A pregnant silence followed as nut brown faces at the bar peered round and, from the scattered armchairs, a dozen hostile frowns appeared above newspapers.

Nursing my bruised hand I searched for a friendly face. From one corner, surrounded by empty chairs as though he were a leper, Patrick Brook winked at me. I joined him with relief and we sat at dinner together, attempting to ignore the others as completely as they ignored us.

He had been on the same Arabic course and was also from a cavalry regiment. We had both been assigned to the Muscat Regiment and the following day Patrick was suddenly ordered to join his Company on a reinforcement convoy to Dhofar.

As he left the Mess to pack his kit I heard the fat officer I had seen at the airport mutter to a friend, "Long-haired cavalry louts. They do us more harm than good. I can't understand why London doesn't stick to sending infantry officers."

I climbed slowly through the dust to a hilltop outside and above the camp perimeter. Sweat poured off me. My shirt chafed so I took it off and white salt-bumps quickly began to form along my shoulders and arms.

Two thousand years before the Persian hordes who invaded

Oman found the heat so great that the jewels fell out of their helmets and the feathers from their arrows.

Beyond the hilltop lay an oil camp with tankers anchored in its bay. Huge storage tanks gleamed silver just below me, their pipes leading towards the Interior. But there were no signs of oil wealth in the land; I wandered down a concrete road from the camp to Muttrah town a mile away and everywhere saw poverty and dirt; disease and squalor. The people jostled past and spat and stared from dark proud eyes, with hate I thought, but perhaps that was just a reflection of my own resentful mood. I noticed other officers in the busy market. They all carried revolvers at their waists. There was no electricity or water, yet this was the largest, richest town in Oman. Muscat, the capital, lay some five miles east, but its importance was mainly historical. Muttrah was the commercial centre but what a sorry place. Futile restrictions were rigidly enforced which added to the misery of the populace. Numerous 'don'ts' governed dress and smoking in public; there was a ban on civilians seeing films and, in Muscat city, a nightly curfew.

The next day I was taken to join my company at Bidbid, a small camp some miles inland from Muttrah. A sinewy Major with sun-blackened skin and the features of a Greek bandit came to collect me. He had no escort and drove fast along the gravel track which was the main road into the Interior.

Major John Cooper was Second-in-Command of the Muscat Regiment and a man of wide experience. Like David Bayley, he had fought with the Yemeni Royalist guerrillas. Before that he had served in the crack 22nd Special Air Service Regiment from its inception by the Phantom Major in North Africa through the years of sabotage raids in occupied France, to the post-war campaigns in Malaya and the Radfan. He was also Oman's only ham radio operator and sometimes spoke to Hussein of Jordan, another keen ham, on the far side of the great sand deserts.

Soon the mountains closed in on us, grey, gaunt and arid. This was the vast Hajar Range into which but a few valleys give tortuous access. It rises to over 10,000 feet, hiding an airy plateau with its own tribes and climate. John Cooper told me that this interior plateau had not been seen by European eyes until 1835 when two British lieutenants from the Indian Army first climbed the Hajar and had been lucky to escape with their lives from the fierce mountain tribesmen. A handful of others had travelled within the Interior but it was always risky and seldom permitted by the ruling Sultans, for the tribes were forever at war with one another and the Sultan had little real control. Aggressively Muslim and mostly of the fanatical Ibadhi sect, these plateau Omani were liable to execute trespassing infidels without qualms: nor did they pay much heed to the edicts of their coast-bound Sultan. As late as 1950 Wilfred Thesiger, the greatest of European travellers in Arabia, was unable to enter inner Oman.

In 1957 the Imam or religious leader of the Interior provoked a minor revolt directly against the Sultan himself which proved beyond the scope of the small Omani Army to suppress. Looking to his long standing Friendship Treaty with the British, the Sultan called on Whitehall. At that time John Cooper had been with his Special Air Service squadron—just returning from Malaya for leave—when a signal from London diverted them to Oman.

Now he pointed over the lower limestone ridges to the hazy peaks above and beyond: "We scaled those cliffs by night, sneaked behind the rebel machine gun posts and took them by surprise. Since then the Sultan has kept an Army outpost up there permanently manned. You'll be climbing it before long yourself to train for Dhofar."

Rusty Toyota Land Cruisers lay smashed in gullies usually where the road took a sudden bend. Omani drivers evidently overloaded their vehicles with every hitch-hiker they passed for there were no buses and few civilian lorries. Their ignorance of centrifugal law blended disastrously with their fervent belief that the only honourable position for an accelerator pedal was pressed firmly against the floorboard.

After forty miles of climbing, the mountains fell away to a valley of great beauty: gleaming pools formed a silver thread along the valley's wide riverbed. In the monsoon rains this would be a raging torrential flood but now children splashed in the shallows. Soon we swung off the track into a wired-off army camp of low white buildings. Built on a cliff above the riverbed, the outpost commanded the pass into the Interior. This was Bidbid, headquarters of the Muscat Regiment and my home until the regiment moved south to Dhofar.

The Major showed me my room, one of six in a block; a tiny bare-floored place with fly netting windows and an air-conditioner let into the wall. The machine was switched off and the room smelled stale. Just opposite was the European Officers' Mess; a sitting room well stacked with *Country Life*, *Motor* and *Playboy* magazines next to a small dining room live with the chatter of Goan cook-wallahs. Strange cooking smells and the crunch of bare feet on cockroaches came from the kitchen beyond. It was mid-afternoon and the other officers, whoever they were, were not about.

"Don't forget to take a Daraprim tablet now and once every week. Then you won't get malaria." John Cooper went off. I could tell his room by the two tall aerial masts. The heat pressed against me and sang in my ears. Any man, I thought, who stays normal out here as long as he has, must have a very absorbing hobby to distract him.

There were five others at dinner. Ties were worn and sleeves rolled down. The food was good and the talk of happenings in the south, of sex with the oil-girls in Muscat and of trouble brewing in a nearby district called the Sharqeeya. They were polite enough to me and I kept quiet, listening hard. Omani words punctured their conversation which meant nothing to me. After coffee they sat and talked, drinking quite heavily but with little visible effect.

I left soon after the meal for my stomach was heaving and the room swayed about. Reaching a narrow monsoon ditch I vomited violently and staggered to my room. Someone in Bahrein had said the Bidbid water caused havoc with visitors. They were right: for two days I was forced to keep close to the Mess lavatory. There were no others in camp since the soldiers are accustomed to using stones – not paper – and no European flushing system can cope with such jetsam.

Wanting a shower, I pushed back the plastic curtain at the back of my room and yelled as a large spider jumped onto me. Landing on my head, it slithered down my neck and inside my shirt. Frightened at first into immobility, I lost control, tore my shirt tails out of my trousers and clutched wildly for the loathsome thing as it climbed back up my neck. Knocked off, it jumped onto the wall and with great speed reached the highest corner of the shower cubicle where I hit it with a clenched fist. It was tough and leathery but it fell stunned to the concrete floor where I trampled it to pulp as it had black hairy legs, fully seven inches in span, and a curved beak for a mouth.

21

I slept badly, unused to the dry conditioned air. In the morning an Arab brought me tea. He saw the spider's body on the floor and unstuck it from the concrete to hold in the palm of his free hand. He spoke English.

"Did you kill this, Sahb? It is no good thing to crush such an insect for there is a chapter of the Holy Book given to its honour." He glanced at me disapprovingly and removed the corpse on his tea-tray.

There was a captain with brass red hair, a mass of freckles, and the lanky sort of body that moves with ease on mountain trails. He was Peter Southward-Heyton and I liked him because he was friendly and shared his enthusiasm for Oman with me.

The Colonel, he said, had asked him to show me around. He'd been with the Muscat Regiment for two years as a mercenary then left for a job in the city. After a few months he had ceremoniously burnt his bowler hat, using a pink newspaper for kindling, and returned to Muscat.

Soon he would be dead, but that morning his happy personality pulled me through the gloomy mood which settled on me when I met my men. As we approached their billet Peter explained the make-up of a Reconnaissance Platoon.

"What there should be and what there actually is are not related, I'm afraid, and that will be one of your main problems. You should have five Land Rovers; each with a driver, signaller, and five soldiers. But recruiting has lapsed lately and now there are only fifteen men in all. Some are Omanis, others Baluchis. Basically they dislike each other and this can lead to bad trouble if you let it. Never show the slightest favouritism for either crowd or the pot will start boiling."

Peter returned salutes to three smartly dressed Arabs, exchanged elaborate greetings and shook hands with each of them. This ceremony happened several times as we walked between the billets.

"Let me give you an example," he said. "I was driving south through the desert last year when one of my Arabs shot a *dhub* lizard, eighteen inches long with much rank meat. They skinned and cooked it but the Baluchis got in an ugly mood. The Prophet they said, forbade such food. Nonsense, said the Arabs. He meant another type of lizard, *Dhubs* were a delicacy and they would damn well eat this one. When a Baluchi corporal began to load his rifle I thought it time to intervene. I poured petrol on the wretched animal and buried it. But the men looked daggers at each other for days."

We came to a hut by the compound wire. Inside flies and wasps swarmed where dates lay on dirty tin plates. The place smelled of sweat and tobacco. Hair oil bottles from India lay about without tops so that wasps with clogged wings waded drunkenly in the white grease. A rifle hung unattended from a bedstead and a Baluchi soldier squatted by a Singer sewing machine chewing quietly and picking his nose.

"Well, here you are, Ranulph. These are your trusty men." Peter grinned wryly. "In just six months you'll be let loose in Dhofar and, between you and me, it would be suicide to go anywhere near *adoo* territory with this bunch in their present state . . ."

"What's *adoo*?" I asked.

"Arabic for enemy. When I was last down there – a year ago – they were hard to find. Now things have changed with a vengeance. As soon as the Brits left Aden last November the *adoo* were presented with a safe base. Now they are multiplying, and they're good. My God they're good. They move around like invisible gazelles; they know the country because it's theirs and they can smell any army presence a mile away upwind. Once you're in the mountains you're being watched. Put a step wrong, move carelessly and they cut you off. Without well-trained soldiers you'll be asking for trouble down south."

Peter sucked at his knuckles in thought. "God knows why I came back. I saw enough last time to put me off this country for good, but it has a fascination which grips you without your knowing it. Then, when you're far away back in England, it's the good things you remember, the company and the desert nights when you feel free. No old johnnies and dogs' muck on the pavements. No strikes and stinking air, traffic jams and endless talking about nothing in stuffy pubs. That's largely why I came back but now I'm here the other memories waft around like spooks trying to scare me off again."

He was speaking to himself as much as to me.

"Alan Woodman was a nice fellow. I remember his voice coming over the radio the day they ambushed him out on the cuds.

23

He was lost, I think, and his men had run out of water. Some of his lads were dead and others moaning. He had a bullet somewhere in his stomach but at first he seemed O.K. Then his voice got muzzy and he said he was going blind. No one could help him. There are no helicopters in the Army and he died bravely some time later without water."

The Baluchi had begun to pedal his Singer, sewing up a *dishdash* skirt of printed cotton. He ignored the flies and us. We sat on a tin trunk in the middle of the room. There were two lines of these trunks running down between the beds and containing all the belongings of the soldiers.

"Hamish Ainsley was luckier for he died quickly. He took his Land Rover deep into the scrub of the northern mountains. It wasn't the first time and the *adoo* were waiting with a 3·5 rocket launcher. The first rocket struck the radiator and Hamish must have copped it. The *adoo* closed in then. They slit white officers' throats when they can—but Hamish's signaller wasn't yet dead and fired a single burst that killed the *adoo* leader. A sort of Old Testament justice, don't you think!"

A bundle of clothing stirred in the shadows and a little man swung his legs over his bed rubbing his eyes awake with a grimy headcloth, red and white chequered like a Kashmiri shawl. He saw us and sprang to attention on his toes, bring his mop of wild black hair to a good four feet ten inches above his bare feet.

Twin layers of fine white teeth showed in a wicked grin. Pointed ears and pointed beard with a bulbous Punch-nose set among deep crinkles of humour.

"This is Private Ali Nasser," said Peter, clearly pleased to see the beaming Arab, "Ali's from a mountain bedu tribe: small but tough."

"*Salaam alaikum, Ali. Kaif haalak?*" Peter greeted the little man.

"*Alaikum salaam*—Hello, Sahb," Ali replied, showing off his ability to speak at least one English word. There followed the normal spate of greetings; then Peter introduced me as the new Recce Sahb. Ali smiled disarmingly and asked polite questions which I nodded hard at. He made us stay for coffee—heated on a little paraffin burner. He chatted all the while. I understood very little and Peter explained.

24

"He was asking about Tom Greening, the last Recce Captain who left some months ago. They all liked him. He speaks and writes Arabic fluently. Also he enters their minds somehow and they tell him their inner thoughts. You'll meet him soon because he's to come back as an Intelligence Officer before long. I was at Sandhurst with him and so was the Sultan's eldest son Qaboos." Peter looked about him and dropped his voice. "He and Tom got on very well together and last year the two of us were sometimes allowed to visit Qaboos in his private house beside Salalah Palace. The Sultan keeps his son under virtual house arrest there you know. Probably because their dynasty, the Albu Saeedi have ruled Oman for two hundred years and nearly all have died at the hand of a close relative. Keep this to yourself but I heard Tom and Qaboos discuss some very delicate matters. It got me quite scared because if the old man had had that house bugged, we'd all have had our heads chopped off. I sometimes wonder quite what Tom is up to these days. He's a dark horse."

Ali poured coffee from a battered *dhille* coffee pot, brass with a curved beak spout, and placed a tin of dates crawling with wasps before us. The wasps were over an inch long and looked aggressive so I shook my head politely when Ali indicated the plate and made encouraging noises.

Peter prodded me.

"Take some or you'll offend him. But watch the *dibbees*. Their sting is as bad as an African hornet's."

Two men with black beards came into the room wearing white *dishdashes* and cotton *shemaghs* wrapped around their heads. Ali and Peter stood up to greet them and I followed suit.

"*Tafaddel*," said Ali, meaning they must be seated and eat with us.

As the men talked they watched me from grape-black eyes which at first moved too quickly to meet my glance.

One of the newcomers was Mohamed Rashid, a machine gunner of the Platoon. His dark features were finely moulded with the nose and chin of a hawk. But his eyes were gentle.

He is a man to trust, I thought.

Others arrived to join us and everyone rose to greet them. Their manners were gracious and natural but no Baluchis came near though I noticed a group of them in another part of the room.

Peter went and the conversation withered. Ali Nasser smiled nervously at me and offered the dates around to cover his confusion. I tried to think of a question to ask in Arabic.

"How many are there of you in the Platoon?"

They all answered at once and all, it seemed, gave a different figure so I nodded and muttered "*Al Hamdu lillah*" which means 'to God be the Praise' and can be repeated as often as one feels inclined. I did not remember feeling so awkward for a long while and they seemed to sense my embarrassment. The atmosphere hung heavily so I shook their hands and left as though I had business elsewhere. Behind me I could hear their chatter break out again. I should have greeted the Baluchis but they looked away as I passed them. Anyway they doubtless spoke no English, like the Arabs, and I knew no Baluchi.

Already my shirt and the crutch of my trousers were wet with sweat. A handsome Arab with a paunch and well-creased uniform greeted me in good English.

"I'm Salim Abdullah, Staff Sergeant of the Reconnaissance Platoon. Most happy to meet you, Sahb. For many months now we have had no officer and when I ask the Major for new equipment or more men I get nothing. For this reason Recce is not happy. You have met the men in our room, Sahb? Come, the others are with our Land Rovers."

The 'others' were a motley crew of five drivers all of whom were sat in the back of one jacked-up Land Rover smoking Benson and Hedges cigarettes. To a man they wore dark glasses, grime-caked overalls and frayed gym shoes with no laces.

One had his legs dangling over the tailboard. He peered at me over his glasses and said 'Hello, John'. They stood up one by one, finding it an effort. The Sergeant seemed uncomfortable. He told me their names which I forgot—they were all Mohameds or Hameds or Mohmeds. But Murad I would remember; he was the cheeky one. He could swear in English and wore a floppy khaki hat at a rakish angle.

His face was triangular with a Conquistador chin tuft and the hard brown eyes of a bedu. He was noisy, I soon learnt, only because he was unsure of himself and often he brooded in silence. He was half Baluchi and tried hard to find favour with the Arabs whilst being friendly to the Baluchis; not an easy life.

Of their five Land Rovers, only Murad's worked.

26

"I, Murad son of Adam, am your driver, Sahb. Our *Lund Rovver* is Number One, the most speedy in Oman."

The Sergeant drew me aside.

"He has a big mouth. To be sure he is good with motors when he has to be, but otherwise he is lazy and the drivers all follow his ways."

He held my hand earnestly, anxious that I should understand.

"In the new season the Regiment will move south and the word is about among the men that many hundreds of *adoo* will come from other lands to fight us. People say the *shooyooeen*, the communists, from China and Russia have sent them deadly guns and many instructors. They are strong and we of the Sultan are few."

The Sergeant pointed his long aristocratic fingers heavenwards and then prodded my stomach. He was evidently coming to the point.

"The Companies will be safe perhaps, God willing, for they are a hundred men each with mortars and Vickers machine guns. But we can survive only by stealth and cunning. This means good training and good heart. But, Captain Sahb, this Recce Platoon has neither. They are rabble, they are too few in number and worst of all they quarrel bitterly among themselves."

He paused but I said nothing so he continued in a low voice.

"I will tell you why there is bad feeling. It is simple. The Recce Platoon was always of the best Arabs in the Regiment, such men as could drive better, signal better and shoot with a straighter eye. They were hand picked from the Companies and they came because in Recce they no longer need walk over the mountains and through the sands carrying their water. In Recce our Land Rovers carry us everywhere. And, Sahb, they came also because in Recce they would not have to live with wretched Baluchis beside them. Baluchis who moan like women at pain or discomfort; who must drink twice the water an Arab needs; who are unhappy if they have nothing to complain about. They are men even who speak evilly of their companions behind their backsides. Ugghh!"

The Sergeant ended with an interesting noise and wiped his little beard expressively as though cleaning his mouth of foul words. He seemed to have finished his peroration so I asked him how we could get rid of Baluchis at a time when the platoon was already well below strength. Also, remembering Peter Southward-Heyton's exhortations, I remarked on his prejudices.

"Surely, as a Staff Sergeant you should treat all the men of Recce as one, whether Arab or Baluch? How can you discard all Baluchis as useless unless you show open favouritism?"

At this, he threw his hands up high so that his *dishdash* rode up above his shins.

"Never, Sahb, I am always of a remarkable fairness to all the men. I see them all only as fellow Muslims under God, all of whom are naturally afflicted with one evil or another but the Baluchis, praise Allah, are more gravely afflicted." His fawn eyes stared at me with hurt.

I gave up and returned to the Mess. Lunch was sandwiches and three pints of ice cool *loomee*; limes boiled with sugar. Oman is the greatest exporter of limes in the world though she is more famous in Arabia for her camels and dates.

In Oman I discovered that dogs, Arabs and Englishmen disappear into the shadows at the first sign of the midday sun so I followed suit, lying naked beneath a rough cotton sheet.

I woke with a start to find two Arabs I did not recognise standing about my bed. My lack of clothes prevented me from springing up.

One was very dark with black negroid hair, the other small with harsh features. Both wore white *dishdashes* and carried bamboo camel sticks.

They greeted me, shook my hand and seated themselves one on the bed, the other upon his haunches on the floor. The darker man ran his camel stick over my sheet in a manner that I found unpleasantly intimate. Their eyes wandered around the gloom of the room, meeting mine every now and again to give quick smiles with their mouths that did not touch their eyes.

For ten minutes they remained saying nothing and seeming quite content.

I thought of a number of courses of action but all were stultified either by my nakedness or my lack of Arabic.

Peter saved the situation, banging on the door and asking if I'd join him for a swim. Coming in he saw my problem and spoke quickly to the Arabs who left.

"They're both bedu from Adam beyond the southern mountains. Good fighters but troublemakers. They've been in Recce longer than the others and rule the roost. They pay no attention to the Sergeant."

I followed him along a dust track down the valley to where reeds rimmed a deep pool. Around us date palms shaded vines and fields of fresh lucerne.

"There were puff adders here and water snakes which made swimming a touch risky till we dropped some grenades in last month."

The water felt wonderfully cool and afterwards we lazed on the warm rocks above the pool.

Walking back, the sun set slowly in the Hajar sending waves of changing colour over the land.

The valley moved with life. Women met their lovers in the date groves. Others, balancing water jars, walked sinuously from the pools to their square clay homes. Their laughter and the spicy smells of cooking reached us moving through a long deserted village dark with shadows from the ruined houses.

"Bidbid was here not long ago but the pox came and those who didn't die wandered into the mountains to starve for they feared to go near the other tribes. Sometimes lepers sleep here. Never come here by yourself without a gun. The Sheikh of the Sharqeeya, who hates the Sultan, has many agents around to cause trouble and there are others too about whom we know less but from whom there is more to fear."

As we scuffed through the orange dust beyond the compound gate, Peter continued soberly,

"It's not just those outside you must beware of, Ranulph. There are some within the Army who hate us too. Don't ever give them an excuse. You can throw a stone in jest at a British soldier if he's lagging and he'll laugh. Throw one at the wrong Arab and you'll be shot through the back, maybe two years afterwards."

I resolved to check and purge my own men very carefully before the time came when we would enter the mountains of Dhofar.

2

FROM 1968 until 1974 carefully selected Dhofari guerrillas were sent abroad for military training and Marxist indoctrination in Russia and China. Some of these men later defected, and I came to know them well. Not only did they tell me about their experiences whilst I was in Dhofar, but I was later able to interview some of them in the summer of 1973 in a small village in south-west England. From the notes and conversations I have attempted to put together a description of events *on the other side*. To do this I have adhered completely to the facts told to me, to the feelings and the thoughts which they explained to me but I have reconstructed them so that it reads more coherently. In this way, throughout this book, I shall try to give the other side's viewpoint, as well as my own. I hope by doing this, to give the reader a much clearer picture of what was happening, of those we were fighting and of what motivated them.

In many cases intelligence reports, eye-witnesses and defectors all gave accounts of the same scenes so that it is possible to put them together to make a well-rounded three-dimensional account of what happened. There are also photographs to corroborate evidence and facing page 33 you will find a photograph of Ahmad Deblaan with his fellow guerrillas at the training school in Peking.

Ahmad Deblaan was well known to me and he gave me some long and vivid accounts of his time in Peking. He remembered first that hazy day when a uniformed guerrilla had come to his village in Dhofar with a letter from 'the leader' in faraway Aden.

Ahmad had packed his belongings into a leather shoulder bag and walked to Hauf in the People's Republic of Yemen, with two other recruits. After that it had been confusing. Twenty others from different tribes had joined them: men from clans that his own tribe had hated since the beginning of time but the commissar harangued them whenever they stopped: telling them that they were part of the People's Front for the Liberation of the Occupied Arabian Gulf (PFLOAG) now, that the sheikhs and the tribes were no more; that old loyalties and feuds had ceased and that old ties of blood and lineage had now given way to those of the class-struggle.

An ancient jeep had taken them, ten at a time, along the hard coastal sands to Qith'a and then a tattered Dakota DC3 had taken them to Aden, where they had met Al Ghassani, then military leader of the revolution in Dhofar. A Boeing 707 of Middle East Airlines to Karachi, Pakistan Airways to Shanghai and a smart Illyushin 14 of Internal Chinese Airways to Peking.

Then a week in a plush city hotel with daily visits to gardens, schools and so on. Insidious patter about the wicked Mings and Chings as they toured the Emperors' palaces and tombs. After that the work began, politics and guns, politics and knives, politics and karate. The 71 mm field gun, the 25 mm RCL, the Kalachnikov. Marx, Engels, Lenin, but mostly Mao. There is no Allah but Mao ... The Soviets are revisionists as evil as the imperialists ... War is the continuation of politics by other means ... When you meet larger enemy forces, shout "*Hujoom, hujoom*—Attack, attack" and immediately withdraw ... We communists oppose all unjust wars that impede progress but we do not oppose progressive just wars ... In Dhofar you will have no bases and you will have many, centred on the local population, from whom you will gain temporary succour. Your only real base, in the present state of operations, is across the Yemen border which is immune from attack ... special emphasis must be laid on night fighting operations ... above all else your principle is to attack and destroy isolated enemy forces on your own ground ...

Ahmad Deblaan remembered the endless indoctrination lessons for the Chinese instructor had spared no pains to see that every word was lodged firmly in his head. He would be able to repeat them for the rest of his life:

"What is the Koran and who is the Prophet, comrade?"

"The Koran, the Prophet and all other manifestations of Islam are inventions of the British imperialists who are running dogs and lackeys of the U.S."

"Why did they spread about such inventions in Arab lands?"

"They wished to poison our society with the class-ideologies of religion. To cloud the Arab mind with Islamic ritual — leaving no time to ponder the injustice of our suppression ... To make us place all inequalities at the door of a make-believe God when in reality the British and their puppet Sultans were to blame. In Arabia more than any other country in the world religion is a tool used by the regime to terrorise and mystify the people ..."

Dressed in simple overalls with a red Mao button provided for his right lapel, he had spent three months in school whilst the teachers droned on and on. As well as Dhofaris there had been Africans, and North Koreans. They had been told not to expect that all the people in their country would immediately, on their return, believe all the new truths that they had been taught. They had also been told to work with fellow comrades of differing views in order to use them to further their own ends. For Marxist-Leninists should strictly observe the principle of using different methods to resolve different contradictions.

Ahmad himself knew perfectly well inside his brain that Allah was Allah and always would be. He wondered whether the other students and other Dhofaris really believed that there was no God. He could find no reason for disbelieving the Chinese people about the British fabrications but somehow he just knew that there was more to Allah than a cunning imperialist plot.

However, he continued to learn what he was told, to stab model figures with the short bayonet attached to his AK47 rifle, to scream and kick out his legs when attacked, to chant in unison the necessary slogans and to remember the ethics of Mao: "Be fair in your dealings with people ... Do not bully them ... Do not ill-treat prisoners ..."

When they had arrived it had been March: ice cold winds had blown from the Gobi Desert bringing clouds of airborne grit like an Arabian sandstorm. They had been taken by bus from Peking to the Peking Military School beyond the city suburbs for eight months. Later a convoy of lorries took them north

Mubarreq

Mussabba of the Wild Hair

Mohammed Rashid of the Beard

Said Salim

Fat Hamid of the Browning

Ali Nasser

Ahmad Deblaan (*front row fourth from left*) with his fellow guerrillas
at the training school in Peking

Dead *adoo*

through high mountain passes, past the snaking Great Wall of China to a place of forested hills very similar to his own Dhofar mountains. Here they trained hard until they became expert in practice at all those guerrilla tactics they had so assiduously learnt in theory. It was a strange country, full of contrast yet the people were all the same. Someone had said there were 600 million of them yet to Ahmad all seemed exactly similar in their white gauze health masks, their baggy blue trousers and faded jackets.

He remembered the guided Peking tours in groups of three or four.

In the fields between the Forbidden City and the great compound of the military school the peasants worked ceaselessly like ants. Barefooted in the dry dusty fields tilling the earth with ancient hoes and man-pulled ploughs heaving and straining . . . and around them the red fluttering pennants.

Seated on hall floors in geometrical patterns of blue and serge, the political cadres listened and were exhorted, roared chorused quotations, and sung the revolutionary songs . . . and above them the wall placards featured the great Mao Chu-si, Chairman Mao; godhead to the godless.

There were cheerleaders: "What do we do to the Black Gang and the bourgeoisie?" From the body of the hall the massive chanting response. "*Shah, shah* . . . Kill, kill."

And the interpreter, in whose Warszawa saloon car Ahmad and two others were taken around, explained that the bourgeoisie were those selfish Chinese people who still considered themselves as individuals, who wore tapered trousers, applied scent to their bodies, kept a pet cat, wore long hair tresses and so on. That the Black Gang were the capitalist intellectual clique who dared to mislead the proletariat into thinking they were superior just because they were teachers and professors.

The interpreter explained that fortunately these menaces had largely been dealt with since 1966. That was when the great Chairman had begun a Cultural Revolution to purify the Republic of such filth. Throughout the vastness of the land they had been eradicated one by one, humiliated, villified, beaten, and then executed by the elite corps of Red Guards specially formed from youths whose devotion to Mao was proven.

This 'cultural revolution' had known no bounds, purging the

33

misguided from the lowest workers to those in the upper echelons of power. Even the President, Lin Shao-Chi, and the Mayor of Peking, Peng Cheng, had been removed and disgraced.

Ahmad's tour had included People's factories, People's communes and People's hospitals. There were few other cars; only endless streams of cycles and pedal-rickshaws. Street loudspeakers blared the news from Hsinhua, the masters of propaganda, also called the New China News Agency.

He marvelled at the gilded curves of golden roofs, of palaces and temples. The Working People's Palace of Culture known to the subservient peoples of the Ming dynasty as the Imperial Ancestral Temple. To its west the Gate of Heavenly Peace led onto the vast Square of that name.

Ahmad remembered with chill unease that morning in the first week when he had asked why the peasants were so poor in this enlightened society. The instructor had a ready reply but Ahmad felt that he was watched especially closely after that and had sometimes been kept behind after classes to be questioned closely on his beliefs.

None of the students could leave the compound without a supervisor and then only on Saturdays. In the city they saw a group of Egyptian students. Their request to speak to their fellow Arabs was turned down without reason.

With nine months of indoctrination under his belt, Ahmad Deblaan passed out with honour, his early indiscretion forgotten. Proudly he joined his comrades in the Great Hall of the People to receive congratulations and two hours of exhortation from the local Chief of the People's Liberation Army. At this meeting he was presented with a bound copy of Mao's Thoughts in Arabic. He had already received five identical copies over the preceding months: the Chinese Republic were most generous.

Intelligence reports from sources all over the world informed us that not far to the north in the Shantung peninsula some 700 special couriers were under a different sort of training: they would be sent to Hong Kong to obtain employment on board European freighters travelling to European ports. In Europe they would collect information from a network of agents who had themselves received training in China; mostly at the intelligence school of Mokanshan in the province of Chekiang.

These agents came from many countries but mostly from

India, Vietnam, Thailand, the Philippines, Laos, Latin America and the United States, the majority of the latter being anarchist students and negroes. Each year over a thousand such agents graduate from Mokanshan.

One of the methods by which these agents obtain intelligence is through infiltration of cheap heroin and opium into the West. From state-controlled plants in China and North Korea, 9,000 tons of opium are exported every year although world demand for medical opium is only 300 tons a year. The main smuggling routes are from the Yunan province and Burma to Rangoon and Singapore. But there are many others.

A useful side effect of the opium project is the undermining of health and morale in the non-Communist world by increasing drug addiction.

Other training centres are located in Harbin and Nanking which specialise in guerrilla warfare and sabotage techniques.

Ahmad Deblaan was sent back to Dhofar via Kuwait and Aden. At first he was pleased to be back home and fought with a will alongside the other guerrillas. But little incidents began to unsettle him; to remind him of his earlier doubts about Maoism. Things like the shooting of any tribesman denounced by two others as a Government spy. A friend of his had died this way, a man he knew well was no spy. His accusers were simply settling a long-standing feud in a novel manner. And not all the executions he had witnessed were straightforward shootings. People who had acknowledged their Muslim beliefs in public were punished in several ways before being finished off. The soles of their feet were burned away; red-hot coals were applied to their faces, backs and genitals.

It was not so much the pain that these people had suffered as the indignity that disturbed Ahmad. They were after all his fellow *jebali* mountain tribesmen and he knew inside himself that he was still as true a Muslim as they were. By the time two months had passed, he had made up his mind.

When the opportunity arose, he fled from the mountains to surrender to the Sultan's Government in Salalah. They might not be glorious or revolutionary but at least they refrained from burning and murdering folk who believed in Allah.

Among Ahmad Deblaan's Dhofari rebel friends were Kamees,

Musallim Ali and Salim Amr. When I first started questioning defectors, I asked them whom they knew in order to cross-reference information obtained. I was much surprised to find that Kamees, whom I knew well, was a great friend of Ahmad Deblaan's and Salim Amr and was actually blood cousin to Musallim Ali. But the cousins had been separated in their training, Kamees going to Russia with Salim Amr, whilst Musallim Ali merely received local instruction in Kuweit. Kamees and Ahmad Deblaan were, from my point of view, the best at telling me in great detail about events, but Musallim Ali and Salim Amr were the people whom I ultimately came up against as opponents and enemies.

Musallim Ali was of the Bait Qahawr tribe. In 1959 he left his home in the Qara hills of Dhofar to join the Trucial Oman Scouts (T.O.S.) in the Trucial States like many other Dhofaris. They received good pay and excellent training from the British officers who commanded the Scouts.

A third of their monthly pay was collected by two Dhofaris, Corporals in the T.O.S., who worked secretly for PFLOAG and sent the money on to the Kuweit PFLOAG office.

When fully trained many of the T.O.S. Dhofaris went on leave but never returned. They remained in the Qara mountains to spearhead the war against the Sultan's British officered troops.

Occasionally letters would arrive for the two Dhofari Corporals asking them for some men from the Trucial Oman Scouts to go to Russia for courses in guerrilla warfare. Those selected by the Corporals would ask their British officers for permission to go on leave. This granted, they were not seen again.

But Musallim Ali was never selected despite his burning desire to help liberate his people.

In 1967, frustrated, he returned to Dhofar and helped the guerrillas operating from Qum, the headquarters nearest to the rolling downs of Bait Fiah where his family's camel herd were wont to graze.

A year later he was moved to Kuweit. He had at last been chosen for a political course.

Musallim's wife Noor, which means Light, was exceptionally beautiful. They had married when she was thirteen, a nubile fawn as desirable to him as life itself. Now, twelve years later, they still had no children and but for the deep love and respect they had for each other, he would have divorced her many years ago.

In Kuweit Musallim Ali met Ahmad Deblaan and the other Dhofaris on their way home after the long course in Peking. They stayed for three days only awaiting their onward flight but the fire of their newfound convictions was infectious. Musallim Ali hung on their every word, gratefully accepted little red booklets, and realised that his own Kuweiti course was very small beer compared with what these men had experienced in China.

Although at heart a deeply religious man, his thoughts from then on grew less and less involved with Allah and even with his beloved Noor. The Maoist spark had kindled in his breast. In the course of time he was to regret it.

Salim Amr, scar-faced and bitter from birth, watched the fat-bellied Englishmen with their short khaki trousers. He would often stare at their pink spotty faces as they bicycled about the camp between the RAF control tower and the swimming pool: between their sweat-reeking rooms and the NAAFI. He hated them.

He stole from their rooms whenever he could. They were careless and he was quick. This was not through necessity for his pay was good, setting him above most other Dhofaris in Salalah. He visited the market twice a week to buy an hour of the fat negress's resourceful favours.

One day in the spring of 1968 he left the camp for good, taking with him many watches, lighters, and the collection of torn documents that he had assiduously collected from waste-paper baskets over the months. He had no way of knowing their security value but he felt the guerrillas might anyway be grateful for his efforts.

His tribe, the Bait Na'ath, lived along the Arzat Valley. Most of the guerrillas of that region were negroes, sons of Sultanic slaves, but they accepted him readily enough when they saw the loot. They paid cut prices and Salim Amr soon substantiated his position with them by acts of cruelty amongst the local population. To exhort food from villagers who denied having any — owing to the drought — his speciality was a wood fire. The recalcitrant villager would be lowered over the embers with his legs held wide apart so that his most sensitive parts kippered slowly but surely. If there was a food cache about, its location would soon be revealed. In this and other more refined ways Salim Amr became a respected member of the Arzat *firqa* or guerrilla group and it was a tribute to his reputation that he was selected for more advanced training.

There were five others with Salim, including Kamees, two of them boys in their early teens. Three guerrillas escorted them to Hauf, and during the five-day march Salim watched with admiration as the two lads, staunch Muslims, were encouraged towards atheism.

The march was long and extremely hot. When they stopped the first evening there was no food or water save that carried by the escorts. One of these approached the five recruits.

"You will eat with us?"

They replied with one voice: "*Imshaalah* — God willing."

The escorts looked at one another, shaking their heads. "But there is no God," they said, and sat apart for their meal.

Salim went over to them. "You are right, my friends: of course there is no God. How foolish of me. My error was due to weariness."

At that the escorts bade Salim share their food and water and soon two of the other recruits came over: they too apologised in order to drink.

The two youths were made of sterner stuff and — not having had daily contact with guerrillas as the others had — they were prepared to suffer rather than turn away from the belief that was the source of their existence.

By the second evening they were in a very bad way. Their throats were too dry to do anything but croak hoarsely.

But again when asked if they would like a drink, both said, "*Imshaalah.*"

"It is all very well thinking God will provide," said one of the escorts, "but he hasn't, has he?"

At midday on the third day one of the youths collapsed and motioned desperately for water.

"Will God provide it?" he was asked in mocking tones.

"There is no God." The voice was cracked and desperate.

The other young man broke down soon afterwards. He could go no further but refused to deny his God.

He was dragged behind some boulders by two of the escorts. Salim heard a dozen or so dull crunching thuds, then the two men returned alone and the little group continued, unhindered by such reactionary ideologies as religion.

Later they were flown to Aden, to some new buildings just off the main street in Crater. Here an *adoo* leader, Hassan al Awa, told them they were to be greatly honoured. They had been selected to go to Russia for a long course. But they were told to remember under *no circumstances* to tell the Russians how large or how small PFLOAG was.

For three weeks the five recruits stayed in the Officers' Mess in Little Aden camp—where not very long ago the British had been. Salim and Kamees listened agog to tales of the heroic fighting which had forced the defeated British to flee from Aden and were much impressed to hear that everyone was now prosperous and happy. The NLF government was developing things fast and furiously with the help and guidance of their new-found friends the Russians and Chinese.

What the recruits had seen in Crater did not bear this out but then Crater was probably next on the development list. (They could not know that Aden's jails were daily crammed with new 'political prisoners' for execution nor that 42,000 refugees had already successfully fled through scorching deserts into Northern Yemen leaving a far greater number dead along the way. With Saudi financial aid these refugees were even then forming an anti-NLF army in the Northern Yemen to be called the United Liberation Army.)

A Russian Army plane took Kamees, Salim and the others to Cairo, then on to an airport north-west of the Black Sea. They were not told their destination.

For half an hour a bus drove them through green hilly country to an army camp. They were there for three months with groups from South America, Africa, Vietnam and Cambodia. They wore green uniform and caps with a gold badge incorporating the hammer and sickle.

During this period they received a week's holiday in Moscow; twenty-four hours away by train. They were shown Red Square and inspected the model of the great rocket that took the Soviets to the moon ahead of the Americans, or so the technical jargon led them to believe.

Then on to the Lenin Memorial. They were most impressed. Above them the Mausoleum clock struck sonorously. People moved in and out of the GUM department stores across the way: the wondrous silhouette of St. Basil's giving tone to the bleak lines of Red Square.

The interpreter droned on: each feature of the Square serving to demonstrate some glorious aspect of the Soviet Union or the past horrors of Tzarist times.

He led them to a medieval platform, the old Execution Ground, where they sat to listen further.

It was astounding—when one was privileged to hear the revelations from official sources—how well advanced the Soviets already were to take over the Western powers.

He mustered the facts as he had learnt them ... Already the Russians had conquered one-third of the world's total population and quietly exterminated or imprisoned all those within their own colonies stupid enough to oppose communism. All this they had done without in the long run alienating the Western governments. In the underdeveloped countries they were winning the all-important battles for hearts-and-minds. In non-communist Europe they had crept insidiously into every walk of life whilst encouraging the idea amongst capitalists that to show alarm was to 'look for reds under beds' and melodramatic.

In France they could command thirty-five per cent of the suffrage, in West Germany—where they employed 27,000 spies —they were daily consolidating their control of schools, universities, trade unions, and factories where their efforts were undermining the State by revolutionary violence. In Italy they were already in control of many local councils and challenged the current coalition government. Their street fighters were trained in brigades equipped with steel clubs, special nails to puncture police cars, and portable radios to co-ordinate activities.

In Britain, their members had infiltrated educational, industrial and social bodies to an extent where they could not easily be dislodged and they could manipulate social disorder, strikes, and demonstrations over 5,000 strong at short notice.

And their greatest strength lay in the individual people of the West who were quite certain there was no menace to their free way of life which they knew would carry on as always – though they never lifted a finger to actively ensure this.

To Salim Amr's mind this was most admirable but not half as impressive as the military might of the Warsaw Pact. He remembered the excellent map they had been shown and the brief summary of anticipated events . . .

They would advance through and past capitalist Germany like a knife through butter at a rate far faster than the Nazi blitzkrieg of 1939. Armoured vehicles, totally nuclear proof, would advance 100 kilometres a day along a path prepared with toxic warheads, biological and chemical nerve gases that kill in seconds but disperse quickly so that follow-up is not hindered . . . Major nuclear strikes would protect the flanks causing heavy residual radiation through which the enemy would find it difficult to counter-attack. The enemy themselves have no biological or chemical offensive capacity owing to past pressure of public opinion. Furthermore they are ignorant that sixty-five per cent of all Soviet warheads are either biological or chemical: and so on . . .

After three months at the political camp, the Dhofaris were flown south-west for one and half hours to Odessa where they remained for six months at an army camp in the centre of the city.

They were allowed to have a holiday only on Sundays when they could wander about the town at will. Salim was amazed at the considerable differences between the rich and the poor of Odessa: it was just like Salalah – well-dressed officials, ragged dirty farmfolk and labourers.

The months passed slowly, ending in a final 'passing-out' week designed to test the men to the utmost, as fully trained ideologist guerrillas.

Of the twenty-two Dhofaris who began the course twenty-one were successful. The other man disappeared half-way through the course: the camp authorities later reported that he had suffered a brain seizure from which he never recovered. Kamees found it strange that the passing-out week should take place in the far north wearing thick woolly uniforms and trudging through deep snow drifts. But then the Russians knew best.

3

FROM Bidbid, I drove south with my Recce Platoon, in three Land Rovers, the soldiers chanting as their palms beat the hot metal of the vehicles. They bounced on their bundles of bedding and rations clutching bren guns and rifles. Only the darker faces of the Baluchis were sullen and silent as the wild tune of the Arabs followed the wind:

> Heywah the sun is silver
> Where the date palms shade the land
> And the women carry water from the wells.

> Heywah the men are riding
> on their camels to the war
> And they'll die or kill with honour Imshaalah.

The track wound south through gravel hills and well-worn limestone guts. No other country has the same wild look as though torn from the face of a nightmare. Its mountains sprang not long ago from under the sea so that vast rifts of black ophite and igneous were spewed up beneath a skin of horny limestone. Creeping down the furrows of this jagged moon-scape, we passed by villages of fragile beauty cut off from the surrounding harsh land by the rim of their local watershed. Here clover grew and vines and cress in water meadows. Skinny boys collected melons, figs and mangoes in their *dishdash* folds, and pomegranates ripened beyond the date groves that sustained each village.

Some of the hamlets had several hundred inhabitants usually of a single tribe, others were split in two with men of one tribe living west of a certain landmark, the others to the east. Certain tribes have blood feuds with one another and a few days after our patrol passed through the valley, two hundred men were killed in tribal fighting within the neighbouring Jaalaan province. I knew nothing of this until I read of it in *The Times* a month later.

The entire region, the Sharqeeya, was ruled by a Sheikh, Ahmed Mohamed Al Harthi, whose ambitions were a growing threat to the Sultan. We were sent in armed patrols each year by way of the Wadi Tayyin, the fertile valley in which we found ourselves a day's drive south from Bidbid, in order to establish the Sultan's influence and maintain his recruiting rights in the Sharqeeya.

Before leaving Major John Cooper had handed me a scroll in Arabic signed by a Minister. It ordered the reader to allow me safe passage anywhere within the Sharqeeya and beyond to the land of the Wahibas. But John warned me;

"Don't go too far. If you sense overt hostility, turn back at once, because there's only one way in or out. Your predecessor was badly wounded in an ambush so be careful. Find out all you can in the villages, record any mapping errors, and get recruits if you can."

Armed with bundles of recruiting pamphlets and all fifteen men, we had set out only after a number of petty but violent quarrels amongst the platoon members which had taken a whole day to disentangle. Being unable to understand anything but the most basic Omani Arabic, I was left out of the arguments altogether as words flew, hot and bitter, about the platoon room.

Sergeant Abdullah, far from keeping order, was shouted down by the two bedu and the Baluchis during the brief lulls between their own quarrels. I felt about as effective as a pint of oil in a stormbound ocean. Frantically I had unearthed my Arab grammar notes and tried to memorize those phrases I had lacked to quell the pandemonium.

After much improvisation Chief Driver Murad proudly announced that three of his five 'Lund Rovver' were in good health. Weapons were cleaned and oiled. Some were in a filthy state and the two-inch mortar could not be found by its crew. In the British Army both men would have been arrested on the spot for negligence: as it was, I set to to find a replacement.

Major Richard John was still away recovering from his wound, and there was no other British officer about in his Company so I 'borrowed' a mortar and machine gun from his armoury which, over the next two years, were never missed by their previous owners and saved our lives more than once.

So, in some semblance of order, we had left Bidbid a day later than required and camped by Naqsi where the Wadi Wasit joins the Tayyin.

I cleared a place of stones beside a palm stump and spread out my sleeping bag. I lowered the fine mesh mosquito net over a makeshift bamboo frame and took my shaving kit to the bushes where an inch of water ran though the pebbles.

It was darker in the trees and I stumbled against a fallen palm. Nursing my shin I saw two men squatting by the stream some yards ahead. They were holding hands and defecating whilst they chatted in low tones. Both were Baluchis. I left the trees quietly, without washing, finding the incident unsettling. Perhaps many of the men were homosexuals but their apparent intimacy could equally well be perfectly innocent. I decided to say nothing about it and moved to the fire. Little Ali Nasser was the self-appointed cook, laying sacks of millet flour and rice among the rocks.

The sun sank inch by inch behind the palms and the men separated to pray after washing their faces and hands. Each cleared a little patch for his scrap of carpet and turned towards the direction of Mecca.

The Holy City lay in the path of the setting sun yet some of the soldiers faced north. A different sect perhaps or a little unsure of their bearings. There were many things I wished to ask but Sergeant Abdullah had wandered off and did not come back that night.

We had passed by girls 'beaked' in black masks, but the younger ones wore bright cotton trousers and their ready smiles were provocative as long as none of their menfolk were present. The soldiers shouted greetings with suggestive rejoinders and Abdullah had smiled happily at me licking his thick lips. Even now perhaps he was easing his loins in a nearby village.

44

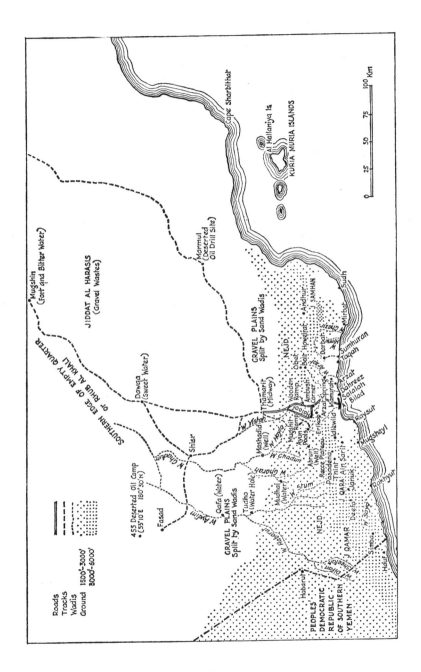

I greeted a massive Baluchi who had prayed longer than the rest, more meticulously following the ritual pattern of Islamic movement. His black beard reached down to his abdomen as he sat by the fire; he was the *moolah* of the Baluchis; their self-appointed religious leader. He did not answer and the others fell silent as I joined the flame-lit circle. Mohamed Rashid, whose fluffy black mane rivalled the *moolah*'s brought me a mug of steaming tea and squatted beside me. He spoke slowly and repeated himself when he saw me hesitate.

"Do you pray, Sahb?"

I saw that there was nothing but curiosity in his question and answered him truthfully.

"I pray when I am in bed, Mohamed, but sometimes I forget, sometimes I am lazy. I pray to the same God as you."

The men were silent gazing into the complex waltz of the fire.

"Raise yourself, Father of the Beard, or am I to cook for all whilst you roast your old bones."

Little Ali Nasser tweaked Mohamed's whiskers and placed a battered cauldron across the firestones.

Murad brought a goat from his vehicle where it had lain tethered on the seat between us for two days. He carried it lovingly stroking its chin and flanks. Then, holding it firmly between his knees he slit its throat with a razor blade and let the blood bubble and spurt into a tin gravy plate that Ali held in readiness, tucking his beard away from the thin red jet.

The meal was good; soft blueish segments of boiled meat and rice spiced with cloves and Indian tomato juice. The wasps had departed at dusk and a soft breeze from the stream kept the mosquitoes away.

Mohamed and Ali ate with Murad. Ali edged them over and waved me into the gap. Like them I used only my right hand to touch the food since theoretically it was clean. Reflecting about this later I felt somewhat guilty that I really ought to amend my sanitary habits so that my left hand took over what my right had, like most Europeans, always been accustomed to doing by way of personal cleanliness. The habit has stuck so that to this day I am left-handed in the lavatory despite my return to the world of cutlery-users.

The Arabs pushed little bits of the best meat from their own portion of the large tin plate onto mine and became annoyed when I returned them to their side of the rice hillock.

The two bedu ate together belching between mouthfuls. Beyond the fire the Baluchis squabbled endlessly, quietened only by the deep tones of the giant *moolah*.

Mohamed Rashid of the Beard poured water onto my hand from his cloth *zamzamia* to remove the grease and rice particles.

"Listen to those Baluchis, Sahb. Yak, yak like Dhofari jackals. Is not their Urdu an exceedingly ugly tongue?"

I agreed, finding Mohamed's Omani surprisingly easy to understand. He cleaned his ·303 bren gun whilst he spoke, his wide eyes, black yet gentle, glinting with humour.

"Those who talk too much will never guard a secret. They would do better to keep silent so that their shortcomings would lie hidden. Then they might pass for wise men. God blessed us with two ears but only one tongue. We should therefore speak half of what we hear."

A violent quarrel broke out across the clearing. The Baluchis had risen clasping their guns; all were screaming at the two bedu. The other Arabs moved over to listen but Mohamed looked worried.

"I told the bedu to leave them alone; now we will have trouble."

The black-skinned bedu swore at the *moolah* hawking a gob of bile at his feet. "You idle sons of pigs. You come to our country for money and to fill your fat bellies. But work is too much for you."

The *moolah*'s great chest heaved and his splayed knuckles flexed over his rifle butt. From behind him a young scarred Baluchi spat accurately at the bedu and the clearing crackled with tension.

I moved around between the men and looked up at the *moolah*.

"Allah has no place for violence. Why do you shout at each other?"

The man glared over my head at the bedu but little Ali muttered clearly.

"The Baluchis will not keep sentry. They say it is for us to do."

I gave the *moolah* a rupee from my pocket telling him to toss

47

it. This did not work for it transpired neither group had heard of tossing coins and all looked at me askance. Taking the bull by the horns I told the *moolah* to watch the east and the dark bedu to watch the west for an hour after which they would be succeeded by mixed roster.

The two bedu looked sullen and moved off together into the dark but the Baluchis seemed happy enough. Ali, who could write after a fashion, made out a duty list and we slept.

In the morning my body glistened with sticky sweat for the breeze had gone long before dawn and the humidity was uncomfortable. Flies came with the first light and whined about my net. The Arabs were already up. Ali brought me tea and fried *chupatti* dripping ghee. I felt dirty and lethargic. The flies, especially the smaller ones, bit the skin leaving red spots.

Not long after dawn we pressed further up the *wadi*. The going was slow for boulders the size of mosques had been strewn about the riverbed like marbles by the force of the last flood. Even so the touch of moving air was a relief in the muggy heat.

Searching for the sheikh of the village Jahi Yadah, clearly shown on my map, I drew a blank and later, in the tiny hamlet of Mudayrah, the *qahdi* or local judge, assured us there was no such place but that Al Badeyah, a thriving community of thirty souls, lay where the mythical map-name should have been.

After this I treated the army maps with as much distrust as the local guides.

Some of the villages showed signs of past riches but now sheltered a single family slowly wasting away with malnutrition. In such places we were welcomed as politely as in the homes of the wealthy. At Mazra 'Ain, no more than a clump of withered palms by a filthy pool, a toothless hag proffered two pomegranates and a cup of green water. Her husband, thin as a stick insect, was too weak to greet us but mouthed the customary *Tafuddel* 'You are our guests. Eat what we have.'

At each palm oasis, the Land Rovers drew up and I followed the Arabs into the trees. The Baluchis seemed content to stay and guard the vehicles for the local people eyed them with open dislike.

The head *Walis* would come from their homes to greet us outside the house of the *qahdi*. The holy men too arrived wearing round white turbans, the symbol of their Koranic wisdom.

48

Qara goatherd

Medical treatment

Qara woodmen await their turn for arms search outside the
wire of Salalah

Qara woman

My information file grew for there was no restraint in the answering of questions until we came to the narrow valley of Zayyan which led deep into the Sharqeeya towards the forgotten port of Sur.

Once a haven for the pirates of the Arabian Sea and the world's greatest slaving centre, Sur sleeps now in a permanent stench of putrefying fish save when the season of the violent Suri wind boils the sea about the port from midnight until midday.

The last slave escaped from Sur in 1950 but the bearded nomads of the Sharqeeya have changed little in their warlike ways since their fathers raped Africa to swell the harems of Omani-ruled Zanzibar with nubile Abyssinian girls and pretty eunuchs from Buganda.

They watched us from the *wadi* cliffs in silent groups high on their she-camels. Five-foot muzzle-loaders hung from their shoulders. Six-inch soft lead bullets held by criss-cross bandoliers of goat leather puffed out their scrawny chests.

It was evening at Zayyan and word of our coming had gone before us.

The *wadi* was a hundred yards across or less and filled with men. Some rode on donkeys, others stood in silent groups resting their hands on the hilt of the *khanja* knife that hung low from every belt and centrally between the thighs in a phallic curve of silver.

At every village shouts of greeting had reached us from the palms before we entered. At Zayyan there was hostile silence and Abdullah cautioned me to stop well short of the boundary trees. The men shook out across the valley with their guns, the two bedu scaling the southern cliff with a bren gun.

The Zayyani were not impressed and none replied when Abdullah hailed them. I counted eighty or more armed with everything from flintlocks to Martini Henri rifles and a few young men with Mark 4 Lee Enfields like our own.

Abdullah glanced at me and I at him. He licked his lips and smiled unconvincingly.

"What do you like us to do, Sahb?" His English was not as immaculate as usual.

"What's the normal form when this sort of thing happens, Abdullah?" He seemed non-plussed so I added, "Just tell them we're friends and want to ask them some questions on behalf of the Sultan."

This he apparently did and by the length of his oration added some friendly remarks of his own, by one of which I understood that we were but the first unit of an entire regiment coming up the valley.

A thick-set villain in a mauve *dishdash* shouted back at Abdullah emphasising his words with much shaking of his rifle. Others joined in furiously. Tempers were rising. Abdullah turned to me.

"Sahb, these are bad people. They say they will answer no questions, nor do they want Sultanate dogs on their land for their only sheikh is Al Harthi who hates the Sultan. I think, Sahb, we would do well to end our patrol at this place for these people are not worth our time and trouble."

Abdullah offered this advice with panache, his rifle resting in the crook of his arm and his right hand tucked elegantly into his belt with its little finger protruding at an angle, like the little fingers of tea-drinking ladies at Women's Institute functions.

Not wishing to cause a confrontation and being unsure of the Zayyani strength I agreed that we should go no further but, to impress them with our superior firepower, I told Abdullah to arrange some shooting practice close by. This clearly pleased the men for even the Baluchis brightened up and there was much noisy cocking of weapons.

A cliffbound area was cleared of goats and two empty oil drums placed a hundred yards from the vehicles.

The ten riflemen, including the drivers and signaller, somehow managed to loose off fifty rounds between them without hitting either drum.

A crowd of Zayyanis had gathered close by and growing mutters on a jeering note began to make me regret my decision to demonstrate our proficiency.

There were still the three bren guns and these I knew could not fail to damage the drums. Abdullah's fire orders rang out clearly and the Zayyanis were silenced. A wild burst of fire issued from the bedu's bren and whisps of rockdust rose along a wide ledge some twenty feet above the oildrums. Ricochets pinged above us and the Zayyanis ducked in alarm. The bedu were jubilant, the more so when they noticed that the other two brens had jammed.

In desperation Abdullah ordered the mortar to fire smoke bombs. After much fiddling with the fuse setting which was clearly beyond the ken of the mortar crew, two bombs were fired in quick succession. The chosen elevation was evidently wrong for both bombs flew over the cliffs and out of sight. They were effective none the less for a great hubbub arose and a flock of woolly black goats stampeded in a dust cloud, descending to the riverbed and trampling through the gardens of the Zayyanis.

The men withdrew to the Land Rovers in high fettle quite unabashed by the undamaged oildrums and the derisive sneers of the villagers.

God help us in Dhofar I thought.

We motored on after dusk to put distance between ourselves and the Zayyanis, camping beyond Ghiyazah. Somewhere behind us the beat of village drums throbbed during the night and Murad killed another goat.

There remained the oasis of Hindarut to check before we returned to Bidbid and Abdullah counselled an early start in case the Zayyanis should outflank us and await our coming further down the *wadi*.

At Hindarut the people knew of our meeting with the Zayyanis.

"Bad folk," said the *Wali*, leading us to his wattle house, "you did well to turn back for the Sons of Al Harthi are murderous and you are few."

The *Wali*'s sons laid out two thick Baluchi carpets beneath the palms. Elders of the village came through the gardens and as each arrived we all arose to shake their hands. After an hour thirty villagers had joined the circle and my haunches were growing tired with the ceremony. Everyone carried their rifle and wore their bandolier but the atmosphere was friendly.

The women of the *Wali* nagged him from behind a screen where they prepared the food. They must not be seen by strangers so the *Wali*'s sons brought plates of fruit and *halwah* — which is the Omani rendering of Turkish Delight. The food as always crawled with insects and the black and yellow *dibbee* date wasps whose needles ever flickered in and out from their abdomens. The larger flies rose in swarms from the faeces about the huts and settled on the plates of fruit.

I had no appetite but refused nothing the Arabs passed me with their sticky hands for the watchful eye of Abdullah was upon me. We sat barefoot on the carpet with legs tucked underneath us so that the soles of our feet could not point at another man – for this would be an insult to a Muslim. I found this position uncomfortable.

At length Abdullah flicked me with his camel stick and, nodding at the *Wali*, I began the questions.

How many inhabitants, goats, *falaj* drains, troublemakers etc. did the village of Hindarut contain?

Much argument between the elders followed each question but finally all answers were agreed upon, complaints were made and noted and Ali Nasser presented our visiting cards to the *Wali*. These were reams of recruiting pamphlets exhorting the sons of the villagers to join the Army. As in all the other villages, the *Wali* and the elders promised faithfully to send their sons straight to the nearest army camp once the date harvest was over. Response to the pamphlets was in reality rare, possibly because in many a village there was no one who could read the contents.

Coffee was poured to guests in order of importance. I came after all the others, for being a *Nasrani* or Christian I rated lower than the poorest Muslim. This was not always the case and in villages of the Sunni sect, less strict than the Ibahdi Muslims, I came higher on the coffee list than even the *Wali*.

Afterwards the sick people came to the Land Rover. We had First Aid satchels but no medical orderly.

A grey-beard with puffy eyelids thrust his face close to me to show his ailment. Pressing his thumb against the corner of his eye he forced a surprising amount of white pus to exude from beneath his lower eyelid. This he repeated with the other eye and I felt queasy, unlike the soldiers who gathered around laughing.

"Give him an Aspirin and he'll be happy," shouted Murad.

There was Optrex in the satchel so I squeezed some into the loose sacs below the man's eyes once I had swabbed most of the poison away. Quite what was wrong with the old fellow's eyes I was uncertain but the population was evidently riddled with trachoma. Even the younger folk were affected, usually in only one eye which was glassy and grey like faded marble.

"Many hundreds of people go blind every year," said Abdullah, "there is nothing to be done about it. To God be the praise."

The filth-carrying flies buzzed everywhere, massing at the backsides of naked babies, crawling around the lips and eyes of children who scarcely blinked. Certainly they never bothered to swat them off. The same flies that visited the suppurating sores of the ever-present pi-dogs.

The racking cough of tuberculosis-ridden lungs was common. Enlarged spleens and other signs of malaria and chronic anaemia were apparent: leprosy was endemic with no enforced segregation of the scaly sufferers.

Oman is larger than Syria, Jordan and the Lebanon strung together yet there were only three hospitals in all the land and eight out of every ten babies died within ten months of conception.

"Why are there so few hospitals, Abdullah? I've never seen such sickness. Something should surely be done about it?"

Abdullah was not impressed.

"The Government have more pressing matters and not too much money. Anyway this is a poor area, Sahb, with miserable people. Illness comes to those who sin." Abdullah was not concentrating: a slim girl of twelve was watching us, her long brown legs shapely beneath the knee-length cotton blouse. Tresses of black hair fell in disarray around an impish face and she fingered her small but shapely breasts quite unselfconsciously.

Abdullah sighed, licking his lips, as always it seemed when gripped with emotion.

"*Al Hamdu lillah*, the Prophet be praised. The Koran says that Heaven is a blissful place where there are gardens and vineyards and girls with firm but swelling breasts of the same age as oneself," he mused and added smiling, "I think, therefore, the sooner I get there the better."

We left the Wadi Tayyin and I never went back. It was a place of beauty and mystery tucked away in a cruel withered land. Our return to Bidbid was the end of a vivid dream. Back to oil pipes and bustle from a place where progress meant nothing and time had stopped for eight hundred years.

I felt confused for a mounting frustration gripped me in those early days. The evidence of my eyes suggested the British were bolstering a corrupt regime where the Sultan and his chosen few

53

lived sumptuously enjoying the first fruits of oil wealth whilst the mass of Omanis lived out their narrow lives in squalor and illness benefiting not at all from the culling of their country's riches.

The Government was doing nothing and planning nothing beyond the confines of Muscat and Muttrah towns. Content that the age-old conservatism of the Ibahdi system would continue to strangle all strivings for change, to smother all revolutionary mutterings, Sultan Said bin Taimur seemed determined only to perpetuate the medieval gloom of Oman. And here I was volunteering my services to the military machine that upheld the old man in denying eight hundred thousand Omanis their rightful inheritance; the benefits of human progress, hospitals and schools; an opportunity for knowledge and experience.

Within the Oman, away from the larger towns at any rate, things were quiet enough. People did not know what they were missing of life and the *Walis* feared change as a threat to their authority. But even the poorest Omanis would soon be able to buy the cheap transistor radios now available from Asian traders on the coast and then the seeds of discontent would spread.

All around us the Arab world was in ferment from Egypt to Jordan, from the Sudan to the Yemen. Oil was changing life radically for our nearest neighbours in Kuweit and the Trucial Coast. Until now the Persian Gulf, the Indian Ocean and the great seas of sand to the west had absorbed the shock waves of Arab militancy buffering Oman against contagion. But the Voice of Cairo and Aden Radio were now beamed east and north at a thousand megawatts and the invisible voice of sedition bounced down through the outer ether to a swelling band of avid listeners in the wattle *barusti* huts of Oman.

"... Throw off the harness of British Imperialism. Take the wealth that is yours but is stolen by the Sultan. Why does he hide from you amongst his harem in distant Dhofar? Because he is ashamed that he has betrayed the Omanis. See what we revolutionaries have done in the People's Republic of Yemen. Here there are schools for our children, hospitals for the sick. With the help of our Russian and Chinese brothers we are building a great future for our people. The road to success is revolt. Our programme will show you how to achieve such success. Tomorrow at the same time Said Masoul, leader of the gallant Omani freedom fighters here in Aden, will speak to you . . ."

I became friendly with Staff Sergeant Abdullah and together we planned the rehabilitation of Recce Platoon into a force of fighting men to be reckoned with. Often in the furnace-heat of the summer evenings we would walk among the palms of Fanjah and he would tell me of the rantings of the local transistor-fuelled revolutionaries. For a while the rumoured conspiracies continued to be vague and disorganised but Abdullah confessed he was worried. There were things he did not understand, he said, but I felt he was hiding much from me. His loyalties perhaps were confused and divided. What, after all, could he say to defend policies that denied his own people a better life; policies about which he himself must be as doubtful as I was.

For two hundred years the Sultan's family, the Albu Saeedi, had ruled wisely from Muscat, surviving the loss of the richest slaving empire in the world. But without slavery and its emporium of Zanzibar, Oman had become inward-looking, eking a living from dates and one million pounds a year from their old friends the British. Without adequate funds no Sultan, however well meaning, could do much for his people.

In the early 1960s the Sultan said to his American friend Doctor Wendell Phillips, "Wendell, just think what I can do for my people when we have oil. The conditions in Oman inherited from the past are not my fault but if I have the means and yet do not improve my people and my country then I should be ashamed for did not the Prophet say 'A King is God's shadow upon earth'?"

But now the Sultan had received mounting oil revenues for three years and still no whisper of progress had reached the Interior. There were vague plans for electricity and water along the coast; for a deep water harbour at Muttrah might please the local merchants who would benefit from such schemes. But reasons of humanity alone dictated that a hospital or two should come first; something to show the populace that their invisible Sultan had their interests at heart, so that they could at least reply to the agitators, "Well, he's trying. We have a new hospital and when the oil flows faster he has promised us another."

The longer the old man cut himself off from the people and the richer the Oil Company's wired-off European compound

55

near Muscat became—with its swimming pools and seaside chalets—the more vexed the Omanis grew.

The People's Front for the Liberation of the Occupied Arabian Gulf (PFLOAG) were well satisfied and no month passed by without their agents entering the Oman by *dhow* boats along the sandy coast of the Batinah. Well trained in subversion, they came from centres in Kuweit, Egypt and Syria and returned to their own Omani villages. After a suitable period they made their way to certain allotted tasks. Some to the Oman Army's recruiting centre at Ghubra to join the Army, others to Muscat and Muttrah to infiltrate the fledgling labour forces, yet others to Nizwa, Rostaq, Sur and Izki where they began to form cells under the noses of the Army garrisons there. These cells received arms shipments from the coast on appointed dates which they cached in caves or buried deep in the houses of well-respected Omanis.

How much of this Abdullah knew I could not tell but he became a worried man and, towards the end of July, said he would have to leave the Army. Our training of the men was not going well, partly because of the heat, in excess of 120° Fahrenheit at midday, and Abdullah promised to stay for three more months until my Arabic improved and I might manage without him.

The Colonel of the Muscat Regiment was a polo playing Grenadier officer and a personal friend of the Duke of Edinburgh. For a hobby he wrote plays, but he was very down to earth. Nothing escaped his eagle eye, and he was fair to all so that old sweats like Major John Cooper respected him and the soldiers served him well. I was summoned to his office on the 1st of August.

He smiled from behind wire rimmed spectacles.

"Sit down Ranulph." He was a chain smoker and inhaled deeply from a duty-free cigarette. "You're to fly south tomorrow and join the Northern Frontier Regiment for a month. They are short of officers and you could do with the experience before I let you loose with our Recce Platoon. Things are hotting up down there, so be careful. David Bayley will also be going."

The following day we flew south beyond the Hajar over a gravel desert that shimmered without a shadow for five hundred miles to the unmarked border of Dhofar.

4

THE Beaver was white but for the blood red symbol of crossed Omani daggers. I tightened my safety belt as the plane juddered violently in a depression. Far below, the desert, shapeless for the last two hours, squirmed under a moving heat haze and took on nightmarish contours where the arteries of a dry watershed split its surface. Gravel hills rose to high mesa plateaux and suddenly a ruler-straight line of cloud moved below us hiding the ground.

For a second, too quick to be sure, I saw a fringe of intense green between the gravel plateaux and the cloud. The pilot spoke over the intercom.

"We're over the Qara *jebel* now. It's green as England below the clouds but not as friendly." He chuckled and switched to VHF for landing instructions from RAF Salalah.

Southern Arabia from Aden to Muscat is a featureless waste but for outcrops of barren mountain and small oases. Yet through a quirk of nature thirty miles of Dhofar's mountains and its maritime plain of Salalah are an exception. Here there are jungles, lagoons, and grassy downs. From June until September the south-west monsoon winds blow over the Indian Ocean from Africa. Skirting Somaliland and brushing Socotra they are sucked against the Qara hills by the vacuum of the scorching deserts beyond. These *khareef* clouds release up to fifteen inches of rain onto the mountains annually so that rivers surge into the *wadi* beds and waterfalls dash 1,000 feet over sheer cliffs.

For a hundred years Omani Sultans have ruled Dhofar as a province but their authority seldom reached into the Qara mountains where the tribes were usually at war. Only Salalah Plain was secure, a flat and fertile region nine miles wide and thirty long. An RAF airstrip and an Omani Army camp lie a mile north of sprawling Salalah protecting the coastal city and its palace against guerrilla attacks from the Qara mountains.

The mountains stretch west from Salalah for seventy miles to the border of the east Aden Protectorate, now called the People's Republic of Southern Yemen. To the east they vanish in cloud where the Samhan Range towers over Mirbat, the only village of any size. Beyond the Samhan Range, Dhofar's nebulous border melts with Oman somewhere about the sands of Cape Sharbithat. In all Dhofar is 38,000 square miles, roughly the size of Wales.

Just off the coast of Oman the low grey island of Masirah wallows like a dead whale.

Over a hundred years ago the ruling Sultan of Oman signed a Friendship Treaty with Britain that still exists. As a result of this Oman has enjoyed British military aid ever since and allows the RAF facilities on the island of Masirah and on Salalah Plain.

The Masirah airstrip is vital, especially since Aden and all other Middle East staging posts of the sixties are no longer available to the RAF. 208 Squadron Hawker Hunter fighters, Victor V-bombers, Nimrod nuclear submarine hunters and many other aeroplanes sprayed khaki and green, spatter the Masirah runways. A powerful radio transmitter, key link to the BBC Far East service is also housed at Masirah.

The Salalah airbase, once busy as a Second World War transit post, is no longer needed by the RAF and serves only as an embarrassment and unnecessary expense to Northwood and Whitehall.

But Sultan Said bin Taimur had every reason for wanting the RAF to keep the Salalah airstrip open. So long as his own tiny air force — (in 1968 he had only two small fighters in Dhofar) — were safely housed and maintained, any guerrilla attack on Salalah would be a risky affair since the plain was featureless with nowhere to hide from air attack.

So the wily old man allowed the RAF the use of Masirah Island only on condition that they maintained the Salalah base too. An added bonus to the Sultan was the assurance, that should the guerrillas attack Salalah, the British would send aid if only by way of ensuring the safety of RAF personnel.

Easing low over the sea and the chequered green of Salalah our Beaver landed neatly by the hangars. A camouflaged Land Rover without doors or hood drew up by the plane. The driver and another man wore faded khaki streaked with green dye. Each carried a Sterling submachine gun slung by their waist. A loaded magazine was taped in reverse to the magazine already clipped into each gun so that sixty-four nickel nosed 9 mm rounds were immediately available. Neat leather sheaths hid the metal of their wristwatches and dappled green *shemaghs* covered their heads, the loose ends hanging about their shoulders. Their arms were darkly tanned. Dust filmed their goggles and everything else in the vehicle.

I thought they were Arabs but David Bayley muttered, "Embryonic Lawrences. I wonder if they all wear fancy dress down here."

The driver pointed behind him with his thumb.

"Shove your things in the back. We'll take you to Umm al Ghawarif camp. It's a couple of miles from here."

Outside the barbed wire of the airfield we bounced along in a dustcloud keeping clear of the dirt-track.

"Mines," the driver shouted. "They lay them by night. Mark 7 anti-tank mines left behind in Aden by Harold Wilson. They make a nasty mess of a Land Rover."

There were sandbags under our seats and on the floor of the front compartment. Scant comfort, I thought, and squeezed my thighs together involuntarily.

Ruins, tombs and single pillars with inscriptions sped by grouped in clusters half covered by acacia and, a mile south, the coconut palms of Salalah—all seen in a fleeting glimpse through the dust.

Umm al Ghawarif camp, headquarters of the Army in Dhofar, had a functional look about it. Searchlights in towers on stilts, barbed wire, and shallow trenches along the perimeter.

Soldiers, dressed like our driver, moved about the camp with purpose. Bedford 3-ton lorries laden with ammunition crates passed us on their way to a tiny airstrip just beyond the wire and Pakistani mechanics battered mangled vehicles back into shape in an open workshop.

It was as breathlessly hot as Oman but not so humid and a fitful breeze from the sea fanned the dusty camp.

The driver's ample belly wobbled as he drew to a halt, spilling out of his open shirt. He unwound his headcloth and lit up a briar pipe. His nose was beaked and very large. A good natured type, I judged by his lazy grin.

"I'm Bill Prince, Second-in-Command of B Company Northern Frontier Regiment, to which you're both attached for a month. We're very glad to have you though I must say your bunch of recently arrived chaps aren't too popular down here after the incident a fortnight ago."

He told us that a Captain from the Queen's Royal Irish Hussars, who had come to Oman with us, had been treating his men with open disdain. "Not cruel or anything, just the wrong attitude," said Bill, "it may have worked with the Paddies or the Hussars but it sparked the Arabs right up their spines and they hated him."

The final straw had come on the overland route to Dhofar when the Hussar officer had been cleaning his pistol at a night halt.

"Somehow he banged the gun off by mistake," Bill told us, "and blew the Mess boy's head to bits, poor chap."

I wasn't quite sure whether Bill Prince was sympathetic to the officer or the Mess boy. The former, he said, had been sent back to England for the boy's relatives were legally entitled to kill him to avenge the death of their kin. Unless they preferred the alternative of accepting blood money in lieu of the Irish officer's life.

Prince and the other officers we met over the next week were keen, slick and efficient. All spoke the fluent *geysh* Arabic of the Army and some spoke Urdu as well although many of the Baluchis could understand Omani. Security was tight; Company convoys left quietly by night, the lorries easing out of the camp gates without lights. They moved slowly for noise carried to the mountains nine miles away warning the guerrillas to be wary.

The Colonel of the Northern Frontier Regiment, Mike Harvey, was a very different kettle of fish to our own gentle colonel. He operated his four Companies on a close leash with an iron fist. He was an expert at counter-guerrilla warfare and his hobby was karate. He had achieved Brown Belt standard and was known by his officers as Oddjob, though not to his face. Serving with the Gloucesters in Korea he had won the Military Cross by taking his Company out of the Imjin River trap by a frontal assault on the Chinese. The rest of the Gloucesters were killed or imprisoned.

Colonel Harvey hated communists and his tactics in Dhofar were described as ruthless by many officers in the other two regiments. To begin with I thought so myself.

B Company had three fighting platoons. All were mixed though mainly Baluchi and the manpower was chronically under strength due to the date harvest in Oman. Once the dates were ripe, many soldiers took leave to help their families cull their only source of income for the year. David Bayley and I were each attached to a platoon, issued with camouflage clothing, three blankets and an old bolt-action Mark 5 ·303 rifle with a hundred rounds in bandoliers and a green headcloth. Also a set of maps of the mountains, quite unlike any maps I had seen before, being 0·63 inches to a mile. There were very few place names and most of those that there were had the words 'Position Approximate' or simply a question mark, in brackets beside them.

By day, when the dank monsoon mists wrapped the plain, the B Company lorries left Umm al Ghawarif camp. Our work was simple, being part of the Colonel's policy to gain intelligence and subdue the local people into refusing aid to the guerrillas. The more patrols I accompanied, the more convinced I became that neither purpose was being achieved. If anything those tribesmen as yet uncommitted were being driven to hate the Army and the Sultan we served.

As the mists grew thicker and a ceaseless summer drizzle drenched the plain, more bedu came down from the mountains where, tough as they were, they found conditions difficult. The monsoon tics drove a man crazy unless he sat all day in a smoke filled cave. By night the mosquitoes settled in millions and the rain, much heavier than the drizzle of the plain, turned the hilltop soil to mush.

In the damp humidity of the mists, it grew noticeably cooler as summer passed by and soldiers fell ill with racking coughs and chest colds. Life was not easy for the bedu, and we did not help since every able male who might conceivably be guerrilla material was taken back to Umm al Ghawarif camp without ceremony and interned for questioning. They might be imprisoned for a few days or for weeks before the Intelligence Officer was satisfied and released them to find their own way back to their families and cattle.

Whilst they were absent, many of their families came close to starvation.

The bedu men collected loads of wood from the mountains. These they took by camel to Salalah where there was no wood suitable for burning. In exchange the bedu obtained enough flour and other basic commodities for their families to live on. Whilst the men were away with the wood the women cared for the camels and goats, keeping them free from the killer flies. Young camels were especially vulnerable at this time for their eyes were eaten out by the flies unless the bedu women were vigilant. Often they lashed sacking over the young camels' heads as they lay hobbled and groaning beside the tattered tents of their owners.

Our plain patrols soon became routine. Spreading out across a chosen *wadi*-bed the platoon moved quietly along its meandering course with the machine gunners on the cliffs that rimmed either side of the *wadi*.

Coming to a cave dwelling the men closed around it in the mist as I moved into the centre with the Sergeant and three men. After a careful search for arms with a mine detector, all males of an age to handle a rifle were herded back to the lorry. Once it was loaded to its limit and the area thoroughly checked, we returned to Umm al Ghawarif to hand the bewildered bedu over to the guards. If belligerent, or suspect in any way, they were hammered into leg irons and chains. Otherwise they joined the queue awaiting interrogation; their accommodation a large dilapidated marquee festooned with coils of barbed wire.

After a few patrols I came to know one or two of the Sergeants by name. Seramad was negroid and built like a post. He was gentle with the bedu and liked to chat to the young girls in the caves when their men had been removed. Sometimes he spent many minutes at this self-appointed task and I noticed his men tittering amongst themselves when he returned. Mahmoud was smaller, squat and beardless; probably a fourth generation Omani Baluch. Quick and sharp, he treated the bedu as cattle. Like most of the Baluchis he believed that every man, woman and child from the *jebel*, or mountain, tribes was a terrorist.

The guerrillas might well have been crushed a long time past through genocide by the Army had the officers been Baluchis. But there had been an air of sport and chivalry about the Dhofar campaign since the earliest troubles in 1964, and the guerrilla movement had spread without firm Army reaction. As late as 1968 the overall commander of the Sultan's Army wrote a letter to the Colonel in Dhofar saying:

'For rebels, as for ducks, we need cunning and good shooting.'

But the Army's list of dead and wounded had lately become alarming. The game was turning sour and a new mood came to the Dhofar garrison with Colonel Harvey. Soon after he arrived in the spring of 1968 he applied killing rules that were sent out to the tribal sheikhs by runner.

In his 'Emergency Regulations Dhofar', Colonel Harvey announced that all people from the Yemen would be directed back there by October 26th after which date the border would be closed. Tracks, wells and passes at the frontier would be blown up where possible and a curfew would apply throughout Dhofar after dark. Soldiers could thereafter fire at and kill any armed man seen to run away – without first challenging him. This also applied to armed groups of three or more men and anyone seen with a Russian SKS rifle, a mine, mortar or machine gun.

During the first week of August we searched the winding Wadi Sahilnawt, well east of Salalah and easily found by the high cliffs that fringe it. When the sun touches these cliffs they stand out pink or golden and visible from far across the plain.

But through the monsoon mists they brooded sombre grey above the *wadi* and in their lower reaches we found a double-tiered cave crawling with bedu. Camel thorn fences lined the bottom half of the cavern in which at least a hundred cows jostled for standing room, coughing in the acrid fumes of a dung fire. Their pale brown skin hung loosely over their ribs so that their haunches, it seemed, must burst through at the least pressure; flies fed on their many open sores despite the smoke. Above the cattle, jutting slabs of rock formed a perch for some twenty or thirty bedu, mostly children. Four women with babies squatted crooning about an old woman lying in rags; a living carcass as emaciated as the corpses of Belsen. Soon they would take her away to a rock shelf in her tatters, her only belongings, and pile rocks against her to keep the vultures and hyenas away.

There appeared to be no men, only the four young women and a filthy tangle of children. Their eyes were luminous in the gloom, frightened and hungry. Sergeant Mahmoud spoke sharply to the women who chattered shrilly back.

He translated, "Their menfolk are in the *jebel* to collect wood. Their cows give them only a little milk and they will not kill them for meat because they have no other wealth."

There was a medical orderly with the platoon. I asked if the women would like the doctor but they were strangely reluctant and fell silent, seeming to wish us gone.

This set Mahmoud's mind at work and he had his soldiers search the cave behind and under the cows.

"Why don't they graze their cows on the new monsoon grass?" I asked the Sergeant, "then their milk yield would improve."

"They say they have already lost five cows because of the grass. Before the monsoon came the cows were thin for lack of grazing. Now it seems their bellies swell and burst if they eat the fresh grass."

There was a shout from above.

"Hey, Sahb. An old man and a youth."

It was Seramad from the far side of the cave. He had climbed into the upper 'room' to fondle a little girl with long black curls. In the dark recesses, piled high with goat dung, his sharp eyes had spotted movement.

Two soldiers clambered up scattering the children and dragged out an elderly man and a boy. Both were sullen and said nothing. They are proud, I thought, despite their rags and the stench of their bodies.

The soldiers took them to the lorries. Two of the young women approached me. They were distraught and clung to my shirt. Both talked at once and I understood none of their bird-like chatter. Mahmoud detached them roughly.

He said, "These women say we cannot take the men away for they will all die if there is no one to collect wood for Salalah and buy food. Also they say that bag of bones there is the old man's wife and that soon she will die. Without him."

As we left, the silent huddle of bedu children stared after us until the mist obscured them like the passing of a bad dream.

There was a sour taste in my mouth. Back at the Mess I drank two brandies with ginger; normally I drank only soft drinks. It was not just the muggy weather and the oppressive mists that hung all and every day over the camp and the plain. I was sick inside, hating myself as much as the Colonel and the others.

Analysing my feelings, I failed to see why we, the British, should be meddling in Dhofar in the first place. The tribes had warred and feuded since time immemorial. Why not let them carry on? If Musallim bin Nuffl and his rebels existed—and I'd not seen or heard a sign of them—why not let the Sultan deal with them as his forefathers had dealt with former rebels over the years—with a handful of Omani guards. Did the British consider what to my mind was a rotten repressive regime better than letting the locals sort out their own petty rebellion? If so, what was the reason behind it? All the oil was to the north in Oman and Muscat, not here in Dhofar. Nor did the RAF station warrant our involvement in the war since a small garrison within the airstrip perimeter should suffice to hold off any terrorist attack. We were only increasing the misery and poverty of the Dhofari people. We gave them nothing and the Sultan was openly determined to keep all development from Dhofar. To him Dhofaris were no better than animals. In 1966 some of them had tried to shoot him and ever since he had turned his back on them with ruthless obstinacy. For all he cared they could starve to death in thousands like their cattle.

The whole affair stank and I resolved to resign from the Sultan's Forces without delay. I had come to the Sultan's Army in ignorance of the true state of affairs. But now that the situation was unpleasantly clear to my conscience I had no wish to stay on. It was not as straightforward as that, however, for the thought soon came to me that others might well mistake my reasons for leaving.

In the Mess I had heard talk of other officers who'd suddenly terminated their service in Dhofar and they were referred to with ridicule. They had been cowards or so the gossips implied. Such talk spread quickly beyond Dhofar to regimental Messes in Britain and Germany. Also it would be awkward since I had just signed on for a two-year attachment: I could picture the faces of the others in the Royal Scots Greys were I to go bouncing back from 'romantic' Oman after only two months.

So I decided to delay things for a while; probably until my month's detachment from the Muscat Regiment was over. To leave from the more peaceful environment of the north would smell less of desertion.

In the evenings the officers at Umm al Ghawarif dined well on largely local fare. Barracuda steaks, pink and meaty, fresh lobster thermidor, crisp fruit and vegetables. The cook was a cheerful Goan who waddled between his pots paternally patting the backsides of the Omani Mess boys who served the food wearing white *dishdashes*, green turbans and waist sashes.

Afterwards there were stacks of back copies of British news-papers and *Playboy Magazines* to remind us of what was not to be had in Dhofar, and as often as not, a game of poker. But twice a week we left dinner early as the pallid monsoon moon dis-appeared altogether. Changing quickly after coffee I would prime the grenades which I kept in my pen-tray, two Number 36 Mills bombs with five-second fuses and a Number 83 white phosphorus grenade. These clipped onto a waistbelt beside the ammunition bandoliers. An oiled green polo-neck sweater kept me warm beneath my combat jacket during these night patrols, but only until soon after midnight, when the drizzle penetrated both and I began to shiver like the soldiers in their thin khaki shirts and smocks.

Our ambushes were sited deep within the foothills amongst camel thorn bushes and man-high clay ant-hills. Bedu 'villages' clustered in clearings in these foothills. All knew the terms of the curfew so any man who moved into or out of the villages by night must be of the *adoo*.

Such villages were not easy to find and there were few reliable guides. Bill Prince knew the plain as well as anyone and he would lead the Company after leaving the lorries well away from the mountains. We would move slowly for four hours to the scrub line where the ground began to rise. For an hour then we groped further into the brush cursing the long sharp thorns that gripped headcloths, tore at the skin and threatened the eyes. We slipped and skidded on the wet clay and made sure to keep the man ahead visible a yard in front. And always, when morning came through the mists, Bill Prince somehow knew where we were in the featureless land of ant-hills. Shivering and stifling coughs the soldiers would uncurl from their wet blankets, shoulder their rifles, and passing hand signals from man to man, close around the village clearing which, miraculously enough, was never far from our ambush site.

We came one particularly miserable morning to an open kraal. There were rifle shots as we cleared the bushes and I climbed an ant-hill to see ahead for the sound was muffled in the mist; the location of its source confused.

"Get down, you bloody fool," David Bayley hissed at me. He had thrown himself instantly behind the cover of a hillock, peering through the bushes with binoculars. His reflexes were controlled after three years in the Yemen killing Egyptians, avoiding their traps and surviving despite the frequent bombing of his cave headquarters with deadly nerve agents and blister gases.

There was no further firing and the men closed in to search the bush *rondaavals*. The portioned meat and entrails of a freshly butchered goat lay among some rocks close by the huts and a soldier found two spent ·303 cases in the mud.

But the *adoo* were gone. Somehow they had melted through the mist avoiding detection by the cordon. All the male villagers were arrested but no weapons were found beyond the usual vintage Martini Henris and a rusty matchlock.

Beyond and above the ant-hills where the gloom grew denser and the foothills rose to silent crags, an army could pass by and we would be none the wiser.

I noticed that the men were much happier at the sight of the empty ·303 cases—the sign that only locally recruited 'militia' were about, not fully fledged guerrillas. In such close bush country, even more than in the open, we were at a great disadvantage to the guerrillas, who were all armed with the latest fully automatic Russian rifles, which could fire twenty bullets accurately in a few seconds.

In any sudden contact it is the side with the greatest initial firepower that comes off best. All our rifles were bolt-action ·303s which had to be cocked after each shot. This had a very dampening effect on the soldiers' morale.

I watched Bill Prince closely during patrols to learn from his experience and maybe from his mistakes. His Arabic was fluent, as heavily accented and as totally devoid of grammar as the soldiers' own patois. I watched how he handled the men and the Sergeants, Arab and Baluch, how he controlled seventy men in thick bush by night, and a hundred other minor things that I might need to know in the days ahead.

5

THE guerrilla camp at Hauf was just inside South Yemen territory, six miles from the Dhofar border. Here Ahmad al Ghassani was now in command. Two years ago he had been one of hundreds of newly trained Marxist Dhofari guerrillas, but now he was their leader and the great nationalist Musallim bin Nuffl, original father of the rebellion was nothing. Al Ghassani had attached himself to tribes who were traditionally hostile to the tribe of bin Nuffl. Old hostilities had come to the fore within the Dhofar Liberation Front when bin Nuffl, based in Saudi Arabia, had admitted that his revolution was purely nationalist and had refused to accept overt aid from communist sources. He had said that he would be quite content if the Sultan would let him and his group back into Salalah to take part in the government and lift the social restrictions now in force. Then he, bin Nuffl, would stop his campaign and recognise the Sultan as ruler of Oman and Dhofar.

But then bin Nuffl had been badly wounded in 1966 and had languished in a Saudi hospital with many of his Bait Kathiri supporters for over a year. During this time the Qara faction, whose leaders were backed and trained by the Chinese and the Russians, had grown increasingly powerful within the liberation movement so that by 1968 bin Nuffl had been forced to stay away from Dhofar for fear of assassination.

Now al Ghassani had plans to quash the remnants of the bin Nuffl faction and to purge the guerrilla movement of all nationalists and radical Muslims, indeed of anyone whose motives were not at one with those of the Marxist class struggle.

But as well as carrying out purges and propaganda al Ghassani had other plans: now was the time for positive action when the monsoon mists covered movement. The pride of al Ghassani's arsenal were huge new guns from China which could be taken apart for transportation; each weapon took four camels or twelve men to carry it when in pieces. Now with the help of his able lieutenant Abdel Tahir, he gathered together four hundred men armed with the most modern weapons the Soviets could supply and enough camels for all his Chinese guns and made his final plans. On the first day of August the men were to split into two equal groups, each with their radios for contact. One group under al Ghassani would move down into the foothills towards the RAF camp: the other under Abdel Tahir would move over the mountains towards Mirbat.

In July I was still with the Northern Frontier Force in Dhofar at the Umm al Ghawarif camp. All day long we scoured the plain for harmless bedu so that we might take them back to be interrogated by the Intelligence Section, who badly wanted information on *adoo* intentions in time to act upon such information. Towards the end of the month, the Intelligence people began to notice a certain tension in the air, an undercurrent of trouble to come. They were unable to place a finger upon its source but indicated that the eastern towns of Taqah and Mirbat were to be attacked during the monsoon by unusually large guerrilla forces. Co-operation with the *adoo*, it seemed, was to be received from fifth columnists within the towns and the Army was advised to search both towns without delay.

To reach these towns from Salalah involved a forty-mile drive on winding dirt-tracks keeping close to the sea along most of its route but descending twice into deep clefts or wooded watercourses.

The Company, with two artillery field guns, moved east by night and threw a wide cordon around Taqah ignoring only the seaward flank where the monsoon breakers smashed against the sand and no man could survive the undertow.

I went with Seramad and his platoon through the gardens of Taqah as veins of green and yellow gave the mist a sickly life and the men moved in silence for the thunder of the sea beyond the palms deadened all sound.

The scent of flowering thorn was sharp in the gardens. On the

70

higher ground were vines and withered fig trees: we slid through patches green with wheat and vegetables. Indigo bushes, from which the tribes obtain dark blue pigment for their cloth, blotched the closely channelled fields.

A Beau Geste fort perched upon the cliff above us, appearing for a while to float on air as the mists broke about it. Its red flag drooped for there was no breeze. Some twenty *askars* formed the garrison of Taqah; all were Northern Omanis of the Beni Amr tribe and performed the duties of civil police without army aid. They received food and a good wage and were of all ages from twelve to seventy. There were similar isolated forts elsewhere in Dhofar but only two had radio contact with the Signals Centre at our army camp at Umm al Ghawarif.

Against a sophisticated enemy with the latest Russian weapons and radios, the *askars* had bolt-action rifles, minimal ammunition stocks and medieval fortresses to protect them. The reason for this was not so much a lack of available equipment as a general mistrust of the *askars* and their moral fibre in the event of their being attacked. The Army commanders thought it likely that any equipment given to the *askars* stood a good chance of falling into enemy hands.

The headman or *Wali* of the *askars* came to greet us, pleased to see the Army for he and his men were not popular in the town and there was little they could do to control the population even when they knew that *adoo* sympathisers were about taking food from the townsfolk. A show of Army strength always strengthened the *Wali's* hand. After exchanging pleasantries he left with his retinue to tour the cordon—now tight about the town. As he went a flutter of colour appeared at the upper windows of his walled house.

Seramad nudged me.

"She is truly beautiful, that one. I have seen her twice before. She has the body of an angel. Look she is watching us, Sahb." He ran his cudgel-like hands over the short fuzz of his head and pulled in his stomach.

A girl no more than thirteen moved onto the flat roof of the building and climbed the stone balustrade to relax upon it. She was lithe and tall; a negroid Lolita with full cupid lips which she licked slowly as we stared. Her fingers drummed against the roundness of her buttock and the silver bracelets around her wrist jingled an invitation.

Within the *Wali's* walled garden were three fine date palms, the only trees of their kind in Taqah and doubtless the original reason for the walls. Their foliage creaked above us forming a whispering arbor about the house and the girl who watched. I was to return there late in 1972 but then the trees bore the shreds and splintering of shrapnel and the girl the scars of soft-nosed bullets.

We left the shade of the palms and walked through the stench and garbage of narrow streets. Soldiers had already taken all the male inhabitants to open ground west of the houses, where they were herded within a hastily erected corral of barbed wire coils. Each house was searched with care in their absence as one by one they were taken to a special tent for interrogation.

Questions flowed; answers were evasive or ignorant. Some admitted having seen the guerrillas whilst collecting wood but they knew nothing about them. Money changed hands and soon it was known that large groups of armed *adoo* had moved into the mountains to the north-east of Taqah and nearby Mirbat during the past week. It was said that they were led by a man from the Al Umr tribe; but nothing was certain.

We knew that the guerrillas sent unarmed porters into Taqah and Mirbat to buy food every night yet none had been caught by the cordon.

A few days later, having learned next to nothing, we returned to our camp at Salalah.

At 07.36 hours on 7th August a Baluchi operator of the Signals Centre at Umm al Ghawarif picked up a faint but insistent message. He had recognised the callsign of Mirbat fort and the twin treble-Dah of an Operations Immediate message. For five minutes he scribbled furiously, translating the broken morse into English which he could not understand.

Five hours later a Beaver circled over Mirbat whilst the two old Provost fighters of the Sultan's air force strafed the hills around the fort. They could not see what was happening below but the Sultan's red flag still flew from the fort so cases of ammunition were parachuted, appearing to land between the fort and the sea.

B Company Commander summoned us to his office. He seemed very sober and said the Company was to move at once to Mirbat which, as far as the Army knew, was even now in the hands of the guerrillas.

Leaving a threadbare garrison in Salalah we reached Taqah late in the afternoon. A lorry overturned on the pass beyond the town and rolled over the edge scattering its load of ammunition. After a two-hour delay we continued and by dusk approached the first defile.

A smell of cordite laced the delicate scent of monsoon flowers; the track had been expertly blown up where it wound deep into the gorge. Acacia and thorn crept thickly down the ravine and intricate corridors of caves split the cliffs above. The men were uneasy but nothing moved on the face of the mountain and the detector group returned without finding a mine.

The Company Commander was suspicious of the place and there was another still deeper defile between us and Mirbat. To continue with the lorries after dark would be senseless. So we drove south to the coastline and left the vehicles in a gully.

On foot it was eleven miles to Mirbat. Fearing an ambush en route Bill Prince sent me ahead of the main body with two machine gunners and a National transceiver.

Slowly, for there was no moon, we crossed the first deep valley and I clicked the pressel switch of the National twice once we had gained the far cliffs. Bill's reply came back at once, three quiet clicks, and the Company crossed to join us. They were well trained, scarcely disturbing a rock as they climbed the loose walls.

We trudged for eight hours through the wind blown sand of the dunes, during which time we lost contact with the others and carried on without them. The crash of the monsoon surf drowned all noise, the night seemed timeless, and dawn found us at the mouth of the Wadi Mirbat.

The Company were still not to be seen so the three of us lay in a cave close by the ruins of a mosque. A few hundred yards to our front, beyond a rough patch of hillocks, the guerrillas withdrew with their dead and wounded but we could not know this. Unlike the U.S. Cavalry, we had arrived too late to cut the adoo off from the mountains.

The Company joined us after two hours. They had moved along the soggy beach itself and going had been slow.

Beyond the hillocks the scene jolted my memory. It all seemed to have happened before but perhaps only in technicolour in an English cinema.

Torn by shrapnel the Sultan's flag fluttered from the battlements of the fort. A ragged cheer rose from the turbanned *askars* along the ramparts, some throwing their rifles high and catching them, others kissing their friends. They streamed out from the wooden doors to greet us, everyone shaking hands with much emotion.

A young *askar*, twelve or thirteen years old, showed two soldiers the grisly evidence of his prowess as a fighter.

"They came right up to the fort with their ladders thinking we had no more bullets. Then I found three rounds by my bedding and rushed to the wall. I saw this *adoo* below me. Bullets came past me and my cousin Nassir was hit. But I shot the *adoo* dead with one bullet. Come and see."

Taking one of the soldiers by the hand, the boy led them close to where I stood with Sergeant Mohamed. He kicked at a huddle of cloth and instantly a cloud of flies rose buzzing. The corpse must have lain there since the first night of the attack and could hardly have been shot from directly above since the entrails were partially exposed with an entry wound in the small of the back. The stomach gases had escaped through the wound and the belly was not swollen. The lad kicked the body over with his bare foot.

"I killed two more last night but they took them away." He grinned with pride entirely unaffected by the sickening sight of the guerrilla's face—puffed and split by the heat. The flies had worked on the eyes and the wounds. I wanted to vomit for the smell was overpowering as the body slumped over.

We signalled Salalah and a Beaver arrived to remove the wounded *askars* and the dead *adoo*. The latter was tied up in a polythene sheet for there is little room in a Beaver. But the sheet was not airtight and the pilot looked unhappy as he taxied away from the flat ground beside the fort.

The *adoo* had used 3·5 rockets and 3-inch mortars. A mortar baseplate position was found on a rooftop behind the fort, evidence of collusion, so the town was cordoned off and searched for weapons or casualties.

74

My search group was guided by the *askar* who claimed to have brought first warning of the *adoo* attack to the fort. He had been down on the beach relieving himself in the moonlight when he heard a crunch of gravel by the sacred tomb of Mohamed Agyl, pirate Lord of Dhofar. A lizard perhaps in the jaws of the puff adder that lived in the graveyard? But when the furtive noises continued, he realised it was men, and men trying to remain unnoticed. Carefully he had inched crablike to the dark line of seaweed and jetsam, then rose and ran for the great wooden doors of the fort. As soon as he had told the head *Wali* what he had heard the armoury was opened, but even as the ammunition boxes were being hauled out an explosion shook the massive walls of the fort.

Proudly he told us how he had seen two men on the beach and shot one of them from the battlements. Then there must have been eighty of them in two groups carrying straight poles to use as scaling ladders. Luckily for the fort, the Sultan's Provosts had arrived on the scene before the defenders' ammunition gave out entirely.

In Mirbat town there were over three hundred houses, some mere wattle shacks, others mud brick dwellings honeycombed with dark rooms and cellars. We searched in groups of four with lanterns and mine detectors. For days afterwards I could smell the stink of the houses clinging to my skin and hair and suffered from the bites of tiny fleas and tics. There was a heady mixture of scent, frankincense, and tobacco in many rooms but it blended evilly with the stench of *oomah* sardines that lay on shelves and hung from strings in the cellars. Outside they dried in millions on the beaches, but there the smell was not so concentrated. We found beautifully carved *khanjahs* and swords, bags of silver Maria Theresa dollars dated 1780 but still used as currency in Southern Arabia. Even in the poorest houses there were chests of perfumed cotton clothes and silver ornaments of exquisite craftsmanship. Everything was kept in chests of teak or tin for there were no wardrobes, no chairs nor beds. Crude urinals shaped from clay were built into the rooftops, their waste pipes leading over the edge of the buildings.

Bags of fish bone hung from many of the walls: like the dried *oomah* they are sold to the bedu and *jebalis* to feed their camels and goats when the monsoon grass dries up.

75

We found three modern rifles, ammunition and a case containing faded photographs of Arabs in uniform together with many bundles of letters.

David Bayley had searched the *sooq* on the far side of the town. The storekeepers had a tale of misery. People were dying of malnutrition. Until recently they had bartered many goods and foodstuffs but, with the hostilities, the trading *dhows* from Aden no longer came to buy their frankincense and the skins of wild animals from the Qara mountains which they had exported since the time of their earliest ancestors.

What could they do to survive? The Sultan's chief merchant, a Pakistani named Khimji Ramdas, had promised to organise their trade but had done nothing for fear of the *adoo*. Furthermore, the shopkeepers hinted darkly, the head *Wali* of the fort and some of his *askars* were running their own small business which was why they, the rightful merchants, could seldom get permission to go to Salalah for new goods.

The search was complete by evening time and I wandered along the beach east of the town. It was little wonder that so many of the townsfolk joined or helped the *adoo*. What alternative was there? What sort of a life could they expect from a government that showed no interest in them and whose representatives were corrupt?

The beach glinted with a kaleidoscope of brightly coloured shells of every shape and curious design that crunched underfoot. Hosts of tiny crabs rushed helter skelter into the surf. The sea was now the only source of food for the folk of Mirbat, the Indian Ocean which had made their great grandfathers wealthy beyond their dreams for the monsoon winds had blown their slaving ships in a few days from Zanzibar to Sur and thence to the Persian Gulf markets.

In 1873 the Sultan of Muscat agreed to outlaw the slave traffic but did not free the existing slaves. Omanis treated their slaves well and they soon melted into the population so that many Omanis now have mainly negroid features and pigmentation. The Sultan still continued to keep his own household of slaves. Those that I had seen in Salalah seemed fat and cheerful unlike most of the Dhofaris.

There were no others about on the Mirbat beach. I bathed at the edge of the surf for the smell of my clothes was unpleasant.

I searched them for fleas before putting them on again. The salt water felt sticky but my many bites stung and stopped irritating.

We left Mirbat after three days, scouting ahead with great care for the *adoo* knew we would be returning to our camp at Umm al Ghawarif.

At nightfall we came to the high cliffs of Kohr Rawhri and stopped to camp by the ruins of Sumhuran.

Sumhuran is the only site in Dhofar showing evidence of civilisation before the time of Christ. Over two thousand years ago it had been the greatest city of south-east Arabia. In 1000 BC the temple of the Moon God Sin had stood high above the creek, guardian of the frankincense stores that fed camel trains to every part of Arabia and later to the Roman Empire. Frankincense was the world's first international trading commodity, sparking off the camel caravans that laced Arabia together despite vast regions of sand. And the first of these was led by the Yemeni Queen of Sheba who, combining business with pleasure, agreed upon the frankincense routes with her northern neighbour King Solomon of Jerusalem.

I walked through these ruins of the Moon God's city and found the open mouth of a deep well above the sea cliffs. The place was eerie in the fleeting moonlight. I heard the distant boom of an explosion above the din of the sea. Others followed and I moved back towards the lorries. There was a rustling in the scrub of the ruins and I flicked my torch on, startled. A black snake, some five feet long, uncoiled and hissed at me. I hit at it with my rifle, splintering the stock and missing the snake. Still hissing it departed into the rubble.

There were no further explosions so I fell asleep beneath one of the lorries, but, a minute later it seemed, David Bayley woke me.

"Come on. We're off. A message has come through. Salalah's under attack."

There was no moon but we could use no lights for fear of ambush. By looking skywards it was just possible to see the vague outline of the track ahead at the lower rim of vision. If there were mines, they would get us for normally all the drivers kept to the scrub on either side of the track. Without light this was not possible. But our luck held and towards 2 o'clock the next morning we approached our camp at Umm al Ghawarif.

All was quiet. The worst had not happened. A mortar attack had indeed been mounted against the RAF camp for the first time but the bombs had done no damage and the expected follow-up attack had not materialised. Exhausted we slept, but not for long.

The next day at 8 o'clock, as on every Friday morning at that time of day, two Pakistani drivers took their yellow sewage disposal lorries out of the northern gates of the RAF compound. They were a little later than usual for they had slept badly after the explosions the night before.

They drove slowly over the plain heading north towards the mountains for the British Adjutant had said the sewage should be dumped as far away as possible to prevent flies. Rajid sang happily in the second lorry for today was *jummah*, the day of rest, and tomorrow the NAAFI resupply would arrive, God willing, from Masirah which meant more Mars bars. Rajid loved Mars bars more than anything he could think of at that moment.

The Bedford's diesel engine growled in his ears as he followed his friend Ashraf onto the last bit of flat ground before the foothills. He hooted for he thought Ashraf was going a touch too close to the scrubline where the ant-hills poked up like brown nipples sunning themselves above the greenery. He had seen a deep rut further back which he thought would do very well for a sewage dump.

But Ashraf didn't hear him and drove on. Then his lorry slewed to a sudden halt and a cloud of black smoke arose from the engine. Rajid saw his friend open the cab door trying to struggle out. But for some reason he slumped over, half out of the cab.

Alarmed, Rajid drew up alongside and jumped to the ground. A vicious slap sounded close by his right ear and the glass of Ashraf's driving mirror disintegrated.

Rajid had never been shot at before but the thought came quickly that the guerrillas could be no more than a few hundred yards away and knew he was alone. However, Ashraf's cab stood between him and the ant-hills so he seized Ashraf's arms and dragged him clear of the cab. It was not until he began to bundle the limp body into his own driving compartment that he saw the terrible damage done to poor Ashraf's overalled legs.

There were five or six separate wounds: both tibia and fibula bones had been smashed. Bone splinters and ligament tissue protruded from the exit wounds. Wiping the blood from his hands, Rajid leapt over his friend and jumped into the driver's seat. Punishing the old engine he roared away bumping over the plain, his lorry still loaded with sewage and all thoughts of Mars bars forgotten.

Bill Prince woke me at 9.30 a.m. He looked weary and his briar pipe, though in position, was not alight.

"The *adoo* have sunk very low," he grunted. "It seems they've had a go at the RAF sewage lorries. I'm sure that must be against the Geneva Convention. Anyway we're to go and inspect the damage."

Pining for breakfast and smelling still of Mirbat, I dressed and joined the lorries in the compound. Bemused soldiers, still tucking their shirts into their trousers, were clambering aboard. Only two platoons were going, each of fifteen men, and a mortar section.

Bill Prince waggled his pipe at his driver who recognised the sign and drove off.

Within twenty minutes we had sped over the plain to the north of the RAF camp and soon we saw a thin plume of smoke by the foothills.

Halting some way back from the burning lorry, Bill set up his 81 millimetre mortars and told me to take the platoons forward to inspect the lorry and search for signs of the enemy's positions.

Both of us, I think, presumed the *adoo* would long have departed for they had never before come down from the mountains by day for fear of the Sultan's Provost fighters.

The men were clearly annoyed at this pointless task after their exertions over the two preceding days. They walked listlessly and close together, Seramad's men to the left and a Staff Sergeant whose name I did not know on my right. Once they were in a vaguely straight line we moved forward. The ground was flat and utterly devoid of cover until the line of bush and ant-hills four hundred yards ahead of us. Strangely no birds arose in alarm as we grew close to the scrub, no grazing camels loped away.

Perhaps one sweating finger pressed involuntarily against the hair-trigger of an SKS. Perhaps the leader, whoever he was, decided three hundred yards was close enough to kill and not be killed as his own chosen target filled the mushroom of his sights.

Had they waited another minute our destruction must have been assured. As it was, the first great barrier of shock waves passed above and beside our heads with a crackle that sent the soldiers instantly to ground. The signaller beside me fired his rifle wildly with his eyes tight shut. I swore at him for the blast of his first round took an inch of skin from my finger and filled my eyes with dust.

I could just make out where they were, well concealed in low sangars camouflaged with clay so that they appeared to be mere extensions of the ant-hills.

The weight of fire was stunning. I could hardly think. Fear had taken a firm hold of my mind. If only there had been a single rock the size of a football to hide behind or some dead ground to try to reach.

I had never been shot at before but many times in Germany and Aldershot I had fired on the ranges from 500 yards and then, moving down a hundred yards at a time, from the 200-yard point. The 'Figure 11' targets were of mansize cardboard Germans and I well remembered the pleasure, when the shoots finished of inspecting my target and noting the score. Two through the face, one in the stomach, a spattering of holes around the pelvis and thighs. "Not a very good group at all is that, Mr. Fiennes," the Sergeant would say. "Just as well you're not a foot wallah."

And afterwards I would take my turn in the butts, crouching under the concrete shelter just beneath the targets as the riflemen got nearer. At 500 yards the earthen ramp would explode with thump after thump as the bullets bit deep into the mound, seldom passing first through the targets. At 400 yards things improved. By 300 yards one in two bullets shredded the cardboard with a high crack. I would flinch slightly and laugh as the Jock next door shouted, "That's my Fritz's ba's awa. What a shot!" At 200 yards there was usually a dramatic improvement.

People seldom missed even if they only clipped the shoulder or outer thigh.

But the cardboard had no veins and no tendons. It was already both blind and impotent. Also the exit holes were always as small as the entries since cardboard has no bones for the shock wave, that precedes the bullet, to flatten and crush into splinters; splinters which spread out taking with them the other delicate body matter and leaving a hole into which a cricket ball or three whole field dressings will fit.

The signaller lay behind his radio set, his face pressed into the earth with horror. Bullets were passing lower now as the *adoo* adjusted their aim by the spurts of mud kicked up all about us.

The Staff Sergeant to my right was up and running. He screamed 'Advance' which means the same in Omani and well behind him his men followed suit.

Automatically I shouted to Seramad's men: "Rapid covering fire, 300 yards."

The man's a lunatic I thought. What good can it do to advance. Just making it easier for *them*. But a feeling of guilt came rapidly. I was yellow – shown up by an Arab. Against all common sense, I kicked the signaller and yelled at Seramad. Weaving low, as we had a long time ago on the Aldershot heath, I went forward until parallel with the little group on the right. Thankfully I dropped to the ground. More than enough heroics for the day.

But no, the little Staff Sergeant was up again yelling at his men who seemed to be stuck to the ground.

"Stop. Get down," I yelled at him but he did not hear. Suddenly he keeled over backwards, his rifle flying away, and he lay still. Thankfully, I took the headsets from the signaller and spoke to Bill Prince.

As he answered the first mortar bombs exploded amongst the ant-hills.

"That will shake them. I've signalled for the Provost. How many *adoo* do you estimate?"

I couldn't tell. I had seen no more than three sangars but muzzle flashes were visible over a front of six hundred yards.

A high whine sounded above us as a Provost fighter dived low vibrating at full throttle. I took out the pocket Sarbe radio that operates to all aircraft on the international distress frequency of 121·5 megacycles.

The ground shook as a 250 lb fragmentation bomb exploded over the ant-hills. Metal chunks whistled by.

Now was the time to advance I felt whilst all was confusion. I rose to move forward but a burst of bullets hummed by seeming to come from well to our left front; to the flank of the main *adoo* positions.

The Provost had climbed for another run-in. I spoke to the pilot, a middle-aged Scotsman, a dour but kindly man with a Conquistador moutache.

Despite our covering fire, a stream of tracer met his second dive and the bomb exploded well behind the *adoo*. They were shooting high now, unsettled by the bombs.

The Provost climbed out of its dive slowly and bullets slashed through the fuselage. One jammed the joystick control backwards with the aerelons fully elevated. The plane climbed steeply seeming about to flip over or stall. Desperately the pilot prepared to parachute. He slid back and jettisoned the cockpit cover. As he struggled to push forward the joystick that jammed him into his seat, it gave without warning and the Provost straightened out nearly throwing him from the cockpit. Somehow by brute force he coaxed the plane to a safe landing at the RAF strip three miles away.

The guerrillas withdrew for Bill's mortars had found their range. Cautiously we moved forward and found well sited sangars for fifty to sixty men. There were heaps of empty cases, machine gun clips and bloodstained rags but no bodies.

Miraculously only the Staff Sergeant was wounded. A bullet had passed straight through the centre of one thigh.

"We'll not be so lucky again," said Bill, as we moved back to the lorries. "Automatic weapons are new to them now but their shooting can only improve."

Six miles to the south, Sultan Said bin Taimur heard for the first time the echoes of fighting from the confines of the palace and signalled to his Defence Secretary, Brigadier Waterfield, in Muscat. Three thousand 7·62 Belgian FN rifles and a million rounds of ball and tracer were ordered at once. Also a Hercules transport plane from Bahrein brought thirty men of the RAF Regiment to guard their camp and fortify the compound.

The escalation had begun and, in his house behind the palace walls, Qaboos bin Said, son of the Sultan, bided his time. All his visitors were closely watched by the Sultan's agents. But not closely enough.

My month on loan to the Northern Frontier Regiment over, I flew back to Muscat.

At midday on 10th August Radio Baghdad claimed that the glorious freedom fighters of Dhofar had suffered six dead and ten wounded but that they had destroyed a Hawker Hunter and killed forty-nine of the British imperialist troops.

The BBC said nothing. After all, most of the British public had never even heard of the place.

6

ONDITIONS in Oman slowly deteriorated during the summer of 1968. At an Army camp close to Bidbid, two Baluchi soldiers climbed a gravel hillock to escape from the airless heat of the compound below. Both were murdered within sight of the camp; shot through the head and chest cleanly and efficiently. The killers were not traced.

There were strikes by previously contented workers. Townsfolk were openly hostile to the Army. Intelligence agents of the Sultan found evidence of trained revolutionaries at work in the oil company and the larger villages. Arms caches were discovered, but only a few.

Shiploads of transistor radios flooded the shops of Muscat and Muttrah. Omanis listened to coloured reports of the world epidemic of violence which spread through the summer in Paris, in Grosvenor Square, London, in Poland and Czechoslovakia, even in Red Square. And in the United States Martin Luther King followed Robert Kennedy to the cemetery.

My decision to leave Oman had not wavered whilst with the Northern Frontier Regiment and in midsummer I returned to the Muscat Regiment at Bidbid.

Before I could see the Colonel to tender my resignation, if such were to prove possible, I visited the men of my Recce Platoon. Murad the driver, ebullient as ever, suggested a coffee party. All joined in, even the *moolah* and his Baluchi contingent. There were remarks on my improved Arabic and my back was patted proprietorially. Little Ali Nasser commented on the 'battle of the sewage truck',

"If we of Recce had been in Salalah with the Land Rovers and machine guns those *adoo* would never have dared descend from the mountains."

Mohamed Rashid of the Beard said simply: "We are pleased you are back with us, Sahb. Now we will begin to train and become strong, God willing."

Staff Sergeant Abdullah joined us. He greeted me warmly. "I smelled the evil smell of Murad's coffee from the other end of camp and knew we must have an important guest."

Sitting on beds, tin trunks and the cool concrete floor we sipped the hot black coffee.

I would like to soldier with these men, I thought; they are like a large family needing direction. Afterwards I spoke alone with Abdullah and, trusting his discretion, told him of my reaction to the Dhofar situation.

He shook his head from side to side as I spoke. When I was finished he gripped my arm.

"No, no, Sahb. You make a serious mistake. I understand your words and your feelings but you must see other sides to our problems. I myself have met these communists from abroad, here in Oman. They are more often than not sly men with silken tongues but their souls are empty and all their talk of revolution is without sound base. You see they try to turn us from our God and that must never be. Communism must not come here, Sahb."

His voice rose with the urgency of his words and his grip was fierce on my shoulder. "Perhaps it is true that the Sultan gives us nothing, Omanis as well as Dhofaris. But he has stopped the fighting and feuds that plagued Oman until he ruled us. With peace between the tribes our life *has* improved." He relaxed his grip upon me, watching me keenly.

"You must not think the British do wrong here, Sahb. They do not meddle with our way of life or our religion." He lowered his voice.

"It is said that the Sultan's son Qaboos will rule before long. With the oil money that now pours into Oman, thanks be to God, he will give us all those things which the communists promise *without* changing our religion. If you British leave before that can happen, then the communists will take over without a doubt. They will force us to leave Islam or kill us."

85

I was impressed by the sincerity of Abdullah's arguments but my mind was still confused. It was several days later, in the garden of the Bidbid Officers' Mess, that I finally came to see things clearly, to justify my own role to myself without misgivings or doubts.

Captain Tom Greening, from whom I had taken over the Recce Platoon, had just returned from training in Intelligence work. He called at Bidbid to see old friends before taking up his new post further east. I sat with him in the small but exotic garden overlooking the wide darkness of the Fanjah Valley, and remembered what I had been told earlier about his special relationship with Qaboos, the Sultan's heir.

None of the other officers I had met had Tom's extensive knowledge of everything to do with Oman and Dhofar nor of its vital implications to the international balance of power. He was dedicated to Oman and deeply involved, far more so than I could possibly suspect at that time. He talked with great feeling and I listened absorbed.

That night in my room I felt a reassurance and sense of purpose which I had lacked since my days on the Plain of Salalah.

I now knew that change was inevitable. Either the Sultan used his oil revenues to good effect, for progress in his lands, within the next year or two or else a more enlightened ruler must take over. The crucial time was to be the period before one or other improvement took place. And, unless the British could maintain the status quo during this dangerous period, the communists would quickly achieve domination of all south-east Arabia which would have huge repercussions on many other independent peoples. For there was no doubt at all that the Russians, and to a far lesser extent, the Chinese wished to dominate the whole area for their own political and economic ends. Not simply by fomenting local trouble but by annihilating Islam which was the 'reactionary' mainstay of people's lives.

Once Dhofar fell, Oman would follow. With the gates of the Persian Gulf under their control, the Russian influenced People's Front for the Liberation of the Occupied Arabian Gulf (PFLOAG) would be able to blackmail the West with oil threats, far more dangerous and long term in their implications than those exercised by the Organisation of Oil Producing Countries in 1974.

So long as the Dhofaris were not given aid or support by their own Government they would naturally be willing recipients of any alternative regime that appeared to offer a more attractive deal. From Tom Greening I came to understand that the best service our officers and men could do in Dhofar was to keep the terrorists at bay—for long enough to allow certain authorities to arrange for the removal of the Sultan and the establishment of a new progressive ruler who would give the people of Dhofar a better way of life.

There remained the question of whether the Dhofaris—and Omanis—would be better off with a 'new way of life' under a progressive Sultan or indeed under a progressive Marxist PFLOAG. Of this neither Abdullah nor Tom had been in any doubt. It was a straightforward question of some 2000 terrorists, subjectively indoctrinated in foreign lands, attempting to bring atheistic communism to over half a million people much against their will and against their basic character.

Arabs are highly individualistic people, with keenly developed ideas about religion, morals, and the inferiority of other beings in general and women in particular. In fact their whole essence is diametrically opposed to the communist way of life.

Nor are they greatly in need of a regime to level out the rich and the poor since differences of wealth among them have never been great. Power within the tribes is concentrated in the hands of their sheikhs, who can be and are changed at the whim of the tribesmen. Land and animals are owned by whole families or even tribes collectively.

As Tom had pointed out, Arabs are not men to accept regimentation whether fascist or communist and it was up to us to see that the Omanis and Dhofaris were not subjected to either.

Security increased throughout the Muscat Regiment, spread out as they were between the outposts of Ziki, Bidbid and Rostaq. I went nowhere without Abdullah and driver Murad.

To Murad, Oman was a good place. His pay was sufficient and he knew he was handsome: the lissom girls of Fanjah had told him so often enough. There was only one cloud on his uncluttered horizon; in four months he and I and all the Muscat Regiment would move to Dhofar where fear, not desire, was the ruling emotion. He had already spent three tours there and each time the fear was more acute. There were always more mines, more sudden ambushes, more dead and maimed friends. And what good did it all do him? He, Murad, cared nothing for the ignorant Dhofaris. He failed to understand why the Sultan should wish to have anything to do with such a troublesome lot in a land where there were no date trees and the women kept their favours from handsome Omanis.

Alarming reports came daily from Dhofar. The monsoon clouds began to disperse in September and army units moved into the mountains. Subsequent fighting indicated that huge shipments of arms had come east from the Yemen and with them new bands of well-trained guerrillas from Russia and China. Their tactics were skilful, their shooting accurate. Weapons such as the heavy 81 millimetre mortar were now being used with precision and soon no army unit was safe to move in the mountains below half-company strength; some sixty men. No Reconnaissance Platoon in the Sultan's three regiments could muster half this number and the very fact that they were vehicle-borne made them especially vulnerable to ambush.

As the last monsoon mists lingered in the mountains I learnt that four Land Rovers of the Northern Frontier Regiment's Recce Platoon had headed back to the desert. Trapped within a rocky gully they had been ambushed between three machine gun groups. The leading two vehicles were shredded like vegetable colanders as were the crews, and a massacre was averted only by mists that crept into the gully giving cover to the survivors.

The Colonel called me to his office. "NFR's Recce Platoon is written off for a while so there is no one to cover the desert north of the mountains. *Adoo* camel trains are known to bring in arms that way so your platoon must take over as soon as it's fit. How long will that be?"

I told him we were under strength, the Land Rovers were in poor condition, and the men were uneasy. Word of the Land Rover ambush had spread.

The Colonel said we should leave by December before the Muslim fast of Ramadan began. During the interim eight weeks, he wanted the men trained on foot so that they would not, as hitherto the practice in all Recce Platoons, move around solely by Land Rover.

I spoke to Abdullah at once. We went to the barrack room that evening and told the men what would be expected of them from now on. Their reaction was not philosophical. It was resentful and hostile. For a while, when I had finished, there was silence. Then Hamid the dark bedu struck a bedstead with his camel stick.

"Why should we act like Company soldiers? Our work is to scout and move quickly. Is this not why we have Land Rovers? We did not join Recce to walk and carry back-packs like coolies. Your talk is not good. I for one am not happy with your ideas."

There was a rumble of assent from the other men; even the Baluchis were in agreement with the bedu. Mohamed Rashid of the Beard and Ali Nasser were silent but they too looked displeased.

The training began at a bad time. The heat was discouraging within the barracks even when we were inactive. Beyond the camp where gravel hillocks shimmered in hypnotic waves and fine choking dust rose under foot, it was not at all pleasant to play soldiers hour after hour, day after day. We started at six in the morning before the flies began their torment and at nine, streaming wet and streaked with salt, stopped for an hour's breakfast. From ten until one o'clock we worked at ambush reaction drills and again for two hours in the evening, when the sun was said to be cooler. During the afternoons, people slept and, outside a conditioned room, the air burned the nostrils and lungs.

The men complained with increasing bitterness but never to my face. Abdullah would come to my room at dusk and sip *loomee*, cooled with ice chunks, a drink of sweetened lime juice that quenches the thirst without bringing sweat as hot tea does. After a short lesson in Omani, he would sigh with meaning and when I was quiet, the day's woes came pouring out. The troubles he passed on to me were but a filtered and heavily censored version of the attacks he had himself suffered earlier from the men.

Many of them put in for compassionate leave with heart-rending tales of their family's plight in their absence: all were refused as they had already received their annual quota of leave. Two of the Baluchis and three Arabs applied for transfer to the Companies, all of which I granted. The two bedu asked for discharge from the Army and I agreed with alacrity, pleased to see them go.

Those who had joined the platoon to land a comfortable job in a Land Rover saw things back-firing with a vengeance and they were the first to leave. The Arabs found no extra favours came their way as they were accustomed for I was careful to allot distasteful jobs evenly between the men regardless of their caste.

At the same time they suffered daily from the same pressures as the Baluchis and for once, their moans were in unison: a measure of harmony crept in for the common denominator was discomfort.

Apart from five years with Centurion tanks in Germany I had been trained in the basic arts of an 'elusive saboteur' by the 22nd Special Air Service Regiment. One of their few hard and fast rules was movement by night whenever possible and my brief visit to Dhofar led me to apply this maxim to the Recce Platoon. But in the SAS there were four men to an operational group, not two dozen, so I began to develop a careful system of control with the soldiers.

The resulting drills were not, so far as I know, present in any military textbook. They stemmed from common-sense reactions to the emergency situations likely to occur in Dhofar.

We trained with live ammunition and there were no stultifying safety regulations to observe. Abdullah, with the drivers and signallers, acted as *adoo* setting up a series of ambushes in a four-mile long deserted valley not far from Bidbid. At each position he placed 12-inch white metal plates and as we advanced cautiously up the valley his men fired over our heads from safe places close to the plates.

After many mornings in the valley the soldiers moved slickly and reacted fast to identify the whereabouts of the plates and shoot them down. Only when each man knew by heart twenty simple hand signals, often practised by day, did we begin to patrol by night. Total silence was essential but at first there were clattering pebbles, stifled coughs, loud whisperings and the clunk of rifle against rock.

Advances over broken ground were practised again and again until they were silent. Whispers were no longer necessary once the hand signals were perfected from man to man, executed clearly since only the outline movement of the arms might be seen in the darkness.

Every item of equipment and clothing was painted green and brown, all watches were pocketed, radio aerials were covered by cloth tubes and their luminous control dials by adhesive tape. When the moon shone the men moved with twenty yards between each of them, presenting no bunched target to a would-be marksman. When clouds came, each soldier closed up enough to see the man in front of and behind him and to identify the hand signals which dictated the types of formation in which the platoon would move through the changing terrain.

Abdullah laid trip flares to represent night ambushes. As by day, each section commander reacted immediately by flinging an 83 grenade in the direction of the ambush. Within four seconds a dense cloud of white phosphorus smoke provided cover for our withdrawal. Furthermore if the *adoo* should be unpleasantly close, the white phosphorus would prove far more effective than an explosive grenade since even the smallest amount touching the skin caused an agonising burn which continued to eat deep into the flesh. A low rock might protect an *adoo* from grenade shrapnel but not from phosphorus particles.

Sweat quickly rotted our clothes, sharp rock and camel thorns cut through footwear and tore at equipment. Some of the men had socks but most wore only canvas gym shoes however rough the country.

The Quartermaster was a good-natured Englishman but his stocks were limited and he kept a tight rein on them so only a quarter of our requirements were met. This happened also with radio and vehicle replacements until I discovered that small scale 'acquisition' worked wonders and seemed to harm no one.

Many of the British officers were on their annual eight weeks' leave. When they left, Arab or Pakistani junior officers took their place. I became friendly with many of those in key positions, exchanging occasional gifts of fruit and cigarettes.

The Quartermaster Sergeant, an amiable Pakistani, was most generous with equipment whenever the Quartermaster was away. Two new signallers and three new BCC 30 radio sets came from the Signals Lieutenant and soon afterwards there followed a supply of spare parts for Murad's Land Rovers so that, by late October, all five vehicles were in working order.

The more serious problem was manpower. Of the fifteen men present when I arrived, seven had left and Sergeant Abdullah would be gone in a month.

With only eight men left not including the five drivers — who were happy enough since their training was unchanged — I asked the Colonel for more men of good calibre. I needed eighteen soldiers, three signallers and a doctor.

All would have to come from the Companies who would not wish to lose any men unless there was something wrong with them. The time was favourable, however, since two of the Company majors were away, one on leave and Richard John still recovering from his wound. The remaining Major was soon to leave the Army so his self-interest in not losing good men would probably be minimal.

The Colonel agreed to my taking five volunteers from each Company and I set off the following day with a selection board consisting of Abdullah, Ali Nasser and Mohamed of the Beard. The giant *moolah* came too in order to vet Baluchi entrants. Murad broke down twice on the Batinah road in Barka and Jammah. In both places he was known to have girlfriends and in each he spent over an hour finding water for the radiator.

After five hours we came to the ancient city of Rostaq dominated by a crumbling fort and the sheer walls of the Jebel Akhdar.

At the camp gates a Land Rover passed us. Behind its dust cloud, glistening with sweat and clad in shorts and singlet, the Company Officer came running up the road clasping a ski stick in each hand.

He stopped at the gate and checked his pulse rate against a stop watch. He seemed pleased.

"Getting slower every week despite the heat. My pulse I mean, not me. What are you up to in Rostaq, Ran? Come up to the Mess; I'm the only one in at present."

Captain Guy Sheridan had been on the Arabic course with me. He was a Royal Marine Army skier and determined to keep very fit. Now he was acting Company Commander in his Major's absence and was quite unconcerned when I told him of my mission.

"Go ahead. I'll get the Sergeant Major to put the word about. Any keen young fellows wanting a couple of years with Recce

Platoon. It might help their promotion prospects. I'm sure the Major wouldn't mind."

We were given an empty desk with a bench on which Abdullah, Ali, Mohamed, Murad and the *moolah* managed to squeeze on either side of me, presenting a formidable array of black beards to any would-be applicant.

The word which went out must have been a much twisted version of my original fairly honest propaganda for a long queue formed outside the office.

A little man with the fine features and wild black mop of hair of a Dhofari came first. After greetings and shaking hands with the Board he stood rigidly to attention; only his mouth and eyes moving to reply to the questions.

"Your name?"

"Saif Musabbah."

"Tribe?"

"Hawasena."

At this I noticed a certain warmth amongst the Arabs. All but Murad and the *moolah* were of the same ilk or of allied tribes to the Hawasena.

"Why do you wish to join Recce?"

"Yes, I wish to join."

"But why?"

"God be praised."

"Is it because of the comforts of Land Rovers or because you have friends already in Recce?"

"God be praised, Sahb."

I gave up. He seemed an honest strong type so I told him what to expect with Recce. How much more training than in the Companies. How little use would be made of the Land Rovers and how much of our feet. How we would be required to move in the Dhofar mountains without help from the Companies and how there would be no discrimination between Arab and Baluchi.

Seemingly unmoved the little man replied simply, "*Imshaalah* all will be well and I shall in time receive promotion."

Abdullah told him to wait outside.

There followed much sickly looking riffraff some of whom were greasily plausible, others who changed their minds after hearing my summary of Recce's role.

93

The *moolah* was unimpressed by the few Baluchi applicants and recommended that we accept none of them.

There were three tough looking Arabs, a swarthy pirate-face with a lopsided mouth, a thin mortar crewman named Said Salim who carried a stiletto in a sheath and a gentle-faced ox named Hamid Sultan. All three stated firmly "*Ureed Recce,* Sahb. I want Recce," after listening to my tale of predicted woes.

Hamid Sultan came back a second time bringing with him a Hawasena Corporal with the bearing of a Scots Guards Sergeant Major and a quick disarming smile.

Abdullah whispered to me, "This man is known for his bravery. All men like him. He is Salim Khaleefa of the Beni Hinna. If you cannot find a Sergeant when I go, this Corporal will surely be all that you need."

The five men went to pack their simple belongings, a metal trunk and a bedding roll, and to take leave of their friends.

I thanked Guy and we left for Bidbid.

At Ziki camp the next day we were received with much suspicion. Although Richard John was away, still recovering from the wound which had necessitated his removal on the day of our arrival in Oman, his Lieutenant, a shrewd Pakistani, spoke English very well and, whilst pouring me a *loomee* in the Mess, said he was quite sure the Major would never allow any of his better men to leave the Company without his direct permission. However, as Richard was unlikely to be back for a while and I had the Colonel's word, I could go ahead.

Alarmed at the influx of Arabs the day before, our *moolah* toured the Ziki barrack rooms with his own line of propaganda. The Recce Sahb, he said, was scrupulously fair to all and had even rid the platoon of the two hated bedu who had long made life a misery for the Baluchis. In the Companies, said the *moolah,* there were many British and Arab officers who loved only the Arabs and gave all the dangerous or dirty jobs to the Baluchis. This, he promised, they would not have to suffer in Recce.

His sales patter was effective for two tall Baluchis, both experienced machine gunners, applied to join at once. Sadeeq Jumma and his friend were inseparable, spoke good Arabic unlike many Baluchis, and were—unknown to the *moolah—* *hasheesh* addicts.

A six-foot Zanzibari with a handshake that crushed my fingers and a head of fine black fuzz wished to join for original reasons. Recce Platoon had more machine guns per man than the Companies. And Mubarreq Obeid—for that was the big negro's name—had been unable to have a machine gun in his Company. With such a weapon, he said, his thick lips compressed in a snarl, he could kill many Chinese *shooyooeen* (communists) in Dhofar and that was his main desire.

I protested that there were no Chinese communists in Arabia let alone Dhofar but he was adamant.

"You are wrong, Sahb. They are behind all the troubles everywhere. Soon there will be many like locusts in Dhofar. In Zanzibar they talked to the African how he must throw out the Arab. Then, seven years ago, they rose and murdered all the Arabs they could catch; slitting their throats by night as they slept. Some of us escaped to the *dhows* but my parents were chased along the beach by a crowd—though my mother was African. They ran into the sea to swim to the boats but some of the crowd followed, caught hold of their hair, and drowned them. So I, Mubarreq, have no parents because of the Chinese rats." When he had gone I looked at the others. All nodded their assent. Two Arabs joined us from Ziki and on the third day, back in Bidbid, four Baluchis from the inlying Company volunteered under the *moolah's* cajoling. One was a regal looking Corporal named Taj, as prudish as the *moolah* himself. Finally a medical orderly from a coastal plain Batinah tribe was sent to the platoon and the billet was full to bursting.

I divided the thirty men into five sections of six allotting to each a Land Rover driver and signaller. The Baluchis, a third of the total, were evenly spread through the sections, and, in the billet, their old practice of sleeping all in one block was stopped. Now they must identify themselves by sections and not by race.

Sergeant Abdullah lived in a separate room so Corporal Salim Khaleefa was effectively in charge. I stressed to him the need for absolute fairness with the Baluch. The Baluchi Corporal was given charge of a section as were the senior soldiers Ali Nasser and Mohamed Rashid of the Beard.

The drills we had practised so often and so carefully were taught to the newcomers and put to the test, for thirty men can be difficult to control silently on a dark night or in thick thorn bush country.

Each section commander carried a small National Panasonic radio transceiver powered by battery and hung round the neck. These allowed conversation up to two miles. For greater distances my own section and those of the two Corporals carried BCC 30 backpack radios with a morse range of 200 miles or more. By day or night the men were allowed to talk on the radio only in a whisper; a modulated whisper not the sibilant hiss that Arabs normally produce which carries far, especially by night.

The upper plateaux of the Jebel Akhdar are as tree-clad in many regions as the Qara mountains of Dhofar and they are nearly three times as high.

In mid-October five Land Rovers bulging with men and equipment left Bidbid ar dawn. For six days we would travel and train on the airy plateaux of the Akhdar and test the fitness of the men in conditions similar to the war zone of Dhofar.

The air was still cool as we moved out, the light a soft pink which touched the mountains and the wisps of cloud around their summits. The walls of adobe houses and the ramparts of their forts were impressive standing out sharply in warm orange relief for the shadows were still long.

By seven o'clock the sun was up and the land lost its contrast, growing hazy and intangibly hostile.

The Land Rovers followed a *wadi*-bed corkscrewing into the bowels of the Akhdar until a boulder barred the way.

Murad grinned at me behind his dark glasses giving a quick twirl to his moustache. "Have a good time up there, Sahb. I will be back to collect you here after six days. It would make me most happy to come with you but of course these other foolish drivers need my guiding hand."

The vehicles bounced off, the red *shemaghs* of the drivers streaming from the open cabs.

At first a mule track followed the *wadi* twining through and beneath huge white boulders. Corporal Salim Khaleefa knew the way, turning left behind a tamarisk shrub. A dizzy climb began up a sheer ravine where no breath of wind disturbed the blistering heat.

After 5000 feet we rested sucking limes, for to drink once

Said bin Geir

Dead *adoo* outside Fort Marbat

Recce Platoon Officers' Mess

Recce Platoon on patrol in Gravel Plain

makes a man crave for more water and it is bad practice to drink often on the march.

My backpack and rifle weighed more it seemed as the hours passed. In a remote gully we drank from the spring of Salut where the Beni Riyam tribesmen water their camels. An old man appeared and asked for the Sahb. Abdullah kept him waiting whilst we filled our *zamzamia* water bags. He squatted patiently in the shade of a palm watching us.

"Come now, old man," said Abdullah, "what is it you want?" The last man had left the spring to replace the sentry picketing the boulders above the water.

"My daughter is dying. A snake bit her yesterday and no man in the village can cure her. *Imshaalah* you have some Aspreen, Sahb."

With four soldiers and the medical orderly I followed the man back the way we had come to a village with amber-coloured chickens and children playing between the clay houses.

The man's daughter, if such she was for she could have been no more than ten years old, lay writhing on a carpet. Dark spittle smeared her cheeks. Her face was a yellow mask creased with fear.

"Where is it so bad, little one?" Salim the orderly knelt by her undoing his medical pack.

She only moaned and retched dryly, her neck muscles standing out in horrible relief; her stomach arching up from the mat.

"The bite is on this leg." The old man indicated twin puncture holes, "I have applied a *wussum* to the other leg, but she gets worse."

The bitten limb was badly inflamed but it was the other leg that held my attention. On it, from the ankle to the knee, were a series of deep pustulous burns that had been brushed over with fresh camel dung; perhaps for mistakenly antiseptic reasons. The *wussum* burn is the Arab antidote to pain. In effect it only eclipses the initial pain with a worse one which itself may cause gangrene and death.

Salim incised the snakebite and sprinkled purple crystals into it. He placed clean dressings on the bite and the burns and gave the girl ten cubic centilitres of morphine through the shoulder muscle. She must not move at all, he told the man, and another doctor would call the next day.

97

After a further 1000 feet climb we came to the army camp at Saiq perched high above the perpendicular crags and sheer grey flanks of the central Jebal Akhdar. The garrison officer and most of his Company were away but I found a medical orderly who promised to visit the sick girl at once. When we returned after three days, he told us the girl had died before he reached her.

The nights were cool and fresh on the plateau, blissfully so after the humidity of the past few months. Abdullah said it had snowed during February two years before.

That night we walked through strange country towards a deserted village shown on my map. By dawn the men had moved in ever changing formations, using only hand signals, over eight miles of broken tree-clad land, without a sound. The men were pleased with themselves and friendly bickering as to who was most efficient had begun between the five sections. We slept until evening and again moved by night between isolated villages, lonely mosques and gullies with deep cave systems.

Beneath us the mountain fell away, not with the usual vertical buttresses but in giddy tiers of irrigated steps. Every layer was fed with artificial channels along which water ran into a terminal pond. From there it overflowed in a miniature fall to the step below and so on for two thousand feet of tiny fertile orchards.

Trees and plants of every shape and size hung heavy with fruit. There were figs, pomegranates, nectarins, peaches, almonds, walnuts and berries. Sugar cane groves bunched on the lower tiers and lucerne spread a green carpet at every level. Massive crags speared above in chimneys and battlements giving a Don Quixote air to the cliff-hanging villages with their vivid splashes of greenery.

Once the land was richer still, supporting a much larger community. Fifteen hundred years before, invading Persians in armour had conquered the mountain tribes and settled in the village now called Shiraija after Shiraz. We descended to the village, through its narrow streets and over flat roof tops where yellow corn cobs ripened. Following cascades of water from orchard to orchard we came at length to arid slopes with signs of long abandoned but extensive cultivation.

The Persians were great workers; irrigation their speciality. Trained artisans dug subterranean channels to take water from springs, underneath the hottest deserts, to distant towns or orchards. Sometimes these channels or *aflaj* were up to a hundred feet deep and over fifty miles long. Despite the heat above, little water was lost through evaporation.

The diggers were called *muqanat* or 'men of the killers' for many died from rockfalls and escaping gases. They were often young boys, blinded soon after birth, who developed an uncanny accuracy when digging through solid rock with simple tools so that the channels ran straight and dipped only imperceptibly to maintain gravity. From the slopes of Shiraija we returned to the spring of Salut.

Beyond Salut a steep scree chute rushes down to the Wadi Muaydin. I persuaded the negro Mubareq and two of the Arabs to accompany me down the sliding scree and the others gazed appalled as we disappeared over the lip of the cliff in a slither of loose slate. It took fourteen minutes to descend and an hour awaiting the others who followed Corporal Salim down the more orthodox track where steps had been shaped in the rock by generations of bare feet and the sharp hooves of the Akhdar donkeys, taxis of the mountains. There are but twenty-two other equally steep and narrow tracks giving access to the upper plateaux yet somehow the Persians had fought their way up past ten thousand Omani defenders hurling boulders and spears.

Using different routes, we returned five times to the mountain to train on the high green plateau which once formed the central citadel of Oman. Three Baluchis and an Arab found life too hard and left the platoon. They were replaced. In this way the weaker elements were filtered away leaving a willing and reliable core.

The fast of Ramadan was due in December by when we must be in Dhofar. Since the men would not see their relations again for a year or more we joined up again with our Land Rovers and proceeded to patrol to the far corners of Oman stopping in remote villages to meet and eat with their families.

Despite their poverty, sickness and the puritanical nature of Ibahdism (their moral and legal code as well as their religion) —the Omanis are a happy people. Their moods, which are frequent and unpredictable, pass quickly like clouds. On those early patrols, I thought I had begun to understand some of the soldiers. Months later I knew I had been wrong; one can no more put a label on the nature and the being of an Omani than pin quicksilver under one's thumb.

West and south of Bidbid, gravel wastes stretch away to the great sand sea. We followed the oil tracks to Fahud where pillars of flame burn high and the pipeline begins that takes the oil to storage tanks above Muscat. And then further south until the Land Rovers met soft yielding sand not far from the bottomless quicksands of Umm al Samim.

From there we drove north along the desert trail silvered by the moon through the crooked night shadows of *ghaf* acacia and thorny mimosa. Foxes barked close by, safe in the knowledge that few Muslims will eat their flesh.

The trail lies along the ancient caravan route where sealed gourds of frankincense travelled north to the entrepots of the Roman empire. This is the 'back' of Oman.

Two of the soldiers were no more than seventeen years old. Both, Abdullah told me, were often visited by spirits. I laughed for in those days I had not witnessed the alarming reality of the desert *djinns*. We ate a newly slain goat with the bedu and sipped bitter coffee as they chanted to the throb of goatskin drums.

Tired and grey with dust we slept in the warm sand until dawn when Murad rose quietly to wash his limbs with sand and pray. The negro Mubarreq brought hot tea and sat close by to drink his own. He was the machine gunner in my section. Already, on the range, he had shown a remarkable accuracy with the weapon: he carried it everywhere, a green handkerchief lovingly wrapped around the working parts against the dust.

"Have you no orderly, Sahb?" he asked suddenly as though this were unthinkable.

"I suppose not, Mubarreq. I have no need for one. There are no boots and belts to polish in this army and no trousers to press for parades."

"But what about your food? It is not seemly for an officer to fetch his own food and tea. I will look after these things, Sahb, never fear." He added as an afterthought, "For so long as I am your machine gunner."

To the west a mesa rose 2000 feet from the scrubland mists, sheer and solitary like Roraima, the 'lost world' of Conan Doyle. We packed our blankets and drove off towards it.

"Soon we will reach the frontier at Buraimi," shouted Murad above the engine noise.

He accelerated past a long line of loaded camels, frightening the beasts and shouting to their startled riders. Just then a rear half-shaft broke and Murad swore quietly, embarrassed as the camels plodded past us. Their swaying jockeys muttered mocking words and remarked on Murad's ancestry.

In an hour we were on our way with a new shaft and entered the sprawling oasis of Buraimi. It is divided into seven separate villages owing allegiance either to the Sultan of Muscat or to Sheikh Zaid of Abu Dhabi whose country forms part of the Union of Arab Emirates. Contraband and revolutionaries enter Oman from the west this way and a troop of Oman Gendarmerie man the frontier fort to prevent this happening too easily.

At the frontier itself Omani Buraimi contrasted poorly with its neighbour, its dirt-track meeting the well-surfaced tarmac of Abu Dhabi's Al'Ain where street lights and modern shops provided a glaring contrast to the dust and hovels of Sultanate territory.

There were no restrictions on crossing into Abu Dhabi for their Army and the Armies of the other Trucial Coast States were led by British or Pakistani officers. A miniature fortress, round and whitewashed, housed the commandant of the Trucial Oman Scouts in Buraimi. He was a polo-playing Hussar officer with a strange double-barrelled name, even stranger than my own, and a number of his soldiers were Dhofaris.

"Hadn't I better keep my men away from them?" I asked in alarm.

"They'll not cause trouble up here. My Sergeant will see to that. You know, I'm glad I'm not going to Dhofar. In my opinion, each of our Dhofaris is worth ten Omanis. They're tough as wire and sharp as razors. You'll find out soon enough."

He admitted that a growing number of his Dhofaris were going on leave once he had trained them, taking their rifles and never coming back. "But of course," he added somewhat weakly, "there's no actual proof that they're joining the guerrillas."

From Buraimi we drove back towards Bidbid. On the way we passed south of the little-known Mussundam peninsula, whose northern point flanks the Straits of Hormuz, through which the oil tankers pass. It is peopled by Shihu nomads who speak only the Zaara tongue and live like animals in caves. Abdullah said that they buried their dead under their earth floors and believed in the spirits of Rock and Sea. He then laughed in a most superior fashion.

The mountains of the peninsula are sheer and barren dropping straight to the sea and forming isolated fjords where inbred families of fishermen live with flint or metal axes as their only weapons.

The Mussundam was known even to the ancient Greek mariners, for the narrow waters of the straits blow into terrible storms without warning. It is an area where a particularly unpleasant form of fraud has long been practised and still goes on unchecked and seldom reported.

I witnessed a mild example of this late in 1972 on a visit to the village of Khasab in eastern Mussundam.

Two hundred and thirty unemployed Indians from Karela, south of Delhi, had each paid £70 in rupees, their life's savings, to the captain of a dhow. Happily they had set sail for a land where there was 'work for all'.

At Khasab they were arrested, fed by the police and deported back to India. They were luckier than countless other shiploads of pilgrims or unemployed Asians who sail every year to the Mussundam. Sometimes the captains land them at a sandbank or a lonely fjord and point over the nearest mountain. "Two miles yonder lies Muscat; a great city of rich merchants." But beyond the mountain there is no city nor even water to drink and when they return for the dhow, it has left. Crazy with thirst they turn mad drinking sea water or drown.

Other captains are in league with local bedu 'guides' who lead the immigrants inland, often with their wives and children, and then disappear overnight. Without guides, the Indians wander on through the heat and the great gravel peaks that lead nowhere.

From Mussundam we drove south by way of Sohar, a sprawling place of palms and long white beaches made famous by the merchant sailor Sinbad who was born there.

Salim, our medical orderly, lived nearby. His parents were dead but his brother looked after their gardens. With his army pay he had installed a diesel water pump to irrigate his palm grove and banana trees. Now his annual date harvest was better than all the neighbours who still used oxen and wooden wheels to bring water from their springs. Salim's brother served us on a carpet beneath the palms. It was a cool dreamy place with shafts of sun dappling the carpet and the faces of the Arabs. Top-heavy flamingoes, tall and stately, peered at us from the reeds beyond the palm grove. They had flown from western Europe for sun and good fishing.

Salim had read agricultural books from Kuwait and knew as much about date and banana farming as about medicine. There were eighteen different varieties of banana he said and all were grown along the Batinah coastal plain. Much of his own crop was exported to Dubai and his dates to Muttrah.

He reeled off an unbelievably long list of names, all of different types of Omani dates. He could crop up to 300 lbs of fruit from a single tree but owned only one male date palm. By artificial pollination, Salim explained, he could fertilize 500 of his female trees from this one male plant.

"I call it King Solomon," he said. We talked for many hours sitting among the trees. Salim told me tales of traditional medicine and surgery in Oman, of practices so horrible and ignorant that I wondered whether I had understood him correctly. When I commented on the barbarism of much he had told me, he only agreed.

"It is true and I know it. I have learnt modern medicine so I understand the causes, the symptoms, and sometimes the cures. But I am only one of a handful in Oman who disagree with the ancient customs. Even today our people will burn and blind a patient through trying to cure him before they would even think of taking him to the American Hospital in Muttrah. That is done only as a final resort when all else has failed."

The setting sun coloured the palms and the sea beyond. It was a beautiful country. Leaving Salim with his brother we drove south and reached Bidbid soon after midnight.

With most of the men away for a week's leave, I joined a fellow officer, recently returned from Dhofar, on a journey to the coast. Close by the wired-off compound of Petroleum Development Oman Ltd, a subsidiary of Shell, there was a keyhole cove with soft sand and a beach club hut. Muscat and Muttrah sweltered a few miles down the coastline but here, by the PDO 'village', one might well be at Saint Tropez on the

Côte d'Azur. PDO secretaries stretched their brown limbs selfconsciously. Their tanned and sometimes handsome escorts were fighter or transport pilots from the Sultan's airbase at Bayt al Falaj.

I watched from a rock beside the club house disgusted at the whiteness of my body. My face at least was darker than most but a khaki shirt and long trousers had kept my skin pale and clammy throughout the days of training. Had I at any time removed them the soldiers would have been embarrassed and disapproved.

The water was warm; alive with tiny algae and spawn. People said the sharks and barracuda never came close into the bay. On the beach two men with hairy chests and moustaches threw a beach ball and laughed like children; and people with aqualungs wallowed about the rocks where technicolour fish might be seen.

An Arab orderly laid out sandwiches and cold beer from a hamper by the club house. I wondered what he thought of it all. If he were unmarried he would probably never have seen a developed female body before; except below the ankles and above the shoulders.

The cove was called Blackpool Beach, nestling below the oil village of Sahil Mahla where PDO officials led the life to which they were accustomed. Many had their families with them and a car to take them shopping in Muscat or Muttrah, the only places other than the desert oil heads where they might travel in Oman. Each employee had his or her own prefabricated bungalow with air-conditioning, deep freeze, and a view over the bay. Fresh food reached them weekly in refrigerator ships from Australia.

Pay was high with the extra bonus of 'hardship' money for working in a tough climate, and the technicians had to spend eleven days up country at the oil heads followed by four days' rest at 'home'. Many of the wives became bored during the periods of separation. Some yielded to temptation for after all the weather was so hot and there were so many romantic young bachelors down on the beach.

Local Omanis were employed within the PDO compound and they watched the behaviour of the Europeans. This did not impress them but neither did it stop them feeling envy since their employers had so much and they so little. They saw too the oil children's schools, the lavish bars and swimming pools. And they glimpsed the magnificently equipped hospital which was kept fairly busy coping with light sunburn cases, stomach upsets and the like. Yet no patients from outside the compound, the thousands of living dead whose life was misery, might come to the hospital. And the employees went home and they talked of these things and of the marvels of piped water and light switches.

If it was Omani oil which gave such opulence to the foreigners, when would they, the Omanis, taste similar fruits? Their transistor radios told them insistently that the answer was never. Not unless they first removed the foreigners and the Government that had invited them to Oman.

I saw Abdullah for the last time as we left Bidbid. In a week he would leave the army to work in his family's orchard; or so he said. He was troubled within himself and grew daily more distant from the rest of us. Several times I asked if he had problems and if I might help in any way. He always replied politely that all was well but his darkly handsome features were sad as our Land Rovers passed out of the Bidbid gates. We were on our way south, driving right across the vast gravel deserts of Oman, featureless for 500 miles to the very foothills of the Dhofar mountains.

7

THE Rubh al Khali or Empty Quarter is the greatest sand
desert in the world and stretches for a thousand miles
from the Oman coast inland into Saudi Arabia. In it
there is nothing permanent; only the wandering bedu, whose
interest is camels and little else. Twenty years ago their lives
were spiced with internecine feuds to the death and camel
raids. Now things were more peaceful though the desert life
was as harsh as ever. The eastern fingers of the sands through
which we travelled, stretched flat and grey to the sea. Here the
surface was gravel baked into a horny crust by the sun.

Had there been oil here much would have changed but,
although forty million dollars had been spent between 1953
and 1961 by the Iraqi Petroleum Company, there had been no
sign of a single major oil source. All the oilfields appeared to
lie to the north.

The oil men had left the jetsam of their search in remote areas
of the gravel desert and even within the fringes of the sand
desert. After two days' driving with my Recce Platoon we came
to Haima, once an oil camp, where there was water and an
acre of rusting bric-à-brac. Then for hundreds of miles we
passed only rock, sand and bunches of dwarf palm or acacia
scrub. By day the heat was oppressive and the glare played
tricks with my eyes. Though there was no wind, sand devils,
many feet high, would spiral suddenly from nowhere and mirages
of lakes stretched across the horizon.

Heading south-east over gravel and caked pans of gypsum
we passed pools of oil where prospectors had struck a surface

anticline of no potential. Close by was water with a sweet fresh taste and Said Salim shot a *dhubi* gazelle from the Land Rover. He skinned it deftly with his stiletto having first slit its throat. After washing the beautiful pelt, he rubbed it with rock salt and rolled it into a tight scroll.

"Tomorrow, I will dry it for you, Sahb," he grinned, "then when you have ten such skins, you may join them together for a rug."

We came to the camp of Thamarit at dusk on the third day, thankfully for we were weary from the journey. When the oilmen left Thamarit, which they called Midway Camp, they abandoned everything. Air-conditioned huts, generators, radio aerials and derricks all surrounded by many thousands of lorry tyres and 45-gallon drums known by the Arabs as *burmails* —a corruption of Burma Oil.

It was dark as we drew up between the huts. The place seemed deserted although it served as the only storage and re-supply camp between Oman and Dhofar. A dust track, made by the Sultan's coolies in 1953 for the oilmen, led south over the Qara mountains and down to Salalah. Other tracks, seldom used, went out into the desert in every direction. Since there is seldom rain to the north of the Qara, these gravel trails have remained usable.

An evening breeze, scented by desert shrub and heather, rattled the wires of radio masts which chattered like yacht burgees: doors creaked to and fro and a fluctuating whistle, the whispering of an unseen crowd, filled the place with ghostly animation. Said Salim touched my shoulder;

"I will see, Sahb." He moved into the gloom of the huts and returned with a Baluchi in a dark *dishdash* and a white *shemagh* wrapped around his jaw as though he had toothache. He was one of the few men stationed here permanently on garrison duty.

I followed the Baluchi to a low green shed with two rooms and the luxury of a lavatory cubicle, quite open, on a platform between the two rooms.

"This is Officers Mess," said the Baluchi proudly and handed me a note from beneath a pebble on the floor.

It was from an officer in the Northern Frontier Regiment.

'I trust your journey was a good one. Please go direct to

Habarut. There is an injured *askar* at the fort there. Radio Salalah for a plane to evacuate him when you have secured the Habarut airstrip.' There was no date on the letter.

Corporal Salim and some of the men had been to Habarut before. It lay on the border between Dhofar and the People's Republic of South Yemen. By the time we reached Habarut we would have driven non-stop from one end of Oman to the other.

"It is eight hours from here," said Murad. "Better we travel by night when the going is cool and the track is hard."

Wearily we loaded fresh cans of fuel and water. Said Salim killed a goat to eat on the way. After four hours a Land Rover broke down, its electric system faulty. It was pitch dark so we carried on. They had a radio and must make their own way to Habarut. The men were tired: in three days we had already driven through six hundred miles of desert. At night it was uncomfortable and cold in these southern steppes; scorching by day. My backside ached from the continual bouncing. My lips were cracked by the dry wind though the ends of the green *shemagh* covered all but my eyes from the sting of the wind blown sand.

"Soon, perhaps tomorrow, the new moon will show herself in the east," said Mubarreq. "Then it will be Ramadan, a month of hardship for Muslims. No food nor water by day. *Imshaalah* we will rest much during Ramadan, Captain Sahb?"

Unsure whether Mubarreq was offering veiled advice or asking a question I replied, "*Imshaalah.*"

'*Imshaalah*' is a godsend to an officer with Arabs. It is both non-committal and yet denotes finality so that further questioning is pointless. After all, 'God willing', which is as near a direct translation as any available, implies that all matters of the future are in God's hands alone and therefore cannot be altered by any official decision one way or the other.

At dawn we rested where a wide *wadi* cut south floored by pure white boulders. In grey blankets we squatted around the fire watching as little Ali Nasser prepared tea and chupattis fried in butter. The sun climbed fast and shadows soon fled. Gazelles bounded away from desiccated salt-bushes at our coming. Ahead lay the water of Habarut; sweet springs by a scattered oasis of date palms on Dhofar's southern border.

Guarding the water on the far western cliffs was an outpost originally built for the Hadhramaut Bedouin Legion of the East Aden Protectorate. British Aden was no more, nor were the HBL, but the fort had a new garrison and modern weapons left behind by the British the year before. The tricolour of the People's Democratic Republic of South Yemen splashed the battlements.

Five hundred yards to the east on the opposing cliffs of the *wadi*, our newer fort, freshly whitewashed, stared back below the Sultan of Oman's bright red duster. It was built in the best traditions of the Foreign Legion by a British architect in 1966. Unfortunately it was not to last long: when I returned in 1972 it had been demolished to a heap of rubble by the communists.

Driving between the forts I felt uncomfortable. I viewed the P.D.R.S.Y. fort through binoculars. An officer stood along the ramparts. He seemed to be watching me through binoculars. Beside him a machine gun barrel stared skywards.

We drove up a steep ramp to the Sultan's fort. *Askars* rushed out to greet us. Behind them, through the open gate, I saw a man limp fast across the compound and lie down on a stretcher.

This must be the 'injured' man we had come for. I swore under my breath. I would see the Chief *Askar* and inform Salalah by radio. But Hamid Sultan, my thick-set machine gunner, was watching me and grasped my shoulder.

"Hey, hey, Sahb. No good can be done by reporting that the sick man is not sick. He is not your worry. Only we of Recce Platoon are your concern. Perhaps this man has other important reasons for leaving Habarut."

A Beaver landed at the short airstrip three miles from the forts once the soldiers were positioned along the surrounding cliffs. The 'injured' *askar* was lifted aboard and I told the pilot he was a malingerer.

He laughed, "So are fifty per cent of the fellows I fly back with to Salalah before Ramadan. And who's to blame them? I think *I'd* prefer to fast in a hospital bed than this fly-ridden spot."

It was noon and over 115° Fahrenheit without a breeze. Yet the little plane rose up from the loose stones of the runway with fifty yards to spare and spun away east over the forts.

My signaller brought a message just received from the army

camp at Salalah. A camel train smuggling arms was expected to cross from the Yemen shortly. We were to search for recent tracks in the waterless steppes to the south where there was thought to be an infiltration route. If found the trail was to be ambushed.

From Habarut a spider's web of *wadis* wind south into a wilderness of deeply incised hills over 1000 feet high. Slashing through them, the map shows the border as a straight line to Cape Darbat Ali on the coast.

Travelling in this harsh land there are no signs to show where the border lies. There are but a few scattered bedu, fierce goat herders of the Mahra tribe who believe the land is theirs, belonging neither to the Government of Aden nor of Salalah, but to the long defunct Sultanate of Qishn and Socotra.

We selected a wide valley named Sheetah that ran deep into the southern steppes and cached all but the most necessary equipment to lighten the vehicles.

Painfully we wriggled through storm gullies, between giant boulders and edged yard by yard through rifts of soft sand. Corporal Salim stopped by a grove of tamarisk shrubs and walked over to my Land Rover when we halted.

"Tonight the new moon will come. We should stop now before we come to the *gatn*[1] hills where there may be *adoo*."

Ramadan was an important time for the soldiers. About one in five British soldiers admit to some belief in a God. One in fifty might regularly attend church. But the Omanis have fewer material distractions. Religion forms a secure base to their lives, socially and mentally, so the feasts and fasts of Islam have a special meaning for them. Ramadan means 'to be hot'. It is the ninth month of the Muslim year but each year it is later by fourteen days for its advent depends upon the first appearance of the new moon at that season. The fasting lasts for a month ending when the new moon is again seen.

That night there was much meat for all as Mohamed Rashid had shot an ibex. Afterwards we drank coffee and climbed a high hill above the boulders that sheltered the vehicles. We watched the orient. The *moolah* and some others prayed with extra care and attention to ritual.

---

[1] *gatn*—the region where the gravel plateaux that rim the southern sands rise up to meet the Qara Mountains.

There was a light breeze that kept the mosquitoes away and the men chatted together in low voices.

Said Salim picked his nails clean with the point of his stiletto and listened to the gruff voice of Hamid Sultan who cited the Koran theatrically into the void beneath us.

"Three *moolahs* or other religious men must sight the new moon before Ramadan begins," whispered Said. "In Oman it is already in force. Our signaller heard it this morning."

"In Pakistan," muttered Sadeeq the Baluchi, "the three chief *qadhis* fly up in an aeroplane to be sure of spotting the new moon in good time. Once they have seen it, it is Ramadan for all."

It began to get cold. Hyenas howled around us and the echoes of their cries came back from the deeper ravines.

"I see her." Corporal Salim stood on the highest rock and craned his neck to stare intently to the west.

A sigh ran through the line along the hilltop. I too felt strangely affected. After prayer the men moved around shaking each others hands and mine. This warmed me for, after all, I was no Muslim. "There will be much festive shooting in Oman and even Salalah tonight," said Hamid Sultan. "It is a shame we too cannot fire off some rounds but it is better not perhaps. Who knows what moves at night in these hills."

Many minutes later I saw a tiny crescent rise above the horizon, rimmed by a skim of stars. I wondered how many an atheist would doubt his dead, scientific theories on a night like this.

Under my feet fossilised scallops and cephalopods lay where the plunging waves of cataclysmic change had left them millions of years before. And neolithic arrowheads of well-flaked flint were easy to find for early Chaldeans and Azdites had lived in these parts.

These men must have watched the sickle moon of Ramadan, knowing nothing of Mohamed or Christ, but they had felt the primitive urge for unseen Gods: someone to protect them from their primaeval fears. And they had sacrificed animals or other men.

The bones of these men lay around us jammed into cracks in the cliff walls and covered by stones. Along the base of the cliffs and around the boulders of our camp were grave mounds marked by upright stone slabs.

Kamis Ali, a bedu, no more than eighteen years old, had spotted the graves and asked Corporal Salim to move elsewhere but by then the camp was settled. Kamis slept clutching his rifle beside the fire.

For two days we pushed further south until only three Land Rovers were in a fit condition to continue. Huge white boulders blocked our way and the *wadi* narrowed to a deep corridor.

The men had begun to complain. It was Ramadan. All day no food and no water. To push vehicles through long veins of sinking sand, to change tyres in the blistering heat; such things should be kept for other months.

The *moolah* was especially vociferous but I told him there was no way of avoiding our orders. I too had drunk and eaten only during the sunless hours so my position was the stronger to argue from.

The map indicated that we had reached 17 degrees of latitude and yet there had been no sign of camel tracks nor even natural ramps into the *wadi* down which a camel might possibly have climbed. So we loaded haversacks and filled our *zamzamia* water bags from the remaining jerricans. Then we left the Land Rovers with Murad and his drivers.

For six hours, on the morning of the third day, we moved south-west over a high gravel plateau, zigzagging continually to avoid the deeply incised valleys on every side. Twice it was necessary to cross such gullies which was tiring and the desire to drink was great. By noon I could clearly see the ridge line of the Qamr mountains and the high bald mesa called Gants' Hill on my map. In front of us a sheer cliff line fell away for hundreds of feet into a *wadi* that ran south with wide serpentine loops. No camel could cross such terrain, especially since the grooves of all the *wadis* cut to the south. None could be used to travel east against the lie of the land. A closer look through my telescope confirmed this and we turned back.

Two bedu appeared with goats as we crossed a ravine. They approached us asking for water which we gave them. One limped and I noticed that the front half of one foot was squashed so that the toes were webbed, black, and crumpled like old porridge. I asked if he wanted medicine but he said no, the wound was an old one: his foot had been crushed on a rock by the hoof of a camel.

Mark 7 anti-tank mines left behind in Aden; they make a nasty mess of a Land Rover

. . . we found the driver over 100 yards away

Terrace irrigation

Sur

The other man had a blind eye that stared only upwards. He was excited and asserted that we were in the *wadi* Deefan which did not belong to the Sultan of Oman. He also remarked that the soldiers from Aden had not been in the Deefan for six weeks.

Thoroughly alarmed, I forgot my thirst and quickened the pace. My head would roll if we were spotted on the wrong side of the Yemeni border: the region took on a new unfriendly aspect and I cautioned the section commanders to move well spread out and silently.

After three hours there was a sudden fusilade of shots to our front. Breaking into a run we crested a ridge and saw two armed men running fast along a gully below. I cocked my rifle and took aim but Hamid Sultan knocked it aside.

"It's Murad and the drivers, Sahb. We are back at the Sheetah."

They had been shooting at a gazelle. I had told Murad there must be no noise in our absence. There were but six men to guard the vehicles and they would do well not to attract attention to their whereabouts.

I was annoyed with Murad and told him so. He was unrepentant and proud of himself. He had taken two drivers to hunt further down the narrow Sheetah and after a while they had found a path up to the plateau. For a while they had wandered south finding gazelle spoor and the droppings of dassie rabbits, the hyrax of the bible. Then, said Murad, they had come upon a series of parallel trails running to the north-east with fresh *athar* or prints of camels on all of them.

Being few in number they had returned to the Land Rover. Now we had only a single jerrican of water which was required for a leaking radiator and the nearest water was at Habarut, many hours drive away. I decided we must turn back at once. At that point the nearest men to our south were the rebels over the border in Hauf.

Slowly intelligence information we received built up a picture of the sort of training and equipment these rebels had, where they went and what they did. Sometimes intelligence information came through sources in Cairo, Israel or Baghdad which often tied in with other data gained direct from our rebel contacts. At one time information reached us that Musallim

Ali had been in Cairo. As his cousin Kamees too knew all about Musallim Ali's visit to Cairo, he gave us a vivid personal account of how impressed and yet confused Musallim Ali had been with it all.

It was on 20th August 1968 that orders came to Kuweit from the Dhofar Liberation Front in Hauf, where Musallim Ali was taking a course, that he was to act as a temporary courier to Cairo. He was to collect vital documents and details of forthcoming financial aid from China and Algeria.

Musallim's Middle East Airways plane from Aden was diverted to Abu Qurqas the military airfield of Luxor. Here Musallim was met by an Egyptian liaison officer and shown with pride the huge SAM missiles on their way to Shellal and the Aswan Dam. Each was 37 feet long and $1\frac{1}{2}$ tons in weight. Let the Israelis who dare oppose Gamel Abdul Nasser shudder.

They travelled north by train to Cairo and Musallim marvelled at the great brown Nile and its lush fields. What a river! It would take a million Dhofari monsoons to feed such a monster.

In Cairo, Musallim was treated as a privileged guest. All revolutionaries, it was explained, were V.I.P.s. He was shown around the smart offices of TASS, the Soviet news agency which, by providing free, if one-sided, news coverage for the Egyptian press, has undercut all its rivals including Agence France Presse and Reuters.

Then downtown to a guerrilla training school for a tour of the multi-national courses in progress there.

Everyone was buoyant. There was a great air of purpose, of dedication and, above all, optimism. This was the golden age of the Palestinian resistance movement and therefore of all patriotic Arabs. For years they had suffered humiliating defeats at the hands of the Israelis, culminating in the Six-Day War. But then, on 21st March 1968, the young commandos of Fateh managed to withstand a frontal attack by the Israeli Army at Karemeh.

The fact that the Jordanian Army helped them considerably was easily forgotten and the 'Fateh victory' was applauded throughout the Arab lands. Arms, money, and recruits flowed into Fateh and Nasser began his war of attrition across the Canal.

King Hussein had behaved with deceptive submissiveness as

Palestinian guerrillas swaggered through Amman in their thousands and the first inklings of international terror to come were spawned in Cairo: Musallim Ali was honoured to witness the fathers of Black September at school.

There were twelve of them, each with a particular reason for attending the six-week course which dealt with intelligence and security.

None of the men turned around as Musallim and his guide entered. In a reverent whisper the great activists of the Arab cause were pointed out to the humble Dhofari ... Fakhri al Umri, the man who four years later was to open a left luggage locker at Munich railway station and calmly shove in seven Kalachnikov rifles, ammunition and ten grenades. With these eleven Olympic athletes were killed.

... And in the front row was Abu Jihad, who later inspired the international terrorist meetings in Lebanon. Although a pure Maoist himself he sought 'unity in terror' with such widely differing groups as the IRA, the Baader-Meinhof anarchists and the Japanese Red Army (Rengo Sekigun).

Musallim Ali's guide pointed to a dapper fellow who frequently interrupted the lecturer. This was Ali Hassan Salameh who, said the guide, always slept with three women, one tall and black, one fat and yellow, one small and white. The same Salameh who was later to serve as deputy leader of Black September, who organised a daylight assassination attempt in the London borough of Kensington – when the Jordanian Ambassador's Daimler was riddled with bullets. The same Salameh who blew up oil storage tanks in Western Europe during 1971 and 1972.

To see such men made Musallim Ali realise his own insignificance. But it also posed the first trickles of doubt to his over impressionable ever-sensitive mind. For had not Mao damned narrow-minded nationalism as reactionary – and were not these great Arab fighters motivated entirely by nationalism?

And again, the figurehead of hope for all those he met in Cairo was their leader Nasser who, by comparison with Mao, was an earthy capitalist. He remembered the great Red dictum that had sounded like music in his ears when first he had intoned it:

... Capitalism will be relegated to the museum; the communist ideological and social system alone is full of youth and vitality, sweeping the world with the momentum of an avalanche and the force of a thunderbolt ...

In his hotel room Musallim Ali read much about Nasser and the Arab-Israeli war. Strange, he reflected, that the Dhofari guerrillas he had met on their return journey from Peking had so slated Islam, the one creed and way of life which bound the Arabs together in the face of adversity.

Reading further, Musallim became hopelessly confused. Even Nasser it seemed was the source of diametrically opposed contradictions. At the same moment he was sending troops to Northern Yemen to crush the Royalist cause under the Zaidi Imam, and guerrillas to Northern Oman to revive the Imam in that country. Both policies he claimed to be following in the name of progress and enlightenment. Revolution was indeed a complex affair: not at all the straightforward path of light which Mao suggested.

The following morning a phone call came from the Chinese Embassy. The documents were ready. Musallim collected them at once and flew back to Kuwait that day. On 29th August he took them to the office of the exiled Imam of Oman who was at that time on friendly terms with PFLOAG. The office staff were all exiled Omanis. Musallim was met by one Achmed al Selini who had worked there for three years. Achmed al Selini took Musallim down to a well-lit basement room in the centre of which stood a squat Japanese H.F. radio transceiver unit. It was then explained that with this transceiver they were in direct contact with Omani insurgents in the Mussundam peninsula and with the Dhofar Liberation Front in the Wadi Naheez. Another link had recently been established with Baghdad where the Arab Liberation Front trained guerrilla fighters. Only a few weeks before al Ghassani had attacked the Sultan's Forces near Salalah and within four hours of the battle he had been able to broadcast his results which had then been relayed to Baghdad and the world press.

Al Selini lectured Musallim on Russian and Chinese political involvement in Dhofar and the Middle East. Nasser certainly favoured the Russians but it should be remembered that the Russians were helping the Dhofaris with the ultimate aim of denying oil to the Western powers whilst the Chinese wished to help the revolutionaries regardless of oil politics.

Bemused but intrigued by his experiences in Cairo and Kuwait

Musallim felt himself to be part of a great and powerful network. He was then flown back to Aden and there joined the crew of a motorised sailboat bound for Port Sudan and Hauf. At Port Sudan they took on a heavy consignment of arms. The skipper had drawn up by a warehouse containing arms crates for various destinations. There were small crates for Eritrean rebels and considerably larger ones for Frelimo. Some had harmless addresses and were labelled as farm equipment for Zambia. Others were openly addressed to two guerrilla warfare camps in Zanzibar where, Musallim was assured, there were 150 Chinese instructors training members of various African liberation movements.

8

Recce Patrol had spent the month of Ramadan patrolling the empty sands and gravel wastes of the Dhofari desert, then when the new moon had risen again, the month of fasting was over and the days were somewhat cooler, we were recalled to our old northern camp at Bidbid. Here we settled down to the daily round of garrison duty and further training. In February 1969 I left Oman on my annual leave which I spent attempting to ascend the river Nile by mini hovercraft. Shortly before I left Bidbid, an over-excited Baluchi had crushed one of my fingers with his rifle butt during a night exercise and the wound later turned gangrenous in the Sudd swamps of the Nile. For two months back in England I received therapeutic treatment but the finger refused to function normally. Then one day a letter came from Dhofar. There had been alarming but unspecified changes. The soldiers were on the verge of mutiny, and all absent officers were needed badly. The letter was vaguely worded but its meaning was clear enough. I decided at once to return. My overdue absence must look suspiciously like malingering in view of the worsening situation in Dhofar. No one spares sympathy for a finger: a smashed leg is a reason but a crushed finger is merely an excuse.

I flew straight out to Dhofar. My Recce Platoon were again operating desert patrols from the base of Thamarit (or Midway).

As the plane taxied in by the rusty oildrums which formed a stockade around the camp, a ragged crowd ran out from the shade of the huts.

They surrounded me, grabbing my bags and gun, and pumped

my hand in joyous greeting. I felt greatly moved by this welcome. It was so unexpected. I remembered coming back to the Jocks after leave from Germany; to the occasional welcoming grunt and "Back to some hard grind, eh, sah, after all that living it up in Blighty."

It was good to find my Arabic was not forgotten and to put names to the thirty brown faces after four months away. At least seven of them were Mohamed and three were Hamad.

They called me Bachait for reasons which I never discovered. It is an Arab name with no English equivalent.

Yet there was an undercurrent to their chatter. They were not at ease and Corporal Salim Khaleefa confirmed this in the evening.

We walked beyond the *burmail* stockade into a gravel wasteland pocked with the craters of *dhub* lizards, the great sand monitors with clublike tails.

"Is all well, Salim?"

"Praise to be God, everything is well, Sahb."

After many minutes' talk of this and that he admitted that things were amiss.

"Soon after you left, a Sergeant was posted to Recce in place of Abdullah and he has been with us ever since. He is a Hawasena and a good Muslim but there is something wrong in his mind. He drives the men too hard. And he is not just with the Baluchis. They hate him and they no longer sleep and eat amongst us Arabs as they did. So long as this man is with us, I fear the platoon will not be happy."

Salim coughed and palmed his beard. He was embarrassed.

"You see, Sahb, when this Sergeant was earlier in Dhofar, the *adoo* ambushed his platoon and his *zoob* was shot off from the hilt." Salim continued sagaciously, "This is not good for any man and I fear it has turned his mind a little."

I thanked Salim for his information and later met the Sergeant in the camp; a charming man with finely chiselled features and quiet manners. His reported failings were in no way apparent.

The weather was unpleasant. Searing hot winds blew fine sand through the camp for days on end so that the eyes stung and watered and tiny sores begun where one tossed and turned naked at night, sweating on a gritty blanket.

When the winds went it was worse, the heat unrelieved by

the slightest breeze and the flies breeding on the faeces of the soldiers beyond the stockade.

A British Captain, with an Indian Army moustache and Jeevesian mannerisms, had come to Thamarit to look after the garrison and the ration stores which were centralised there for the various outposts. He never stopped talking so long as there was someone to talk to. He complained that my soldiers had been using the disused huts in order to defecate without having to brave the sandstorms.

"Just like animals they were till I put a stop to it. Made them clean the huts out themselves. That soon cured their dirty habits. You should keep a closer rein on them."

It was too hot to train most mornings. I lay on the metal bedstead on a towel and sipped the foul Midway water, swatting flies. But the Captain did not share my apathy. He stalked about the camp in baggy khaki shorts, knee length socks and desert boots discussing the defence of Thamarit at length. The likelihood of its being attacked was highly remote since it was over forty miles from the mountains. But he prepared for the worst. *Burmail* drums along the stockade were filled with sand, sandbags were mounted into machine-gun posts around the camp and a gong was sounded from time to time to practise defence reactions. One night my Land Rovers returned late from a desert patrol and, on approaching the stockade, were illuminated by parachute flares. An unmistakable voice hailed us.

"Halt, who goes there?" in English, to which I replied that it was only me and was ordered to advance. The Captain stood stiffly by the *burmails* in his shorts with a drawn cavalry sword. I might have been an invasion force from the Yemen, he complained. In future I must let him know by radio whenever I anticipated returning to camp after dusk.

On the hottest days in the cramped two-roomed Officers' Mess, he talked away non-stop. I cannot remember the topics he discussed but one especially baking hot day I had a bad bout of diarrhoea and sat sweating for long painful hours on the open throne between the two little rooms. The Captain, finding his audience trapped, came and chatted in front of the throne ignoring my grimaces. Finally, exasperated, I suggested that he removed himself before the atmosphere became untenable.

"Oh that," the Captain laughed. "Don't worry about me. I can't smell a thing. Never have been able to since an accident I had."

A deputation of Baluchis under Corporal Taj came to me during a sandstorm.

"We want to leave Recce, Sahb. We cannot stay any longer with this Sergeant. He favours only the Arabs. Soon there will be trouble."

The problem was solved for me by the Sergeant himself. He had had enough of Dhofar and decided to leave the Army. Once he was gone, I reinstated Corporal Salim Khaleefa as temporary Sergeant and relations immediately began to improve between the men.

Towards the end of May, our Colonel decided to attack the suspected *adoo* headquarters south of Deefa using Simon Sloane's Company from its mountain outpost along the Midway Road to support Patrick Brook's Company already at Deefa. Simon Sloane was from the Argylls; Patrick had been on the same Arabic course. He was an old friend from Germany. With the 300 men and a troop of artillery based at Deefa camp, it was hoped a major blow could be struck at the guerrillas in Western Dhofar. Recce Platoon was to go too to guard Deefa camp.

Simon Sloane's men called at Thamarit for petrol on their way to Deefa. Their morale was high and they chanted battle songs as their lorries roared through the old oil camp. Our Land Rovers followed them to the west through dead gravel land. Late on the second day dense scrub closed in from the south. We edged warily by for an hour but there was silence. A bald hill lay ahead spattered with faded tents and rock walled trenches. This was Deefa.

From the jungle ridges that lapped close to the camp all must have been painfully obvious to the guerrillas; even without binoculars. Army reinforcements with heavy guns had arrived, soldiers scurried about the camp in a business-like manner. It could only mean an impending attack and we learned later that an alert and a warning went out to all the *adoo* groups of Western Dhofar. All had Soviet pack radios and by nightfall they had come from their designated regions to meet the attack.

Six hundred or more of them fresh from the guerrilla training camps of the East.

In the Officers' Mess I listened as the Colonel briefed us all. Simon Sloane and Guy Sheridan looked eager; over the past month their men had killed several guerrillas in their own region of the central Qara. They were confident of great things on the morrow. Patrick Brook took notes in silence. His Company commander had left a few weeks before: he suffered from a serious stomach illness due to the bad water of Dhofar. His replacement was new to the western sector; a Royal Marine, extremely tall and thin and quite without fear of the *adoo*. Perhaps, as events later showed, this was not a good thing.

I watched the Companies leave Deefa in file. There was no moon and little noise told of their going but the creak of rifle slings and soft plunk of gravel under the hooves of the donkeys. But the *adoo* were cunning and they would soon learn that only my thirty men were left in the camp. I visited the scattered trenches around the fringe of the hill. Corporal Salim and Ali Nasser guarded the north. Taj and Mohamed Rashid of the Beard had their men dotted around the rest of the perimeter. They were alert and all knew the Company password. Tendrils of *khareef* mist caressed the darker mounds of gloom outside and stressed the silence.

At eight o'clock the next morning a series of explosions triggered off long bursts of machine gun fire, echoing from the ravines to the south. Twenty minutes later the camp signaller reported that the Army had met large groups of *adoo* on every side. A soldier had been shot through the stomach and was dying. Throughout the next two days we watched and waited listening to the rising tide of battle. At night the mists crept up from the trees but no attack came.

The men of Patrick's Company returned to Deefa on the second day. They moved as though retreating from Moscow. There were few smiles: eyes were averted as I greeted them. Sounds of commotion came from the cooking tent: a young Arab who had stayed behind rushed out to meet the slow moving column. He was grasped by two men and broke into a wild dry scream.

"Nassir! O my brother. Where is he? My only brother." He seemed to choke on his tears and sagged into a shuddering heap scraping the sand with his nails. Men arrived with a corpse on a stretcher and the brother's wailing began anew, cutting through the camp and the silence of the soldiers.

"What is wrong with these men?" I asked Said Salim who was quietly carving a stick with his stiletto. "They look as though the world has come to an end."

"To them it has," he replied, "for their new Major Sahb has a *djinn*. The *moolahs* have said so. And now it is proven. There are some who say they will not leave camp again with this *Major Taweel*. Also the Baluchis hate him for they say he favours only the Arabs. There is even talk that they will shoot him. Sometimes he throws stones at men who are slow on patrol: that is surely a *djinn* at work in him."

Taweel meant tall and is a nickname often applied to tall men. It was an apt name for the new Company Commander. Trained by the Royal Marines, he towered like a beanpole above his soldiers and treated them as though they too had been trained on the tough commando course at Lympstone in Devon. He was fit, fearless, and likeable but he was not good at making allowances and jumped upon those who did not measure up to his own standards. This authoritarianism held no appeal for the Arabs and that was not all. His downfall was his rotten luck. The *adoo* seemed to outwit him at every move and the soldiers were quick to notice this. When, during the following weeks more of them were killed, the symptoms of mutiny that I noticed at Deefa ripened and burst.

On the third night at Deefa we were called south into the scrub to cover the retreat of Simon Sloane's Company. We manned the crags dominating a sheer-sided ravine. As dawn came Simon Sloane's men scrambled along the boulder-strewn *wadi* below us. Stretchers creaked in the pale light. The soldiers were exhausted, their clothes tattered and their skin torn by camel thorn. One man grinned up at me from a stretcher. A morphine label was tied around his neck: it lay across his beard like a price tag. A bullet had passed through his upper thigh and his genitals.

But these men were in no way cowed like B Company: they were proud and pleased to be returning.

The day before, their water supplies had run low and a Beaver aeroplane had risked heavy fire to drop 200 sackcloth water containers. All but 30 had split open on landing so tins full of ice were then dropped. These took eight hours to thaw in the hot sun but solved the water problem.

The Sultan's two jets had been of no help whilst the *khareef* mists crept between the jungle and the clear blue sky. Whenever this happened the guerrillas saturated the Army positions with mortar bombs and heavy fire: their strength and their efficiency were totally unexpected.

The operation had been intended to last five days but was curtailed to three. This was to be the last time we penetrated the western mountains: the *adoo* grip on Dhofar was tightening from the west and soon afterwards the Army withdrew from Deefa altogether. Within eighteen months of the British withdrawal from Aden, Chinese and Russian trained guerrillas accompanied by Chinese advisers had crept from the South Yemen border over most of the Qara mountains and soon would encircle the vulnerable Plain of Salalah with its back to the sea.

Deefa camp was tense after the operation: groups of soldiers sat together in the shade talking in low tones. The following day the *adoo* crept close in the surrounding scrub and shot up the camp. Rays of dancing dust beamed through bullet holes in the Officers' Mess tent.

Patrick's upper arm was bandaged where a bullet had gone clean through between the bones. He told me how it happened.

Not far south of the camp, he had taken a patrol to ambush a known infiltration route. At first all went well. The patrol marched all night and through the following morning seeing no one. Shortly before noon they cautiously eased into ambush positions above a deep valley and settled down to brew tea once the machine guns were sited and the mortars unloaded from the donkeys.

Patrick chain-smoked Consulate cigarettes as he spoke.

"It was five past eleven: I remember checking my watch. After that bloody night march it all seemed so green and peaceful. We were sipping tea; just like a picnic in a park really." He laughed at the memory.

"Then one of my machine gunners saw something below us. One moment there was damn all . . . Then, not 200 yards away, a dozen of the bastards appeared. You could see every detail of their kit, the sand-coloured floppy hats and khaki shirts. There were some camels behind them I think. And their rifles were automatic Simonoffs.

"One of my men fired before the order was given. Then everyone opened up. But the *adoo*'s reaction was incredibly quick. They sheered into the bush and three seconds later there wasn't a sign of them."

Patrick was silent for a while then he shook his head slowly, looking sideways at me.

"You know, it was all so sudden, almost like a film. I've been in the Army playing soldiers for eight whole years but nothing prepares you for the real thing when it comes. One minute peace and cups of tea then the whole world crashes and the blood lust comes so quickly out of nowhere. Anyway we searched and found one corpse with a bullet through the face and two in the chest. We put him on the donkey for the boys didn't want to leave a fellow Muslim around for carrion even though he was an *adoo*."

Then the patrol had made a fatal mistake. Their presence was known and they were deep in *adoo* country. Yet for half an hour they delayed, loading the corpse and talking. The kill had made them elated, over-confident. Taking the simplest, most direct route back to Deefa they set out in two files with fifteen yards between them and moving on either side of the main footpath.

"We paused every five minutes to listen, but I suppose we must have made a hell of a din pushing through the scrub. I was leading with my compass because there are so many tracks that without a direct bearing you're soon lost. The scrub hides all landmarks. Quite suddenly we ran into a close ambush: no more than thirty yards ahead. The noise was terrifying. Not only the guns in the close confinement of the bush but the incredible sound of branches splintering all about you and the whine of ricochets from the rocks underfoot."

Patrick was flung to the ground. A bullet passed through his upper arm and another smashed the Sarbe radio he carried on his waistbelt. He crawled to the bren gunner behind him. A bullet had passed through his skull and out behind his ear. Patrick took the ·303 bren and wriggled back to the next man, a Sergeant. He had only one eye; the other was a mess without a socket. The fellow was writhing among sharp stones and Patrick passed by a third casualty to a Baluchi who took the bren and began to fire back.

The *adoo* did not follow up their attack for there were over a hundred soldiers. Sticking to Giap's doctrine, they faded away unseen. A smaller army unit would not have been so lucky.

Making stretchers from rifles and headcloths the patrol took twelve hours to limp back to the camp and the blinded man died en route.

"I dread to think what these mountains will be like when the monsoon comes," Patrick reflected, "and that's in less than a month's time."

The next day we left with Simon Sloane's Company to return to our respective bases. But just before we left one of Simon's men approached me.

"You have no Sergeant, Sahb, and I would like to join Recce. You tell Major Sloane to let me come, and we will both be happy." He patted my shoulder conspiratorially and winked like a pocket Machiavelli. He had a scraggy tuft of beard and was even smaller than Ali Nasser.

Corporal Salim Khaleefa and others of the Hawasena tribe in Recce had gathered about the little man beaming their delight.

On the way back to Thamarit, Mubarreq the negro shouted in my ear.

"Salim Khaleefa and Ali have tongues of honey. All last night they talked to Sergeant Mohamed of the wonders of Recce Platoon. Every man likes Mohamed. It will go well with us if he joins us."

In early June we drove south over the Midway Road from Thamarit to Salalah. The Land Rovers moved along the mountain trail whilst the men scouted ahead and to the flanks with great care. The Qara hills are quite different when seen from their upper plateaux. The gaunt cliffs are hidden by the upper slopes of rock-strewn grass, tinder dry in the pre-monsoon season but not unlike the rolling down of Sussex. Wild fig and tamarind trees grace each hillock like parkland and the labyrinth of jungle-clad ravines that split the land are invisible from on top, so steeply do they descend, like hidden ha-has.

126

Four miles along the track we came to the heavily fortified camp of Simon Sloane's mountain base. He was not pleased that his Sergeant Mohamed, whom he valued, should join Recce and reminded me that I had earlier whisked away five good men behind his back. But he relented at length and a happy Mohamed left with us when we bade Simon good-bye and continued warily beyond the safety of his camp and along the track. We were lucky that day and descended without incident to the Plain of Salalah.

Back at Umm al Ghawarif (the army camp near Salalah), the Colonel told me that various intelligence sources agreed that the *adoo* awaited only the coming of the monsoon to bring new Russian weapons east into Dhofar. Some of these had been seen by informers; metal tubes over 20 feet long which fired rockets.

There was an Australian mercenary officer at Salalah nicknamed Mike Muldoon who had fought in the Congo and along the Zambezi. His speciality was weapons and he believed the metal tubes were probably 140 millimetre rocket launchers of the type much used by the North Vietnamese. Made in Russia, the rockets weigh 70 lbs each having a range of over 9000 yards. This would allow the *adoo* to bombard the RAF station and Umm al Ghawarif camp with impunity from the safety of the *khareef* covered Qara; a necessary preamble to any all-out assault across the plain. But the monsoon had made the mountain trails so slippery that arms-laden camels or men would find it impossible going. They would have to use the more gently sloping trails through the foothills and this, said the Colonel, we of Recce must prevent.

"The monsoon will begin in earnest by the end of June. When it comes you must keep the foothill trails well covered. Ambush the villages where the *adoo* go to get food and the wells where they drink. And always vary your routine or *they* will get *you*."

Night after night we drove towards the mountains without lights. Where dry gullies fissured the plain, a guide moved ahead of each Land Rover waving a white towel. If the winds blew noise inland from the Indian Ocean towards the Qara we stopped six miles from the foothills leaving Murad and his drivers with a machine gun and a radio. When the north wind blew it was safe to approach much closer. Then, on foot, we moved up the mouths of the great intermontane valleys where they debouched onto the plain: the Jarsees, the Arzat and the Naheez, all wide and densely forested.

A maze of footpaths wend through the bush and the ant-hills, some laterally and others leading off into the valleys. Camel spoor and droppings were fresh on many of these trails mingled with the footprints of *jebalis* who never wear shoes despite the heat of the ground and the inch long camel thorns. The soles of their feet grow thick horny scales and their toes often split like old wood.

The grass of the previous year's monsoon lay flat and withered. *Jebali* herdsmen had come from the mountain tops with their families to live in tattered tents by the *wadi* floors where water flowed and there was still some grazing. But not enough. In the Naheez we met a Bait Qatan tribesman half of whose cattle had already died. Two of his ten children were dead from malnutrition and conditions in the mountains, he said, were worse than ever in living memory. Over a third of all the Qara cattle had starved to death and the *adoo* were no longer paying for the food and milk they took from the *jebalis*.

Naseeb, our guide, interrogated the man in his own tongue. Naseeb's own brother was of the *adoo* but he still hated them.

"Have you seen the guerrillas?"

The *jebali* hesitated. He was frightened but we were well screened by bush. To help loosen his tongue Sergeant Mohamed fetched a bag of rice and gave it to him. There was no sign of gratitude since, to *jebalis*, all gifts come not from a human agent, but from God. He placed a finger on one nostril and blew hard through the other: the result being effective but not pretty. Then he spoke to Naseeb, his voice warbling shrilly like the lead-bird of a dawn chorus.

He was afraid, he said, for his wife's family was related to Said bin Ghia one of the chief *jebali* agents of the Government. And of late the *adoo* had arrested a growing number of suspected informers and their relatives. The fate of those arrested was not known but he had no difficulty in guessing at it.

He would like to make a firm stand against the *adoo* but how could he? No one would help him. Certainly not the Government who gave nothing to the people and whose army was too feeble to offer anyone protection. He had no choice but to give food and milk to the *adoo* whenever they visited him. If he didn't they would take it anyway and might suspect him of being a Government sympathiser.

Naseeb talked with him for a long while and watched as he drew a map in the sand. Afterwards they shook hands. *"Saad da'ah Q'ass,"* said the *jebali* with his hand on his heart and then disappeared with his bag of rice.

Naseeb told me that the man was willing to help but that since the *adoo* kept to no set route nor schedule, he had suggested we ambush a large cave further up the *wadi*, where he had twice seen *adoo* groups visiting the bedu who lived there, for milk and for sex with their women.

Two nights later we came again to the Naheez valley and Naseeb took us through dense bush to a long deserted village where fallen pillars indicated great age and past wealth. A black void gaped within the ruins; a huge well with no visible bottom. Beyond it, the hillside rose steeply and we climbed to the mouth of a pitchblack cave. The floor curled beneath layers of goat and bat droppings. Dry wings scrabbled above as we entered the cave and I flinched as a bat blurred past inches away from my nose. The air thrummed with a high pitched whistling as we crept inside. There were muffled voices further within the gloom. Naseeb beckoned me to halt and in a little while I heard him talking with a bedu.

He returned. "The people here agree to stay inside the cave tomorrow but they cannot say when the *adoo* will next come."

For eight hours we lay in the mouth of the cave behind rocks that had doubtless fallen from its high arched roof. The smell of the place was foul and I passed the time scratching myself, for goat fleas infested the dung and small ticks dropped off the rocks onto us.

We could not use torches but as dawn slowly lit the cave, I pulled off the ticks one by one leaving their front claws and heads dug into my skin. Stalactites and stalagmites took shape behind us like teeth in a shark's mouth and finally the wattle huts of the bedu were visible deep inside the cave amidst a sea of small white goats. Naseeb came from one of the huts and offered me his water bottle full of warm goat's milk.

We stayed for two days in the cave but no *adoo* came. I was fairly certain they had not seen us for no one had moved but to crawl backwards into the dim recesses to pray or to defecate. But somehow they had known and kept away.

The men were patient enough during our many ambushes. They lay on narrow ledges or squeezed behind rocks waiting interminably but time after time no one came into our selected killing ground. If we could not capture a rocket-laden camel train, we might perhaps snare a prisoner who would provide us with information. In the wider *wadis* like the Sahilnawt and the Naheez and in other nameless valleys crossed by tracks, we lay in hiding, always in well-spread positions so that between five sections, we covered a wide area of trails. And each time we left Umm al Ghawarif, there were fewer little errors, the men moved ever more quietly, freezing at once to the least noise in the foothills. Sometimes the boredom of the long hours of waiting was alleviated. After twenty-four hours sitting motionless behind a bush, I began to notice little things that would normally have escaped me.

I remember the fascination, even the emotion, of watching a miniature cycle of nature's cruelty, a facet of the ecosystem of life and death in the Qara mountains. A violent buzzing attracted my attention to the feathery web of a spider with a black and yellow abdomen. A large hornet was caught by the wings and the spider hopped onto its under belly to inject its poison. The hornet buzzed furiously and both insects fell to the ground. The spider seemed paralysed but the hornet flew away to die elsewhere. Occasionally the spider moved its legs. Perhaps it would have lived but a red ant ran over the earth and seized it by one leg with fierce saw-edged jaws. The leg came away but the ant bit again into the spider's abdomen and began to drag the larger insect off struggling feebly.

The drama did not end there for the red ant in its greed dragged its intended meal across a black ant trail.

At once the spider became a seething black mass and was eaten alive. The red ant too was stripped of its legs and abdomen though its jaws clung to the spider to the last.

By mid-June the first gossamers of the *khareef* filled the summit downs of the Qara and we laid an ambush deep within the Wadi Dut above a chain of pools where fresh camel prints spattered the sand. My position was some fifty yards above the largest pool in a low ceiling'd cave. Mubarreq the negro and Hamid Sultan sited their machine guns and we lay back. Just beyond the flowering lianas that fringed the nearest pool I could see the shadowy outlines of Corporal Taj and his men, but only through my telescope. A hyena limped by a few yards from them —and presumably upwind since I had still not succeeded in preventing Taj from using a powerful Indian hair cream called Jungle Petal. Even ebullient Sadeeq Jumma and the other Baluchis had, after much exhortation, stopped applying hair cream to their slick black locks. But not conceited Taj: even though he conceded that the *adoo* had powers of smelling as keen as a dog's; being able to smell an Army ambush half a mile away. His line of logic was that since the *adoo* were neither meat-eaters nor smokers they would, if the wind favoured them, smell any ambush of meat-eating, cigarette-smoking soldiers whether their hair was coated in Jungle Petal or not.

Hamid Sultan touched my knee. I followed his gaze and saw three dark shadows moving through the indigo shrubs beyond the pool. Said Salim adjusted the range setting on his rifle.

They were young bedu girls, probably of the Bait Jaboob tribe whose cattle graze the Wadi Dut.

A warm wind blew powerfully from the sea rippling a shower of scented pods from the giant tamarinds about the pool. The girls' laughter came up to us as their dark blue sarongs rose high with the breeze. They unwound the cloth from their shoulders hitching it about their hips. Long black hair fell about their shoulders and breasts as they entered the water splashing each other. There was an animal suppleness to their movements.

They bathed each other carefully using handfuls of fern and burst into gurgling laughter. At length they were finished and squatted on the low bank where the sun soon dried their skin. Humming-birds like kingfishers whirred in the shrubs.

Two of the girls left by the way they had come. The other dallied arranging her hair by its reflection in the pool. For half an hour or more she stayed by the water plaiting reeds and looking around her. Perhaps she sensed the nearby presence of Corporal Taj and his Jungle Petal.

Then she rose and ran into the indigo shrubs; visible only above the shoulders. She clasped a black skinned *jebali* around the neck and rubbed her nose against his. I glanced at Hamid and the others: no one had seen the man come. Together they moved away from the pool climbing the mossy incline towards us and lay together in the deep shadow of the tamarinds. The man was half naked already. He flicked aside the girl's blue cloth and beneath it she wore black leggings. These were dissimilar to European tights for they ended at the upper thighs without covering the genitals. There was much movement but no noise for a minute or so. Then the man stood up quickly and wrapped his loin cloth about him. He stooped once to touch her then left, quickly melting with the dappled shade of the shrubs. The girl lay still for a while before walking languidly to the pool. She washed her face but not her body and disappeared behind the rocks where Taj's men lay hidden.

I looked at Hamid Sultan. He rolled his eyeballs towards heaven and winked evilly. I was glad no *adoo* came to the pools that day; we never returned there and my memories are of a little piece of paradise tucked away on the edge of the great sand deserts.

Naseeb the guide spoke to me when we returned to the Land Rovers.

"Sahb, did you see that wicked girl? If her brother or her husband finds out he will bury her alive or cut out her genitals and throw them into the sea. Such an act brings great shame to her family."

"She could always maintain she was raped, couldn't she?" I asked him.

"True, in which case her family would find a girl of the offender's family and rape her in exchange. That would be lawful."

Later I became friendly with Said bin Ghia, a sheikh of the Bait Qatan tribe who had defected from the *adoo* and become the head intelligence agent in Salalah.

I learnt much from him about the *jebali* tribes. Their lives were not easy but they were hard like Qara rock and their deep-rooted Muslim beliefs, although blurred with many more ancient superstitions, enabled them to accept the hardships of their environment.

Considerable confusion now tangled the minds of these people for with the drought, a worse famine than even the older folk had experienced, came a new terror that unsettled the basis of their being.

Young men whose long hair and beards—the age-old symbols of their belief—were crudely shaven, came back from abroad. They came as strangers to their families and tribes to preach the Anti-God.

Many of the older folk tried to stir the communities against these new doctrines but this ceased when two especially vociferous old sheikhs of the Eastern Mahra had their eyes burnt out in public.

The ceremony had been conducted with a fire-heated pocket knife by the nephew of one of the two sheikhs. The nephew had but recently returned from Iraq and was especially talented at converting his kin to Marxism. After the operation on his uncle and the other patriarch, neither of whom died for several days, he had made the words of Karl Marx heard above their screams. And the gathered *jebalis* listened without understanding the new phrases of politics and the ranting of the khaki-clad youngster whom everyone remembered as an idle child, good only at shirking his duties with the cattle. They failed to see why they should stop praying, why Islam should be discredited, nor why such happenings as they had just witnessed should lead the way to a new and glorious way of life. But they understood the meaning of the young men's gleaming weapons and bandoliers. So they began to concur.

What little food they had saved in this year of hunger they gave to these young and sleek-skinned 'defenders of the people', and they watched the weaker of their children die with distended bellies. And when the young men went away to fight the Sultan's soldiers they did not talk of dissent for they soon learnt to distrust one another, not knowing to whom the communists had promised food in return for quisling services.

Said bin Ghia had foreseen these troubled times four years ago when the *adoo* first contacted him in Bahrein. Born a sheikh of the Bait Qatan tribe, he had emigrated to earn money in the oil states. He learnt some English, married and became head gardener at an American Forces golf course. Then back in the winter of 1963–1964, Musallim bin Nuffl, searching for expatriates to recruit for his fledgling Dhofar rebel group, had coerced Said into a training course with 100 other Dhofaris at an Iraqi Army camp. In Basrah they learnt unarmed combat, rifle drill, and vehicle mechanics. They jumped off speeding lorries into the sand and marched on tarmac parade grounds. They posed in uniform for photographs with their Iraqi instructors and in 1965 they loaded six Dodge power wagons with arms and ammunition. King Feisal of Saudi Arabia was still smarting from the shaming outcome of the Buraimi border dispute with the Sultan of Oman, so he allowed these anti-Sultanate rebels to traverse Saudi Arabian territory from Dahran to Dhofar.

It was an incredible journey though Said gave me his account of it in simple tones.

In three weeks they crossed the Empty Quarter through the heart of the dunes. Their food was always mixed with sand, their cooking utensils were lost in the first week in a sandstorm, two of the Dodge wagons had to be towed and a third was ingeniously repaired by battering a metal coffee pot to replace a piston ring. There was squabbling and attempted murder. For a while they were lost and for five days they drank hot rusty water from the wagon's radiators. Two of the radiators which leaked were fixed with flour and sand. When there was no more water, the men shot gazelles and shared out the stomach water and urine between them.

When at last they had skirted British-occupied Aden and reached the sands of Dakaka, they were betrayed by their leader's uncle. The Sultan's aeroplane destroyed all the wagons and most of the arms were later seized. Said bin Ghia himself then deserted and made his way to the Plain of Salalah to join the Government.

"My people," Said told me, "lived for centuries stealing cattle and killing one another. Then, ten years ago, the Sultan came from Muscat to live in Salalah. The fighting stopped and our young men went abroad for education. If bin Nuffl had not begun the fighting there would now be no bloody communists and no bloody trouble." He rubbed his enormous paunch and looked very merry despite the troubles.

Said still had contacts with his tribe and knew of any event in the Qara within a few days of its occurrence. He stopped me in the camp one day late in June and warned me that the *adoo* of the Central mountains had taken two of the bedu, whom I had been cultivating with food and medicine, away to the Yemen. He said that the *adoo* were satisfied that the Companies were of little danger to them since they were under permanent surveillance; their every move noted and so easily countered. But as Recce moved only by night to ambush a wide and unpredictable front, we were not so easy to avoid. Also we came into close contact with those bedu who were less under the *adoo* thrall being plains dwellers—at least during the spring and summer months—and such people were more susceptible to the friendly persuasion of our food bags and medical chest. Therefore specially appointed *adoo* armed bands had been sent to eliminate us in the course of our operations.

I thanked Said bin Ghia for his warning and forgot it for the intelligence agents were known to be alarmist.

That week chance took us into the mountains to lay an ambush near the village of Darbat. At dusk we drove to the plain above Taqa.

Sergeant Mohamed and a number of the soldiers had coughs. One cough in the mountains might be fatal so only sixteen men left the vehicles and climbed through the foothills. We crossed a gravel track, built by the Sultan in less troubled times when he had married a woman of Darbat. Their son was Qaboos, heir to the Sultanate.

The moon sped by tattered banks of cloud, vanguard of the monsoon, and the slopes above the track were thickly wooded. The men closed up automatically. Said Salim was in front, moving wraith-like with sure-footed ease. He stopped without warning and knelt, taking care to make no noise against rock or branch with his bren gun. I did likewise as did the men behind me. For moments there was no sound save the breathing of the branches in the monsoon breeze.

Then from the hills above twigs crackled. The noise grew louder. There seemed to be a host of people descending the mountainside directly towards us. Behind me a soft click sounded as the signaller eased off the safety catch on his submachine gun. The noise was all about us and a black-and-white cow moved past a yard away. I relaxed and felt my rapid heartbeat ease. The herd moved by and then the sharp tac-tac of the herdsmen's sticks tapping trees to keep the cows moving.

In the gloom ahead one of the herdsmen stopped. Said turned to look at me, passing the heel of his hand across his jugular, followed by a questioning thumbs-up sign with his stiletto. I shook my head and a moment later regretted it for the man gave a falsetto cry similar to that used by the goat herders to marshal their flocks. But the soldiers understood little of the *jebali* tongue and we had no local guide with us. From the rim of the mountains above came a faint reply; the warbling trill of a woman. When the herd was gone Said Salim moved close and whispered softly into my ear.

"That man smelled us in the dark, Sahb. He cried out not to the cattle but to the *adoo* watchers around Darbat. The wind blows tonight from behind us. It will carry our smell to the villagers unless we disguise it."

Finding the liquid green spattering of the cattle, we smeared it on our shirts and trousers. There was little enough about for the wretched cows were thin as rakes but what there was smelled evilly.

"They must have heard the Land Rovers," Said whispered, "and sent the cattle down to cover their search for us. Usually the Qara graze only by day except during the late monsoon. We must be very careful, Sahb; these *adoo* are cunning as rats."

The escarpment was steep. The men were fit and, unburdened, would have reached the plateau above in an hour. But none of us carried less than thirty pounds. Every other man had a machine gun, 500 rounds or bombs for the mortar. Climbing the rock-strewn slope, it was too easy to slip. A single clash of metal against stone or a dislodged rock bounding away down the ravine would betray us. So we eased upwards slowly, furtively, making no sound but the faint slop-slop of the contents of our water containers.

Said Salim and Mubarreq the Zanzibari were somewhere ahead for both were uneasy, sensing that our presence was known and awaited. They were our tentacles. If there were an ambush, they would spring it giving us time to escape. Both carried white phosphorus grenades in their hands with well greased and carefully spliced pins.

At length we reached the shoulder of the escarpment and traversed to a vantage point close above the village of Darbat. Corporal Salim moved by with his seven men.

Through binoculars I watched them separate into two groups and melt into the moonshadow of the rocks. My section split likewise; Mubarreq, Said Salim and the signaller staying with me.

From above a wild cat snarled. A low chill sound that set my teeth on edge. Laying my kit on the ground I began to move rocks into a protective mound, checking each one for snakes, spiders or scorpions before sliding my arm beneath to lift it. The others helped, leaving only the signaller to watch the night.

An animal screamed close by as our sangar wall neared completion. Mubarreq lowered his rock and grabbed his machine gun. "That is no *senoor* cat, Sahb," he whispered. "That is the *adoo*. They are Zingibari slaves escaped from Salalah and they rule the Darbat region with great cunning. Their night signs are those of their forefathers from the rain forests of Usumbara and Ukambani." I had not seen Mubarreq frightened before. His black fists tightened about his machine gun as he crouched low behind the makeshift rocks.

Said Salim was calm. "They know we are here, Bakhait. They will move around us to cut us off and in the morning they will attack. This is a bad place to defend."

I had seen and heard nothing to suggest we were detected but Mubarreq's fear was catching and I trusted Said's keen senses. I pressed the pressel switch of my walkie-talkie four times and waited. Corporal Salim Khaleefa replied likewise and very soon he came back with his men. Mubarreq fetched the other half of the section led by Sadeeq the Baluchi. In a low voice I told them our position was bad. We were overlooked here and must move quickly before dawn and before we were cut off. To our south the sheer abyss of the Darbat cliffs cut us off from the safety of the plain. Behind us the *adoo* moved unseen and to the north spread the forested ravines of the guerrillas. Our only course lay west, through the village itself, to the escarpment beyond the cliffs where it again became possible to descend to the plain.

Corporal Salim had, through long practice, switched off his National transceiver before coming close to me to avoid the possibility of electronic 'feedback' screech should one of us activate our radio by mistake. It was a shock then when, quite

137

clearly in the tense silence, a rapid whispering sounded from my receiver.

Mubarreq stiffened, listening. "They speak in Zingibari on their radios. Quick. Give me the National." But the whispering stopped as quickly as it began.

Not knowing how close were the *adoo*, we edged one by one down the wooded slope towards the village leaving only Said and Mubarreq to follow well behind us. Corporal Salim's men went first. As we awaited their going, Sadeeq the Baluchi showed me a small bottle.

"It is the Jungle Petal, Sahb. I bought some for my hair and by luck it is with me. Perhaps if we leave it here the *adoo* will think we stay all night."

Feeling a little ridiculous, I smeared the seductive Jungle Petal grease over rocks and in the foliage about the sangars before leaving.

The wind combed though the silver scrub playing tricks with the moon and with my imagination. Each rock and stunted thorn held menace, magnified by the silence between the waves of monsoon wind. And in each lull the clouds of mosquitoes sang again rising from the leaves to the hypnotic scent of our sweat.

A demoniac shriek cut into my thoughts coming from the outskirts of the village. I hurried forward passing the men one by one. Where the scrub grew thin and the fields of the village began Corporal Salim and Hamid Sultan struggled with a writhing body. It was the young bedu Kamis Ali. Streamers of froth swung from his chin and he struggled with surprising strength for a slim lad. Hamid's great hands held him firmly by the jugular and across the mouth so that, though the spittle continued to ooze out no sound escaped. Corporal Salim strapped the bedu's threshing limbs with his *shemagh* headcloth and Hamid forced his shell dressing into the young man's mouth. His eyes, bulbous and filled with fear, darted hither and thither beyond his control. His state of terror seemed to effect the men nearby who cowered away covering him with their guns.

But Hamid hoisted the pinioned bedu on to one shoulder easily managing his machine gun with his free hand.

"Hurry, Sahb. I will carry Kamis. Dawn will come soon and we cannot delay."

The sky seemed already a lighter shade of dark. I was worried.

It was vital to hurry yet hurry we could not. The village stretched on and on but we had to walk only where the ground was rock hard. Corporal Salim's section moved unseen away to the right. Sadeeq removed his shoes and carried them down the front of his shirt: the rest of us followed suit for there were few thorns in the open fields. Sometimes glancing back, I saw dark figures flit among the shadows behind. I presumed these belonged to Said Salim and Mubarreq. I had drunk too much of my water already and, passing the rim of a dank pool, replenished my *chagul* water container.

A rocky ledge of limestone took us to the very edge of the abyss where the monsoon floodwaters fall away for 500 feet in a thundering chute when the Darbat river overflows — the only perennial river in Eastern Arabia.

But now the pools were low and lips of the chasm dry as we passed in silence along the brink leaving no sign of our passing even for the practised eyes of the inhabitants of Darbat.

Every ten minutes I signalled to Corporal Salim and heard the two soft clicks of his reply. He could see us outlined against his horizon crouched though we were. The odour of burning dung was strong from the village so our own body smell was safe enough for the present. No dogs barked among the conical mud huts. Perhaps there were no dogs now in Darbat since food had been scarce for the people of late.

Ahead I could make out the rising lump of a hillock but there was still no possible escape to our left for the cliffs fell away sheer without the least ledge or cranny. I lay flat along the edge to check. It was growing lighter quickly now. Glistening white walls fell away to a grey channel far below with truncated stalactites lancing downwards like icicles in tangled columns. At the base of the abyss a dark confusion of huge castor oil plants curled and swayed in the down-draughts. These cliffs, called Dahaq, are rich in legend of human sacrifice and mystic oracles.

I shuddered and kept my distance from the edge. Soon we would be seen from the village. There was no chance now of reaching the plain before dawn. We must hide in the thick vegetation of the hillock close ahead. It was not itself overlooked and commanded a good view of our escape route to the escarpment.

I signalled four times to Corporal Salim who soon appeared and squatted beside me. The evil spirit, he told me, had departed from Kamis the bedu who was now recovered.

Again we split into four groups to find cover on the hillock; Salim's men to face west towards the plain whilst we looked back towards Darbat. The mosquitoes closed in as we left the winds of the cliff edge. Said Salim appeared from behind with the negro. No one, they said, had followed us.

Crawling on hands and knees, we dragged the guns and ammunition beneath a web of liana and thorn close to the crest of the hillock. A fissured rock formed a shallow cave above us and we slept where we lay. Except Said Salim who squatted to listen and to watch.

The heat awoke me and an intolerable sting on my thigh. My eyelids were heavy and my throat dry as parchment. I swilled some water around in my mouth and swallowed it slowly. Said sat motionless like a Buddha by his machine gun. He smiled briefly and lay back when I motioned him to sleep. He was asleep in minutes disregarding the seething mass of black ants that ran over the floor of our tiny cave. I moved carefully and rubbed Antisthan on to the red weals on my side where the ants had bitten me. Using my map I brushed a clear space to sit on. The crushed and injured insects were soon taken away by their cannibalistic brethren. I was bitten again and again and yearned to get out of the hot little hell-hole but any movement would give us away.

People were moving about in the village; mainly between the huts and about the large lake to the north. Others drove flocks of goats and cows into the slopes above the houses. I saw no one with a modern rifle, only the ancient matchlocks which were status symbols rather than weapons.

A foul stench permeated through the cave and I heard the angry buzzing of massed flies at the cave mouth: the remains of an animal festered close by.

I soon grew accustomed to the smell and ate some hardtack biscuits. I was hungry and sorely tempted to open the corned beef tin that made up our rations. But its smell would be alien to the local people and therefore dangerous. My hunger grew and prevailed over common sense: after all surely the stinking carcass outside would out-smell a bit of corned beef. To further salve my conscience I awoke the others, except for Said Salim, and all agreed it would be safe to eat the corned beef. We divided the tin's contents into three and spread the pink meat on to the biscuits after burying the tin and biscuits paper. The flies from the carcass outside seemed to have retained their discerning taste for we had to wipe clusters of them from each mouthful.

The morning passed by slowly and there was ample time to admire if not to appreciate the fine view through the curtain of foliage.

It might have been a scene from a Nile explorer's travels a century ago. Some of the village people who belonged to the Bait Maashani wore loose shoulder-hung cloths and leather thongs bound their shaggy hair: they were true Qara folk with fine features. But most of the villagers were negroid; escaped slaves or freedmen from the coast. Less lazy than the Arabs, they had tilled the fields about the long narrow lakes and between the forests. Even their houses were conical African kraals, quite unlike the square limestone dwellings of the Maashani.

The lakes stretched beyond my view into the Darbat Valley which split the higher plateau. These lakes were now but thin lines of water in wallows of cracked orange mud. The irrigation channels into the fields were dry and only the thicker clumps of forest were green. Small birds and herons gorged themselves on minnows amongst the dry bulrushes where even the smallest puddles were fast disappearing. Cotton and maize fields, dead and brown, were carefully channelled right up to the cliff edge and, above the village, cave dwellers screamed at their goats driving them out into the dry scrub.

Twice goat flocks combed the hillock where we lay hidden and each time the women that drove them searched every thicket and hollow as they passed. But the goats avoided our cave, put off perhaps by the smell of putrefied meat. The second flock passed us in the late afternoon driven by a single hag in tattered clothes. Despite the carcass she seemed interested in the ground about out refuge, examining the earth minutely and casting covert glances directly at our thicket.

I glanced at Said whose face was impassive. An ant bit the soft skin of my armpit. I swore viciously to myself but remained motionless and tense. The minutes passed and the old hag continued to nose around our cave. For a while I lost sight of her then a rock scrabbled faintly above me and a shadow flickered across the lattice work of thorns. She stood upon the rocks that sheltered us and screamed a broken trill, perhaps to her goats. Then she went and no more people came on to the hillock nor even moved about in the village.

At dusk I signalled Corporal Salim and received his whispered reply so, when darkness came, we crept gratefully out and found Sadeeq. Together we joined Corporal Salim's men. From the far side of the hillock he had watched our escape route all day, the clear flat ground that lay between our hillock and the point at which the cliffs of the escarpment became climbable. Only cattle had been there, a large herd driven up from the village at midday, and Corporal Salim took this as a good sign since the Qara never took cattle into an area where the *adoo* planned an ambush. But the cattle were still there and this was unusual for there are wolves and cattle thieves about at night. Normally the herdsmen took the cows to their byres by dusk.

Said Salim was uneasy and said so. We must wait and listen, he counselled. I wished only to get away from the place as quickly as possible. But Said's advice was seldom bad so we waited, just below the skyline of the hillock and, as the moon rose, a commotion began below amongst the cattle.

Through binoculars I picked up at least a dozen men moving among the cows. I could not tell whether they were armed or not but they drove the cattle into the scrub between us and the escarpment and then the noise died down.

Quietly we conferred. It was agreed that we had been compromised, perhaps by the goat woman, perhaps by our smell. But the *adoo* could not yet know how strong we were nor how many, if any, army groups were supporting us.

Leaving Said Salim and Mubarreq well concealed we moved due north away from the windy cliffs and into the forest beside the withered maize fields. Birds fluttered wildly in the trailing lianas. Snakes slithered over dry leaves. We made little noise but enough for the listeners to know.

Following the course of the lakes beyond the forest we trod where the mud was still sticky and our prints were clear behind us. For an hour we moved north turning then directly on our tracks to wait until midnight, straining our ears through the frenetic chorus of bullfrogs and crickets. But no one followed so, as the moon inclined to the east, we crept back towards the escarpment stopping often to listen. Soon the dim rise of our hillock stood to the left and Saif Musabe of the wild curly hair whistled high with the call of the *lefeef* night falcon.

The reply came at once from the bushes ahead and we moved into them cautiously. Said Salim and Mubarreq were there squatting in a stone sangar.

Said Salim whispered quietly, but he could not hide his elation.

"Had we moved forward from the hillock at dusk, Sahb, we would now be dead." He indicated other *sangars* perhaps a dozen of them, all covering the ground between hillock and escarpment. "When you left us, we heard nothing for maybe two hours. Then the cows came back and with them many men: we could not see how many for we were well hidden. They moved all over the hillock and down towards the village. They must have seen and counted your tracks. When they discover they are tricked, they will be back for our blood."

We went like the wind, reaching the plain in two hours. Three green flares fetched Murad and our Land Rovers from Mamoorah.

9

ETAILS of the great rebel camp at Hauf filtered back to
us. It seemed that those who had been trained in Russia
and China had set up a carefully trained execution squad
or *Idaara* whose work was not only to eliminate class enemies
but also to do this in such a fashion that each execution had a
profound psychological effect on other potential enemies.

Why shoot a man behind a rock when he can be thrown
over a cliff in front of his fellow villagers? The latter treatment
was far more likely to persuade the onlookers to behave and
to spread the word as to what awaited future transgressors.

Ahmaad Deblaan and Kamees were in the camp at Hauf
and so was Salim Amr who was employed directly under the
resident *Idaara* commander. Now he was established. But
privately Salim Amr had become thoroughly bored with the
dialectics of communism. Odessa was behind him now and all
those excruciating classroom hours had served their purpose.

If he, Salim Amr, earned good money he aimed to keep it.
Why share it with others who were too idle or stupid to make
their own cash? Furthermore these stupid new ideas about having one wife and treating her as an equal were ridiculous. He
would buy at least three as soon as he could afford them and
they would be kept in their place as Dhofari women always had
been.

A sense of power was his at last: there were people who
cringed at his approach, begged for his mercy and paid for
his clemency. Yes, he would go along with the communists
so long as they gave him the key to personal power. He did not

Major Richard John; he was subsequently wounded and his evacuation from the mountains to hospital in Salalah took eleven hours by mule

The Sultan's Navy in the Persian Gulf

From the Gravel Plains we drove to the foothills of Qara. Then followed a ten-mile march through a waterless waste to the ravines where we laid our ambushes

The Midway Road, snaking over the Qara mountains to join Dhofar with the rest of Arabia

see how their topsy-turvy system could survive for long but whilst their star was in the ascendant he would gain sufficient loot to set himself up in comfort when their inevitable downfall eventually came.

The *adoo* camp at Hauf blossomed as the months passed and guerrillas returned from their various courses to swell the ranks of PFLOAG.

When Salim Amr returned from Odessa via Cairo on 12th January 1969 there had been nothing much but scattered tents, makeshift hovels and, in the hills above, a number of sealed off caves known collectively as the Cage: these were for prisoners awaiting execution.

By June however the imagination and drive of the great leader Ahmad al Ghassani had transformed the place. On the cliffs above and to the east of Hauf village was the encampment of the school named after Vladimir Illyich Lenin.

Here some five hundred Dhofari children clad mostly in rag-tag uniforms, recited the Thoughts of Mao parrot-fashion and learnt to count in Arabic and English. Later there would also be facilities for reading lessons but for the moment it was enough to teach the youngsters to hate. To wean them from Islam. To mould them into bitter fighters and fervent Marxists. In short it was a school of the modern *Comprachicos*.

In seventeenth-century Spain there lived a gypsy band, the *Comprachicos* or child traders, who bought three-year-olds from poverty-stricken parents. Metal braces were applied to stunt and bend the little limbs, knives and wire distorted innocent features into grotesque masks, and weights further corrupted the normal course of growth. The resulting dwarfs, horrid to look upon, were sold to royal courts, travelling circuses and zoos for a handsome profit.

The Chinese, who usually manage to backdate any invention of civilised man, also outdid the Spanish *Comprachicos*. For hundreds of years their sorcerers had maintained a far more cultured monster industry.

They would simply place the selected children into porcelain vases designed with nightmarish cunning to twist and mar the growth over a period of years. The top and bottom of each jar was left open so that head and feet were available for imaginative surgery. Since the inmates were human the sorcerers would stand the jars up by day and lay them down at night. After a number of years, depending upon individual recipes, the moulds were broken and the monstrous masterpieces released to short lives of unbelievable misery and pain. Their flesh was compressed, their bones misshapen but their minds were still intact.

The Hauf Lenin School deals only in the minds of children, catching them young, and forcing them, day after day, year after year, to live together, think together, act together. Any individualistic trait is stamped upon and crushed by the pack. And together they are fed with hatred; the only loyalty is to the Front, to the crude negative basics of Marxism which nowhere touch upon nor acknowledge human rights and dignity. In their early teens or younger, depending upon the success of the mindbending years, these carefully nurtured bearers of hate are unleashed to carry on the struggle for 'socialist peace'.

In the spring of 1969, when child recruits were first sought, it had been with parental consent but, when this brought little response, groups of guerrillas were sent out to bring back a set number of children regardless of the parents' feelings.

Salim Amr remembered the morning in April when a weeping girl accompanied the latest batch of children into the camp. She could have been no more than twenty: he liked the look of her. One of the little boys was her son and that evening an *Idaara* member had caught her attempting to take the lad away from the camp.

First they had stripped and flogged her. Then, since she still screamed for the release of her child, the *Idaara* leader had caught her up by the ankles and swung her round and round. The uproarious mirth of the onlookers had effected the man's judgement—he later received a reprimand—for he swung ever faster, moving towards a rocky hummock, until with a final swing, he split the girl's head open like an overripe pomegranate.

Many of the watching children had been at the school for a month or more and kept quiet but the newly arrived batch clung to one another and wept bitterly.

Salim Amr reflected that there had been no more rebellious parents. Severe measures were the only answer with fools. In Aden he had visited the intelligence training centre being run by the East German HVA and their military counterparts the VKF. They had shown slide films of their methods whilst pointing out to their Arab pupils the obvious disadvantages of softness towards prisoners.

Twenty minutes east of the Lenin School was a busy new camp where Salim Amr worked processing prisoners from the Qara, helping to decide how and where they would be executed. Some would have 'show' trials in Hauf village, others would be flung into the Cage and much later taken into the mountains by night to be shot.

In this camp youths from the Lenin School received basic arms training, political lectures were delivered, the latest war reports disseminated and new plans rehearsed. Men from Russian courses joked with friends returned from China or Iraq. It was generally agreed that Chinese-trained fighters were tougher but those from Russian centres such as the Odessa School made better leader material and more accurate mortar controllers.

In early July the War Council summoned Salim Amr to their tent. They were pleased with his record and entrusted him with an independent task in his own home district of the Qara. He was to draw up execution lists for an *Idaara* squad, now being formed, which would be sent to him by October.

There were many individuals amongst the Eastern Mahra of Bait Fiah territory—along the nothern limits of Salim's designated area—who promised to be exceedingly troublesome. It was Salim Amr's responsibility to ferret out and list these people for the attention of the *Idaara*.

Should he need help, he was told, the guerrillas at Qum would aid him through their local administrative officer whose name was Musallim Ali of the Bait Qahawr tribe.

Before leaving, Salim Amr was presented with a brand new Kalachnikov light machine gun. He swaggered about camp with it and cleaned it religiously twice a day: few guerrillas were entrusted with so powerful a symbol of authority.

On 18th July 1969 he joined the army of men moving east to Dhofar following a newly made vehicle track over the border and on to a lofty plateau known as the Khadrafee.

There they camped in green fields between shady pools whilst more than two hundred camels were prepared to carry the heavier weapons and supplies. *Meemtoos*, or U.S. Army M2

·50 machine guns, originally captured by the Viet Cong, were loaded alongside British 81 millimetre mortars under tarpaulins.

Five hundred men moved off from the Khadrafee leaving a like number behind to aid the garrisoning of the western sector.

The camels moved in single file along narrow trails, separated into packs of twenty in case of ambush or air attack. Each camel was hired along with its owner at a dollar a day: they took an hour or more to round up each morning and sometimes an hour to load. But all in all they were better than the only alternative which was donkeys. They made far less noise, carried up to 500 lbs, twice a donkey's load, and needed much less food and water.

Later, in the Wadi Naheez, Salim left the main *adoo* group and went straight to his home in the Wadi Arzat. His mother had died and his father was ill with fever, so he left after a day and travelled to Darbat where he had a girl and where he could show off his new weapon to his friends.

In Darbat he met Mohammed Sali the chief of the eastern sector, a man well known as leader of two major assaults on the Government forces at Marbat fort.

This illustrious leader was not well. All of his men but a few personal aides were away. He told Salim Amr the source of his worries.

A new army unit was operating in the foothills. They were small and vulnerable but very active. They had already seduced some of the people with promises of food and money. He was afraid that soon someone would give away his whereabouts. Also it was bad for morale to have this unit laying ambushes all over the area with impunity. He said that he had had eighty men following their moves and recently, at Darbat, he had missed them by a hair's breadth.

The monsoon closed in on the mountains during the last week of June. For five days beforehand I noticed a growing tension among the bedu of the foothills. They talked little and were sullen, even those who knew us as their friends and had come to trust us. Even the magical Aspirins of our medical orderly were spurned.

At that time a thousand 7·62 semi-automatic rifles and machine guns arrived from the Fabrique National of Belgium and two new jet Strikemasters to replace the antiquated piston Provosts. Morale improved considerably when the men received their rifles: at last we were on the same firepower footing as the guerrillas.

On 24th June, taking the new weapons for the first time, we patrolled quietly over the plain to the south of the Arzat spring, the source of the Sultan's private water supply, and recently the target of frequent visits by *adoo* saboteurs.

Ten of us climbed to a cave in the mountains above the spring and lay in wait for four days.

On the second evening two armed guerrillas ran down a path directly below us towards the spring: then they disappeared. Next morning a herd of cattle came from the west to the aqueduct below the spring. Men went out from among the cattle and searched the old army sangars that overlook the aqueduct. From the sangars they yodelled the musical cattle call of the Qara to the other herdsmen below. These closed in on the aqueduct behind the cover of trees.

Deciding that their behaviour betrayed their intentions I signalled the Sultan's Airforce, and a Strikemaster fighter roared in from the sea within minutes. Its rockets slapped into the fig trees that concealed the saboteurs and the water continued to flow.

Early on the fourth morning the aqueduct was broken in two places and the *adoo* responsible were spotted by another observation group who radioed for the jet and for Simon Sloane's Company, now based at Umm al Ghawarif.

Joining Simon in the foothills beside the spring I noticed four *jebalis* in dark cloaks springing away from the aqueduct to a steep gully. All carried large bundles and continued to run when we opened fire at them. Jumping into the Ferret armoured car which Simon had brought, I used the turret-mounted ·30 Browning. Through the sights I watched the glowing tracer rounds kick dust either side of the fugitives. I aimed above their heads but they moved beyond my range.

Then the jet dived firing Sura rockets that hit the ground at over twice the speed of sound and scatter shrapnel over a radius of fifty yards. The turret radio crackled. The officer in the observation group spoke softly.

"They've ditched their loads ... One of them's fallen under

a tree . . . Now the other two have stopped. They've dropped to the ground."

Simon took his men up the gully and retrieved the three bodies on stretchers.

Curious to see the bodies of the saboteurs we had waited for so long, I went over to the silent group beneath the fig trees. They laid the stretchers down in the shade by the trickling water.

Some bedu from a cattle herd nearby bent over the bodies without emotion.

A tattered herdsman clutching his thin shawl to his chest removed the army blanket from one corpse.

"She is my wife," he muttered.

Simon looked grey, his lips set thickly and his voice trembled.

"They should have stopped when we first fired. Everyone on the *jebel* knows it is foolish to run if you are innocent."

The bedu agreed. It was the will of God.

Simon spoke to me apart from the soldiers. He swore quietly and viciously. "Bloody war. How could we know they were women? Same dark blue cloaks as the men wear. And running uphill with those great bundles like sabotage gear."

The smashed bodies had been lying about when he got up there; their clothes blasted off. It had been a shock to see they were women. One had a breast sliced off by shrapnel, and they were mutilated down below.

As his men took the stretchers to the lorries, Simon confessed to me that he'd found himself shouting at three of his Baluchis who had been sexually roused by the sight of the mutilated women's bodies. "God," he said, "what a way to earn our living."

He shook his head and walked away to the lorries.

We found a rough notice left below the trees where the channel had been destroyed and the water gushed away.

"Socialist people for the emancipation of the Arabian Gulf. This is a note from the rebel liberators to our brothers who are under the colony in a lower state of being, facing terrible pressure and opposed by the reactionary government and the imperialist colony who are always aggressive against the people . . . We shall fight by violence led by the People's Republic which represents the hopes for success and socialist unity to improve justice and standards. We are able to fight a long war and defeat our enemies until we are finally victorious . . ."

Following the example of the Fedayeen and many Asian guerrillas the *adoo* had begun to recruit women and children to fight alongside them: the war was getting dirtier.

10

PEOPLE liked Tom Greening; he was quiet and unassuming. He had done well as Intelligence Officer in northern Oman discovering arms caches and more besides. So no one thought twice about his many visits to Qaboos, the carefully tethered heir to the Sultan Said bin Taimur. Few remembered that the two men had been at Sandhurst Military Academy together.

Tom took over Intelligence in Dhofar in July 1969 and almost at once a harvest of pertinent information reached the army from sources that Tom seemed to acquire overnight. His success was phenomenal.

He spoke *jebali*, the language of the Qara, and was everywhere at once. No one had reason to think that the handsome young Intelligence Officer had the time, let alone the intention, to plot against the Sultan.

Escorting an English official to the Salalah palace, I passed by Tom Greening along the sea front where the monsoon waves crashed on white sand ten yards from the palace walls. I waved and he smiled back, his pale blue eyes flinching from the glare. He had come from the house where Qaboos lived and passed by to the court of Bareik, son of the *Wali* of Salalah. It was no secret that Bareik disliked the Sultan and his feudal dicta. But few people knew what passed between Bareik and the Intelligence Captain. And they awaited symptoms that the time was ripe for action. To act too soon or too late would be disastrous and they all held important positions, in the banking community of Oman, in the oil company, in the army, and at the Foreign Office in Whitehall.

Corporal Salim's Land Rover slewed around the corner covering Tom with dust and Murad fingered his moutache as we entered the royal compound.

Black slaves built like oxen stood aside wearing turbans and long white skirts. Their forearms were smooth and massive against the silver of their *khanjas*.

Rifles hung from wall pegs in the covered passage to the courtyard. Murad drove sedately now sitting bolt upright and glancing in his driving mirror to check his four other vehicles were close behind as he had carefully instructed for this important occasion.

We parked in a line. White shrouds covered the Sultan's private armoured cars all about us and a ciné camera whirred quietly from a window slit above. A polite Omani ushered the Englishman away through heavy doors of sandalwood, beautifully carved, to a labyrinth of passages and anterooms. The Sultan had two wives, one being the Dhofari mother of Qaboos, a native of the village of Darbat. But there were ninety comely negresses within the palace walls and a room well stacked with bottles of Chanel; performance awards.

Close to the perfumery was an armoury of rifles, machine guns and sufficient ammunition to withstand a long siege.

The courtyard trapped the noon heat until we could bear it no more and the men retreated to the covered passage. I waited by the sandalwood door. A slave came followed by two Arabs with flowing grey beards. Both were short men in white robes. One was the Royal Secretary, the other was Sultan Said bin Taimur. I stiffened and saluted. He nodded with a slight smile and shook my hand, his turban at the level of my shoulders.

A furious scuffle sounded in the passageway as Corporal Salim hissed at the men. All lined up along the wall ramrod straight. A single gym shoe remained in mid-passage but no one moved to claim it.

"These are your men?" the Sultan's English was cultured and without accent.

"Yes, Your Highness: the Reconnaisance Unit."

The Sultan descended the steps slowly. He moved as though recently recovered from an illness and his gentle face was pale about the large brown eyes. After an English education in India, he had ruled Oman wisely for thirty-five years in the days when there was no revenue. Now the oil had widened his scope for reforms which he had no wish to implement with undue speed.

He shook the hand of each man and exchanged greetings with them. He stepped carefully over the gym shoe as he greeted its half-shod owner Saif Musabbah of the wild black hair.

There was an unmistakable aura of dignity about the little Arab. I felt respect and loyalty for him, knowing that I would fight for him and die in his service if necessary, for all that I disliked his shortcomings. I had often blackened his name when we were refused food to take on patrols and cursed him when there were only Aspirins for dying bedu.

But after meeting him and seeing the kindness in his fine old face, I found it difficult to associate him personally with the misery and poverty so prevalent amongst his subjects. And yet so much of it could so easily be alleviated. My thoughts about the man were most confused.

An avenue of palms framed the track from the palace, running through fields of lucerne and fruit. Beyond, and encircling the entire town, was a fence of barbed wire manned by civilian *askars*. We left through one of the two gates where they searched the baggage of incoming *jebalis*. A long line of hobbled camels laden with firewood queued outside. Their owners squatted in the dust and stared from brittle eyes. The fence stopped food reaching the *adoo* since only a rationed quota could leave the gates with each departing *jebali*.

To the north a pall of gloom hid the mountains and lay low about the plain. Grass grew thinly everywhere and a million tiny flowers, blue, pink and yellow pricked up, accentuating the dank wastes. Visibility was a hundred yards some days, the jets were grounded and no ship could land in the churning seas which lashed the coastline. Dhofar was cut off from the outside world for the mountain track to Thamarit was already a quagmire quite impassable to vehicles. Soldiers were jumpy by night as the mists clung about the camp. On 1st August the RAF radar, sweeping the plain, detected movement approaching from the foothills. At Umm al Ghawarif we were alerted and manned entrenchments about the compound. The suspect area was shelled but no attack materialised. In all probability some poor camels or cows were blown to bits for, to the radar scanners, all 'blips' heading south were hostile.

Blood-sucking flies forced many of the *adoo* down to the foothills where our patrols became correspondingly more dangerous.

To gain high ground silently by night was hardly possible for the ground was everywhere glutinous and slippery as ice. A man who missed his footing would slide downwards crashing through the undergrowth, his loaded rifle and primed grenade taking long minutes to recover.

One night our Colonel accompanied us on an ambush above Taqa. He had only one kidney and the going was especially hard for him. Next day a flock of goats crossed our killing ground, a clearing beneath the rocks where we lay, and the herdsmen yodelled our presence to *adoo* above us. We left at once for we were few but the *adoo* were too quick. As we reached the clearing below a blistering crackle of machine guns opened up from our old position and four other knolls high above us. Our predicament was delicate but we withdrew in fast co-ordinated groups, slithering through the scrub, and only one of the men was wounded. In the mad dash of the withdrawal we lost the Colonel's backpack containing two desirable tins of Portuguese sardines. Being extremely partial to these I volunteered to attempt a gallant dash forward to retrieve the rucksack. With two others I sallied forward over the ground we had just lost. But a veritable hail of bullets concentrated on us and I reluctantly gave up the search, returning empty handed to the Colonel.

With the mists as cover the *adoo* minelayers grew bold, sewing the tracks of the plain with British anti-tank mines and Soviet TM6 plastic mines. Some of the drivers who became casualties had their feet amputated and recovered: others' spines were broken like dry firewood. We found a Pakistani driver close to RAF Salalah a hundred yards from the buckled cab of his mined lorry; he was quite dead.

We drove on existing tracks as little as possible but few days passed without a motorised patrol over the plain or further west. Information of arms caravans along the coast itself came to Tom Greening and we were sent west to Mugshayl where the coast trails descend to a waterhole.

Men of Richard John's Company led the way from their camp on the western fringe of the Salalah Plain. Richard had returned from six months in hospital with a long livid scar running over his chest and shoulder but his arm was fully functional.

We spent many days and nights in caves and crannies high above the springs of Mugshayl and by night sent small patrols to the beach itself. Edging the sand were black rocks where spumes of spray burst high in slivers of sudden fire for the waves were alive with phosphorescent sparkle.

Some nights the mists cleared for a while and the moon seemed bigger and warmer than ever. On 20th July it touched the heavy sea with orange and a breeze off the cliffs rustled over the sand. But on the surface of the moon, at the Sea called Tranquillity, there was no wind and the astronaut Neil Armstrong used a spring and stiffeners to keep his country's flag unfurled when he placed it in the coffee-coloured moon sand. We would have laughed perhaps had someone told us he was there at that very moment.

Four days later, in Salalah, we heard the news of the astronauts. I told Naseeb our guide. "What!" he exclaimed incredulous. "It cannot be. The moon is a holy place known only to the Prophet. No man can go there. No aeroplane can carry enough petrol." I explained as best I could what a space craft was and when he saw that I was definitely not joking, Naseeb grew angry, glaring skywards. "The blasphemers! How dare they trespass on holy ground. I will pass the word about and tonight we will shoot many rounds at the moon."

The sea about the Mugshayl cliffs was very deep, the noise of the monsoon fierce and hypnotic. Nature concentrated all her superlatives in this part of the Indian Ocean: the dorsal finned Indian rorqual, over a hundred feet long is the largest living creature in the world. By day they blew spouts of water close by the cliffs and cried like humans.

The great whales and even the vicious hammer-headed sharks provide food for fifteen-foot long sawfish with six-foot saws. These attack with speed and rip their victims' bellies out. Then they feed at leisure on the entrails of the threshing monsters. Whip and sting rays grow to great size and even the local fishermen seldom swim in these waters.

We saw no one at Mugshayl but later Richard's men ambushed a column of thirty *adoo* close to the waterholes.

We were recalled from Mugshayl on receiving news from an informer that a key guerrilla leader had arrived on the Yemen border close to the Sultan's fort at Habarut.

Nine of us were landed as discreetly as possible at a desert airstrip by Habarut. At dusk Sergeant Mohamed and Said Salim crept into the oasis and later we met the informer, a leper. Our bird, he said, had flown to the Yemen only a few hours before our arrival.

There were many such disappointments but any excuse to escape the misery of the monsoon belt was always welcome.

The guerrillas blew up the Sultan's aqueduct from the spring of Arzat again and again until the Colonel lost his patience. There was a network of caves overlooking the spring and no more than a cricket-pitch length away from it. It was decided that small groups of soldiers should hide in these caves for twelve days and nights, changing over every third night.

David Bayley led the first group. I met him when he came back to the Mess after his stint in the caves. He was exhausted; his face a mass of red spots—many bleeding. His arms, ankles and neck were similarly affected and he scratched the livid blotches furiously as I watched.

"The little bastards eat you alive from dawn to dusk," he muttered. "Those caves are a living hell."

And they were. By our second morning in the caves even the imperturbable Said Salim was slapping frenziedly at the humming clouds of flying ticks. We had mosquito nets wrapped around us. But not about the face for we could not risk missing the crackle of leaves or the faint blurring shadow of an *adoo* scout. The ticks were small enough to penetrate the mesh but, once fed, they swelled and burst at the least pressure. At dusk they went and the mosquitoes came. We fed on tea, biscuits and corned beef twice a day. On the evening of the second day two of the Baluchis began to argue; at first in high whispers. Then one started to cry, tears coursing down his swollen cheeks. The flies had driven him to distraction. The *moolah* crept over the floor of goat droppings and patted the soldier's back with one great hand, the other cutting off the cries abruptly.

At dusk on the second day Corporal Salim watched the

cliffs behind and above us. He whistled softly and pointed to the skyline. Concentrating hard I was able to see through binoculars a dark shape in the nook of a lone crag. After a while it moved and disappeared, but not before I picked out the khaki shorts and gleaming weapon. I was sure he had not spotted us but the saboteurs did not come that night.

There was room only to lie down or crouch and the inactivity had made us very weak by the third and last day.

At midnight a new Army group took over from us. We left by way of a narrow ledge and I carried the barrel and tripod of our Browning ·30 machine gun. Without warning my legs buckled under me and I fell. I bounced off a lower ledge and heard myself shout out before my head hit against rock. I was dazed and felt pain in both knees when I tried to get up.

The big gun had clattered noisily on the rocks and Sergeant Mohamed was anxious to get away for there were only nine of us. Hamid Sultan's teeth showed in a wide grin as he slung me over his shoulders. He carried me for a mile wading through deep mud beside the aqueduct channel. Giant frogs croaked and crickets clacked furiously. We passed beneath massive tamarinds and flowering fig trees. On firmer ground I hobbled, aided by Hamid and Mubarreq, and later sent up flares for Murad to collect us.

For two weeks I did little and then flew to the RAF hospital in Bahrein where a surgeon diagnosed strained ligaments in both legs. He advised me to rest for a month but that was not feasible for the Sultan had at last approved our request for supplies. With all the Land Rovers heavily laden we toured the makeshift bedu camps in the foothills. Sacks of flour and rice, sugar and tea, milk powder and spices were doled out family by family. For some the food had come too late, but this did not detract from the bedu's gratitude. We were also given money by Tom Greening; wads of ten rupee notes and, once alone from their fellow tribesmen, many of the *jebalis* were keen to talk. It was the familiar story.

"We do not like the rebels," they would say, wringing their hands. "But what can we do? The government does not help us nor give us protection so we must yield food when the rebels ask for it. Otherwise they beat us or worse."

There was no reply for it was true. The guerrillas ruled the

Qara now. The Army might hold some ground from time to time but once it departed the *adoo* returned. And large tracts of the mountain had never been visited by the Army nor for that matter by any white man.

In 1895 Mabel and Theodore Bent, a couple of English travellers, wandered about the Qara collecting plants and causing quite a sensation amongst the locals with their impractical Victorian garb. Then came Bertram Thomas on his way to solve the last great riddle left to explorers, the mysterious sands of the Empty Quarter. He crossed them by camel in 1931 and thereby proved there was no mystery: in fact nothing but bloodthirsty bedouin and an endless sea of a sweltering sand.

After the Second World War the most avid of camel-borne travellers, Wilfred Thesiger, lived and travelled in the Sands for two years, crossing the Qara mountains on his way from Salalah. Using Thesiger's maps, the oilmen came in the 50s but they kept mostly to the desert and saw little of the Qara. So when in 1964 the first Army patrols probed into the deep valleys, ranged over the high pastures and marvelled at the mountain lagoons they were the first outsiders to do so. There were still many limestone ravines, wrapped with jungle, peppered by caves and deep in guerrilla country where white men were talked of by wandering bedu to marvelling audiences of little Qara mountain folk.

The Qara people's history can be guessed at but with no great accuracy for their ancestors left nothing but scattered graveyards. There are no ruins in the mountains, no carvings nor potsherds of antiquity. Even the oldest *jebalis* know few tales of their forebears.

Like the Dinka tribes of the Nile swamps, the Qara live for their cattle: many of their customs are similar. The eldest son will often be called after the favourite cow—rather than vice-versa. Healthy cows are not killed for food even though the owners' children may be dying of malnutrition. Yet to save a Qara's soul after death, at least half of his herd are slaughtered as a sort of lump death duty.

Two other customs, found also with the Nuer tribesmen of southern Sudan, are still practised by the Qara. Their women, presumably because they are the inferior sex, may never touch a cow's udders and, should a cow go slow on milk production, only the male Qara are allowed to perform the cure which is to apply their lips to the beast's vagina and blow as hard as they can.

Archaeologists, from digs in the Yemen, say that the Qara were not the firstcomers to Dhofar. First came the Hamitic Cushites from Egypt who, in Dhofar, were known as Shahara and built the city of Robat whose ruins lie beside Umm a Ghawarif camp. Much later, they were overrun and enslaved by the Semitic Qara from the Nile lands and Ethiopia. These men came by way of the Yemen as part of the Joktanite invasion. Joktan was a descendant of Shem the son of Noah, and the book of Genesis states that Joktan's descendants advanced as far as the Yemen and those under Ophir as far as the mountains of Sephar;[1] now Dhofar.

Said bin Ghia came with us to question the *jebalis* as we gave them food. He was supercilious about his people, scornful of the *adoo*. Since defecting from the *adoo*, after their epic desert crossing from Saudi Arabia he had grown fat and idle, but he was still useful as an interpreter. The Qara hated him for a traitor, and they knew he could tell when they lied. But they respected him for a rich man, seeing his heavy gold Rolex, his embroidered silk *shemagh* and the glinting golden *khanja* at his waist.

In the Naheez valley where it debouches from the foothills and gouges a deep ravine in the floor of the plain, we found Qara families camped in shallow caves. Smoke from dung fires hung low and drove away the monsoon flies. Without the smoke the cattle would be eaten alive.

We stayed for two days by the caves and gave the families a goat. They boned it and heated the meat in the ashes of a wood fire. We ate with them, savouring their glutinous flour balls dipped in an open gourd of wild honey. This was still in the comb and the bedu ate the wings and abdomens of dead bees caught in the honey without appearing to mind. They mixed fresh milk with the boiled pulp of tamarind fruit. This had a strange taste that lingered in my mouth for many hours.

After the meal the remnants were placed in the bloody goatskin, wrapped up and hung from the cave ceiling. Then we sat back around the fire. I listened to the talk and the belching and rubbed tears from my eyes for the smoke was acrid.

[1] Archeological evidence to this end is not yet conclusive.

The men of the Recce haul a field gun along the new 'road' to the mountains

For days we lay in ambush in caves and boulder-strewn wadis . . . a single careless move would betray our presence

During a lull in the battle in the forest below Deefa three British
Officers share a goat stew

The Arab woman killed by mistake is identified by her husband

The old man of the family called Khalaf arrived with sixty or seventy small goats, none bigger than spaniels.

He greeted Said bin Ghia. They rubbed noses and kissed each other's cheeks. I did not get this treatment; the old fellow looked me up and down and asked Said bin Ghia where he had brought this kaffir from.

His ragged hair was controlled by a long leather thong and a greasy bun at the back. The end of his dark blue cloak hung over one shoulder in biblical fashion and he carried an iron sword as well as a heavy wooden throwing stick. This last was pointed at both ends and he scratched his back with it as he talked.

Conceited as a turkey cock, I thought, smelling the perfume of his hair as he squatted. An odd concoction is often used by the hillfolk consisting of sandalwood juice and hyraceum which comes from the dried dung of dassy rabbits—described in the bible as coneys, or hyrax.

A young lad, perhaps a grandson, put his arms round the old man and tugged at his bun. The boy's head was shaven save for a bristling cockscomb down the centre of his skull. It would be kept that way until he reached his teens and was circumcised.

But old Khalaf's eyes were on the girls, probably his cousins, at play outside—drawing in the mud. The goats flowed around us bleating and treading all over us: they too slept in the cave at night.

The children's faces were delicate, fawn-like and very mischievous. Two of the girls, in their early teens, looked after the goats. They would walk six miles a day or more except during the monsoon to find grazing. Their limbs were slim and supple. Already they were aware of their budding allure and giggled knowingly when Uncle Khalaf winked at them.

They threw stones at the goats which strayed from the cave. Their finger and toe nails were dyed red with dye from henna leaves.

An older woman suckled her baby opposite us; her exposed breast flat and wizened like her face. A single ring pierced her nose below cheeks livid with saffranin and tattooed with indigo streaks. Said bin Ghia saw me watching her. He chuckled, "She is in her young twenties, that one," he spoke in English. "It is the hard work that makes a woman old before her time."

The hard work and the ill treatment, I thought, for women

are far from the first glimmers of emancipation in these parts. They can be bought whilst still sexually immature for a few cows or twelve dollars. The man who wants a girl need only gain the approval of her father or brother and must not already possess more than three wives. When he gets fed up with her he has but to visit the local judge and say the magic words – *Mutallaga bi faladh*. The girl then has no one to support her and often no family to return to.

Despite this they are happy enough and often sing sweetly as they work, their soft silver bracelets jangling and their faces usually free of the beaked mask of northern Oman. Their behaviour is loose and sex is their main enjoyment, made easier no doubt by their goat grazing duties away from home. But the men get their own back brutally enough for female babies are circumcised at the base of the clitoris to blunt their erotic nature. And fear of divorce makes many women place salt in their vaginas after childbirth to cause contraction and so please their husbands. All goes well till the next time a child is born and finds its exit blocked by vaginal scar tissue caused by the salt. Great pressure, agony and death usually follow for the mother. Divorce would have been better.

Old Khalaf took a dagger from his waistband and wet a wad of tobacco with juice from a lime. He had a single tooth, bent and filthy in the lower jaw but he chewed the mixture with evident pleasure and called out orders to the girls.

They entered the cave and took handfuls of fish bones to the family camel, which hobbled outside. It chewed them with relish providing a background accompaniment to the slurping of the old man.

There were other *jebalis* around the fire, listening quietly. Their dark pointed faces seemed to grow and then recede disembodied as the blue smoke curled about.

Sergeant Mohamed told Khalaf we would be back to the caves in four days with food. And money for information.

"In four days exactly?" asked the old man pointedly.

"*Imshaalah,*" said Mohamed.

Radio Aden announced that the freedom fighters of Dhofar had located a group of British propaganda specialists who were attempting to bribe and seduce the plainsfolk of Dhofar.

They were following the movements of these specialists with care and would soon eliminate them.

Said bin Ghia assured me that we were the 'specialists' and would do well to take care.

The night before returning to the caves of Khalaf upon the agreed date, we sent half the men into the bushes in the foot-hills above. There were no ambushers to ambush that time but we could not be too careful.

In other *wadis* we fed bedu families and always we told them a future date when we would return. Many of the men began to catch colds and coughs after successive ambushes in the drizzle and the cold dank air, so I stopped the precaution and started to pay our second advertised visit without a protective cordon placed the night before.

Deep within the foothills and hidden by a green sea of camel thorn were many monsoon camps of the cattle herders. The mountains rose abruptly behind them. In August the area took on a ghostly look in the grey *khareef*.

The Wadi Thimreen wound through this region and close to it we found a huddle of mud and thorn rondaavals. The occupants were in a worse state than most, their cattle as emaciated as their children. We doled out food and medicine as usual and promised to return with more the following day.

Only twelve men came with me next day, including Said bin Ghia; the rest were sick. Corporal Salim and Ali Nasser had three men each. Two Baluchis, Said bin Ghia and Hamid Sultan, with the heavy Browning, stayed with me. We left Murad and the vehicles in the bottom of the Thimreen, our backpacks heavy with food for the village.

Once into the bushes Corporal Salim and Ali Nasser dis-appeared to the flanks. I could see no one but the man on either side.

After an hour moving with great care I smelled the dung fires of the village. The two Baluchis went off quietly to either side. They returned in a while to confirm the other sections had arrived. Then we moved forward.

I approached the thorn enclosures from the south as on our previous visit. Ahead was sparse foliage and ant-hills, then the clearing of the village. There was no one about; not even a cow. I checked through binoculars.

Ali Nasser responded to two finger pressures on my National and somewhere to the east of the clearing his men crept forward; Corporal Salim to the west. I gave them five minutes then got up. On my left Hamid Sultan arose cradling the ugly machine gun, a camouflage net over its belt of bullets. To the right fat Said bin Ghia straightened out gleaming with sweat. He was frowning; uneasy. It was too quiet.

We left the last shred of cover and stepped into the clearing. From the west a murderous rattle of bren gun fire stunned me momentarily. I remember seeing the ripple of earth spurts rising like hailstones landing in a quiet pond.

Then the woodpeckers opened up from the other side of the clearing, Soviet RPD automatics, nicknamed due to their rapid rate of fire and the sound of their high velocity bullets.

I felt the shockwaves slap by very close. Said bin Ghia screamed and fell to the ground.

I twisted, rolled and lurched back to the nearest ant-hill. Hamid was already there struggling with the Browning.

Said bin Ghia rolled over and over, very quickly for one so large in the belly. Flour spilled everywhere from his pack, red with his blood, but he reached an ant-hill followed closely by the woodpeckers.

For a while it was suicide to move a finger behind the tiny mound. Hamid clasped my back and pulled me towards him with the big gun between us. He grinned and rolled his eyeballs in mock horror.

It seemed as though the *adoo* were intent on digging the ant-hill away with their bullets until we were exposed. My shirt tail was loose and a bullet ripped through it. I flinched and felt the fear mount.

Earth sprayed on to our faces, kicked up from the mound. The vibration of the bullets eating deep into the soil came through clearly as our faces pressed hard against the ant-hill.

I turned the National on: my signaller was with Murad and the Land Rovers. They had heard the trouble and sent for the jets.

I took stock of things. We had by the skin of our teeth avoided a well laid ambush. Only the skill of Corporal Salim and his three men had saved us. Outflanking the *adoo* position they must have seen our predicament and opened up just in time.

Corporal Salim came through on the National; his voice high with excitement.

"This is 52. They are closing on us, Sahb. Twenty or more have moved behind those by the houses, and they know we are but four men."

Our hope lay in little Ali. He had three good men each with a bren gun. I told him to close in at once. His acknowledgement was a whispered, "54, *Imshaalah*."

His men opened fire as one and no more *adoo* bullets came our way. Hamid jammed the Browning tripod on the mound. One great hand fed the snake of bullets into the chamber, the other panned the gun and squeezed the trigger back.

Branches flew from the thorn huts and leaves shredded in the scrub beyond.

Then we ran across the clearing. I forgot the pain in my knees. All fear was gone now with the action.

The *adoo* had left but bloodstains and heaps of empty cases remained.

Corporal Salim's voice came over the National, jubilant.

"They are running, Sahb. Shall we follow?"

I said no. They would not run for long if we exposed our total number.

Bin Ghia's wrist was slashed by a bullet. We dressed it as he swore dramatic vengeance on the cowardly dogs, his belly heaving. A bullet splintered the butt of my rifle and ripped on: the *adoo* had reached the slopes overlooking the village and could probably see their error in overestimating our strength. The Baluchis lay out a long flourescent cloth, T-shaped and pointed at the *adoo* positions above us. A Strikemaster roared in and loosed off four 80 mm Sura rockets. There was a malfunction and two exploded close to Ali Nasser's ant-hill, showering it with shrapnel.

We had been lucky; no one but Said bin Ghia was hurt and the men were pleased with themselves. Two weeks later, intelligence sources confirmed that six guerrillas had died that day. We continued to visit the bedu along the edge of the plain.

A dream recurred many times, usually coming to me in the early hours and once when lying in the scrub on ambush. Mubarreq the negro awoke me with his hand on my mouth and a finger to his lips.

In my dream I was back in the medical classroom of the Special Air Service barracks in Hereford but the words of the lecturer formed images. The men of Recce were there stretched out on the demonstration desk. Their faces materialised one after the other and all of them smiled fixedly at me though their shared body lay across the desk, mutilated by the successive images . . .

"When your mate's shot, treat him for shock. Give him liquid except when the bullet enters between nipples and knees. Don't forget that 'cos a bullet going in above the knee might end up in the stomach and the poor feller won't want liquid then, will he now? . . . What if he cops it through the jaw, lads? What then? Often as not bits of bone and other such crap'll end up down his windpipe and choke him. If you can't fish the muck out, slit his throat below the jolly old apple and stick a tube in to by-pass the obstruction. A biro will do—then he'll breathe like a baby."

I remember fighting back the nausea, embarrassed to show my feelings to the others in the class.

"And don't forget those main arteries. When one's cut, you act fast—no time to think. If you don't catch the loose ends and stop 'em spurting then burn a field dressing and cram the ashes in the open wound. Then bind it fast and forget all that rubbish about tourniquets—that went out with rock 'n' roll . . . If you've not got a dressing and you're alone in the jungle or the desert, do like our Lillico did in Borneo. He copped it in the gut and crawled away from the Indos for four days with his middle hanging loose. He knew the bush was mengin' with bacteria, so what does he do? He lets the flies crawl all over him and lay their eggs. Then when the maggots hatch they eat up all those nasty bacteria and keep the wound nice and healthy—that's why they say there's no flies on Lillico. Just keep your cool when you cop it and you'll live . . ."

The dream never changed and stayed with me through the monsoon months until we left the plain.

11

For a month the guerrilla Salim Amr compiled his lists of traitors to the Marxist cause. This he did from the relative comfort of Qum where dung fires smouldered ceaselessly to fend off the *khareef* flies.

The guerrillas there had checked on every tribe and patrolled every valley in Bait Fiah territory. Through them Salim Amr drew up his black book of troublemakers unsympathetic to the cause.

Since so many *jebali* names were similar and because many of the guerrillas had personal grievances against a particular man or family, the *Idaara* list that Salim ended up with undoubtedly included a number of perfectly innocent men and women. But why should he worry? He was doing his job and the more names that he could produce for the execution squad the more efficient he would appear.

He must outdo all contenders, Salim knew, to maintain his job. And with each successive day that passed the realisation grew that his was indeed a plum posting. The word had quickly spread amongst the tribes as to the reason for Salim Amr's presence. People were aware that he had only to point his finger their way and their doom was sealed. Rumours were rife as to the fate awaiting those *jebalis* sent to the Cage in Hauf. And since no one was sure quite what *did* happen to those arrested, the rumours gave full rein to the fertile imagination of the Dhofaris.

Salim played on their fears. He had no need to rape a pretty girl who took his fancy. A word to the head of her family was enough to ensure her favours. Otherwise her family might find themselves marked for the attentions of the *Idaara*.

Sometimes Salim feared he was not doing enough. From Darbat, with those few travellers who braved the *khareef*, there came tales of torture and execution.

Five old folk from a mountain village close by Shahayt had been caught praying in the open, contrary to the new unwritten law that religion was reactionary. The local *Idaara* had summoned a number of villagers from the locality and held a public trial to show that they were just. All five old men were found guilty and held down over red hot coals until their backs were raw and blistered. Then they were beaten and taken to the Dahaq cliff at Darbat, wreathed as it was in mist.

One by one they were thrown over the edge, at hourly intervals, a refinement which Salim could not help admiring. Sooner or later he must make his mark in his own area. He had no cliffs easily accessible but he would think of something.

Towards the end of August he left Qum and went west with several of the local fighters and militia. Crossing the Wadi Naheez, they came after some hours' travel to a great cave in the Wadi Risham. Many *adoo* leaders had already arrived from all over Dhofar and sat about chatting: waiting for the conference to start the following day.

It was not the first such annual meeting and promised to be a lively one for there were several serious rifts developing between different factions of the guerrillas.

Some of Musallim bin Nuffl's original fighters were still influential despite their outmoded beliefs in Islam and their willingness to settle with any Salalah Government that granted minimal democracy to Dhofaris. Then there were those who, though Marxist inclined, were at heart nationalists and cried for an end to all Russian or Chinese influence in the Dhofar Liberation Front. Their ambitions were confined to revolution in Dhofar alone, and they refused to widen their outlook to the liberation of all Arab lands.

The cave echoed with heated discussions, raucous laughter, the bleat of goats and the squeal of bats overhead. The babble continued well past midnight, only to be brought to temporary but instant silence by the occasional thud of distant artillery fire. In such moments there was stillness in the natural rock hall except for the flickering fingers of flame and long crooked shadows that reached into the furthest crannies.

Men were sleeping crouched about the fires when Ahmad al Ghassani came. The leader was alone: his part-albino features seemed to float above the men as he picked his way to the inner recesses, a black-clad transceiver swinging from his neck.

At dawn the meeting was convened without ceremony. Altogether eighty or ninety men and a few uniformed women were present. A ring of unseen scouts settled down on the heights far above the cave but there was little cause for fear. The Risham snaked through sunless ravines in the deepest fastness of the Qara, where no army group would dare set foot in numbers small enough to escape detection.

Each regional commander stood up to declare his presence and his allegiance. Speakers had no need to shout as the bat-infested dome of the cave, fluted like a vast limestone cathedral, amplified each sound.

A tall thin man of the Bait Maashani was up and calling for silence.

His rifle was an ancient ·303 but a recent exit wound discoloured one shoulder giving him a certain authority.

Eloquently he pointed out that they were all dependent upon the people for food and shelter, for security and information. Yet of late a reign of fear had repressed these same folk who were their only hope of eventual victory. They were even forbidden the basic rights of any Muslim, to observe the traditions and prayers which all had performed since they were children. Food was scarce in all Dhofar this year: families were starving. Yet they were forcing people to feed them as though they were kings.

The unknown speaker called for an end to this type of behaviour before the people turned against them as a worse evil than the very government they were struggling to overthrow.

Before the unknown Bait Maashani could sit down, al Ghassani shouted his disagreement. How could they struggle on behalf of the people unless they all suffered together? And what alternative did the people have? A close-fisted Sultan with an army of mercenaries made up of Britishers, Baluchis and one or two deluded Omanis? Al Ghassani pointed out that they were winning; that the Sultan's Army was falling apart due to religious differences and mutinies; that it was short of men and had many deserters.

Sure of his following, al Ghassani took upon himself the role of chairman, reminding those gathered that this was a historic occasion being the prelude to the Third Conference[1] of Hamrir and a crucial turning point for the Front. He reminded them that, only a year ago, it had been decided to re-name the old Dhofar Liberation Front as the People's Front for the Liberation of the Occupied Arabian Gulf. He stressed that this meant more than a mere name change. It symbolised the intention of the Front to fight not only for the freedom of Dhofar but for a united Marxist community from Aden to Kuweit with full ownership of its own oil rights. The leader of PFLOAG's Omani branch, an Arab from the same tribe as the Sultan, was equally determined to follow up these principles. And furthermore the Aden Government had agreed to form a united state with Dhofar as soon as the struggle was won. He explained that the Egyptians had lost the revolutionary struggle in North Yemen through their mistaken attempts at setting the local sheikhs against one another. But that they, the Dhofaris, would accept *no* help from *any* bourgeoisie. When victory came they would throw all foreign oilmen out of their land, because oil meant nothing compared with the genuine class struggle.

Al Ghassani was interrupted by Musallim Ali of the Bait Qahawr. Salim Amr had not met him before: it was his first sight of the man he was to liaise with in the eastern sector with his *Idaara* execution squad.

Musallim Ali's voice rattled with emotion. The long hours of confusing study with the Little Red Book, the frustrations in Kuweit, the contradictions and underlying dishonesty of so much he had almost believed in. All were crystallised in this crude al Ghassani whose power was that of a bully. He could not let this hypocrite blatantly confuse an issue so basic to his beliefs. To think that he had but a few months ago revered this man as a hero of the revolution. His words tumbled out in the cohesive fervour of conviction.

Musallim Ali pointed out that Chairman Mao had said the

[1] The Third Conference took place soon afterwards in the coastal town of Rakhyut.

outstanding thing about China's 600 million peasants was that they were poor and blank. He had also said that this was a wonderful thing since poverty was the greatest impetus to revolution and, on blank paper, the freshest and most beautiful pictures could be drawn. This same Mao then drew his beautiful picture in blood red with the broken bodies of his Chinese opponents. Musallim Ali's finger prodded the air at al Ghassani whom he accused of trying to emulate Mao by destroying the people. Al Ghassani, he said, had claimed to have broken the hereditary system of sheikhdoms, the *shuyukh*. But it was the accursed Sultan Said bin Taimur who had done this himself by seducing all the tribal sheikhs to Salalah where he still kept them prisoner. It was he who had caused the vacuum, taken away the tribal leaders and left the people like sheep. Like dust waiting to blow with the next gust of wind.

Musallim's voice rose to a pitch. The audience were spellbound for this was no leader: this was one of them, old Musallim Ali who people joked about. The beauty of his wife Noor had long been the envy of many, yet he had no children.

Al Ghassani realised that he was being slighted in public by an ignorant low grade commissar. Yet he could do nothing whilst the crowd's sympathy lay with the Bait Qahawr fool.

And the man had not yet finished.

Musallim Ali continued by pointing out that Dhofaris were not downtrodden Chinese. They must indeed overthrow the Sultan and evict the British but they did not need to have Marxist-Maoism thrust upon them. They did not want it for they were a nation of individuals and their system of *shuyukh* was already democratic. If the sheikh was an old fool then they threw him out and elected another. They did not need Marxism to help them do that. Moreover Marxists might say "what is yours is mine" and take it, but had not the bedu always said "take all that I have, you are welcome to it"?

Why could not they use democratic methods of persuasion? Even Mao had said good communists must not use coercion and if he had ignored his own code and crushed the Tibetans, was not this to his eternal shame? Why should they follow a path of terror and oppression suggested to them by a clique of power-hungry leaders? Could not they all decide to work together?

Many of those present, as reported later by Kamees, were

impressed by this speech and many approved Musallim Ali's sentiments. Although the local leader of the Naheez *adoo* sprang quickly to the defence of al Ghassani and the Russians, other factions felt that Musallim had given them a lead.

Hafidh bin Abdullah, bitter rival of al Ghassani, then spoke, pointing out that the Chinese and the Russians might have aided them but it had not been disinterested help, for they did not tolerate Islam. Last year, he said, documents were published by the Dhofar Liberation Front denouncing the British as anti-God and now they were being asked to kill their own people for their beliefs in the same God. He and his people of the Eastern Qara would not tolerate suppression of Islam. They would remain loyal to PFLOAG and its aims only so long as the revolution did not attack their religion.

Some fifty of the *adoo*, those from the Eastern Qara, rose to their feet to cheer Hafidh. Among them Musallim Ali. But not Salim Amr.

Provoked further by the leader of the Naheez *adoo*, who sprang automatically to al Ghassani's defence, Hafidh was finally forced to attack Russia itself: its denial of freedom to its Muslim people. There were eleven million Muslims in the U.S.S.R. colonies. Korans had been confiscated, in Dagestan 1200 mosques had been closed and many Muslim Tartars had been imprisoned for practising their religion. He knew for he had read about it in Lebanese and Kuweiti newspapers and he also knew that *Pravda* had attacked the Muslims in the Chechen-Ingush Republic for their refusal to learn to speak and write Russian. Marxism and Islam were radically opposed to each other. He, Hafidh bin Abdullah, had ceaselessly fought on the *jebel* to defend the people, but in the name of Allah. Finally he attacked all those like al Ghassani who spent their time wandering around the world in aeroplanes and trains talking to foreigners whilst he and his people did all the fighting.

Since no one could deny that Hafidh was a loyal PFLOAG fighter of considerable renown, the opposition were temporarily silenced.

But when the plans for the future had been agreed upon and the meeting disbanded, al Ghassani decided to take steps to deal with this troublesome eastern sector. He instructed Salim Amr to collect further information on dissident ringleaders in the eastern sector and to find out who was loyal and who was not. The men to watch were clearly Musallim Ali and Hafidh.

Now that the west and centre of Dhofar were firmly in their hands, it seemed likely that the east would soon succumb if they could only root out the troublemakers. Then the time would come when they could deal 'firmly' with all religious reactionaries.

There were days when the mists withdrew for a while from the coastline leaving it humid but cool and the Colonel decided the few British and Indian officers in Umm al Ghawarif should spend one *jumma*, the Muslim day of rest, having a picnic on the white sands of Sumhuran.

Three of my Land Rovers provided an escort through Taqa and the hills beyond to the cliffs where the ruins stood above the beach.

The Colonel produced an amazing supply of delicacies and wine from some portable freeze-boxes. The picnic was laid out on a rug over the velvet sand. The sea burst in explosive release, whipped up by the same winds that lashed the Somali horn, and swimming was not advisable.

I wandered up to the cliffs, sticky from the spray, and found Hamid Sultan lying by his beloved Browning among the ruins of the temple of the moon god, Sin.

There are other ruins on the plain but none as ancient as these. Al Bilad, the old harbour city of Salalah, was deserted two centuries ago but its rubble anyway shows no evidence of life before sixth-century Islam. At Sumhuran however the American archaeologist Wendell Phillips found evidence of an impregnable fortress city dedicated to a pagan god.

Over to the west, beyond the pure white sand and the clutter of pink bodied picnickers, the sea-cliffs split in two, where the creek called Khor Rawri once joined the sea. Before rockfalls and silt blocked its mouth it used long ago to form a safe harbour for ships from the Red Sea, Mesopotamia and the Far East. At a time when the Roman Empire worshipped its gods with myrrh and frankincense the lands where the incense trees grew were sought by the legions who, twenty-four years before Christ's birth, sent a military expedition into Saudi Arabia. But they never reached southern Arabia, for they died by thousands in the deserts to the north of the Yemen.

173

The kings and queens of Sheba and Yemen then ruled the tribes of the Hadhramaut as far east as this very Temple of Sumhuran, controlling the myrrh of Yemen and the frankincense of Dhofar. Their people, the Sabaeans and Himyarites, had built fine temples and cities further west and now, in Sumhuran it is possible, though not yet conclusively proved archaeologically, that they built the greatest spice centre of the world, from which the bags of frankincense might go by sea to India and even China or by camel over the deserts to Damascus and Alexandria.

Beside Hamid Sultan and his Browning was a huge stone slab with smoothly worn blood channels, a sacrificial table of the Sabaeans when the city was called Abyssapolis by Ptolemy. Only four miles to the north the great abyss of Darbat, that gave the city its name, gleamed under the grey blanket of the *khareef*, and reminded me uncomfortably of Jungle Petal and a narrow escape.

The picnic over, we returned along the coast road. A week later, with another officer, I removed a newly placed anti-tank mine from the same road a mile from Taqah. The guerrilla watchdogs had doubtless reported on the picnic and were hoping for another.

In early September the monsoon began to shift its clammy grip and Salalah felt relief. The *adoo* had not taken advantage of the mists: no close attack had materialised.

Once a week, if I was in camp, I borrowed a film spool from the RAF camp and set it up on an open-air projector within the compound. One night it was *Bonnie and Clyde*. The soldiers enjoyed it for they could understand the fast cars, the guns and the beautiful girl, though the words were lost on them. Before the film ended I saw Sergeant Mohamed beckoning the men of Recce from the crowded audience. Fifteen minutes later the Land Rovers slid up to the compound gates and I joined them.

The night was deliciously cool as we inched through the darkness to the coconut groves of Umran. Two days later, weary from the patrol, we met Murad again by Mamoorah and sped back over the plain towards camp. Idly I looked back to count the spumes of dust rising high behind each vehicle for, even during the monsoon, there is much erosion on the plain.

Three other dustclouds only: one of the sections was missing. We stopped and the others caught up, nodding with the fog of sleep.

"Where is Mohamed of the Beard?" I asked Ali, the last to arrive.

"Perhaps he is broken down, Sahb."

I checked on the radio. There was no reply.

"They have a new driver today," said Murad. "Perhaps he is in difficulty."

Sending the others on, I returned with Ali's men.

We found the missing vehicle near a narrow *wadi*-bed. It was upside down with acute skidmarks behind where the driver had obviously tried, at the last moment, to avoid the runnel.

Only Mohamed Rashid himself and the young driver were standing and unhurt.

Mohamed looked vacant. He was badly shaken. Other men lay about dazed and bloody. There were groans from beneath the vehicle.

We flung ourselves at the Land Rover and heaved until it swung up and over. An Arab with a smashed leg and bleeding chest wound was dragged free but Hamid Sultan lay still where the vehicle had been.

His face was a dented pool of blood, unrecognisable save for the little curling beard. He seemed so much smaller than before. I felt his pulse and, tearing his shirt back, pressed my ear to his sternum. He was dead. Four of the others were badly injured. We returned slowly along the bumpy track not caring whether there were mines, and the injured men were flown out to Muscat. They never came back to the platoon.

The monsoon cleared a few days later on 14th September but we did not share the high spirits of the Companies.

12

Aфтер a death, the Arabs would ask anxiously, "Who was
it? Was he Arab?" If the reply was, "No, he was Baluch,"
they would sigh through their teeth and say, "Thanks be to
God."

The Baluchis' reaction was usually similar but not after the
death of Hamid Sultan. The *moolah* and Sadeeq Jumma led a
deputation of the other Baluch to Sergeant Mohamed to express
their grief at the loss of so fine a comrade who was a friend to
all.

The Arabs watched silently, surprised at this unprecedented
behaviour. But they were grateful and the two groups were
knit the more closely by the needless death.

Only Corporal Taj, whom they called Abu Jungle Petal,
was too proud to join the others and he left the platoon shortly
after the monsoon ended. I had noted for some time his ten-
dency to develop sickness and a noisy cough whenever patrols
were planned. No one was sad to see him go.

The Regimental Sergeant-Major called the platoon 'Qabila
Recce' meaning the Recce tribe; for their clannish behaviour
was noticeable amongst the Companies where hostile feeling
often ran high between Arab and Baluch.

The weather grew cooler as the mist clouds began to withdraw revealing the Qara, all waving grass and steaming jungle;
greener even than Sussex in spring. And now unpleasant things
began to happen, setting a pattern for the future.

Along tracks and in sangars much frequented by our patrols
we found little plastic mines no bigger than torches but sufficient

to blow a man's leg into his stomach, to tear off his scrotum and to blind him. And a worse matter close to Salalah set people on edge within the confines of the city wire.

Tom Greening summoned me to his office one morning. Various Arabs whom I did not recognise were sitting about him sipping coffee, as he told me that something would happen shortly to the east of Salalah. He could give no further details, but urged me to keep a watch by night on the Dhofar Force garrison and the village behind it.

Every night we motored quietly over the plain till the search-light from the Dhofar Force fort was five minutes' walk away. Then the men spaced out in groups of two in a semicircle about the fort and the village of Arzat. Returning to the vehicles shortly before dawn, we slept by day at Umm al Ghawarif.

The men were uneasy about the task. Ali Nasser, who had been in Dhofar in 1966, whispered to me one night, pointing his thumb at the dim outline of the fort.

"The soldiers of the Dhofar Force are *jebalis*. One day soon they will attack Salalah with their armoured cars for they support the *adoo* not the Sultan. Three years ago they tried to shoot him while he was inspecting them. But he has a charmed life. Two of his slaves were killed and the Pakistani commander of the fort was hurt protecting the Sultan's body. Thirteen of the *jebali* soldiers then escaped. They are no better now, Sahb. If they see us here with their searchlight, they will shoot us and afterwards say they thought we were *adoo*."

We lay in wait around Arzat for many nights. Tom had not explained why he wanted us there. Night after night, nothing happened.

Then, without warning, we were moved away to the mountains on another task and, four nights later, it became apparent what we had been waiting for.

Following the course of a dry streambed the six men went quietly to the line of palm trees that leads to the village. For a while they followed the wide track under the trees with water rushing quietly beside them from the spring of Arzat. The village is named after the spring although it is nine miles away.

All six carried Soviet weapons in their right hands and moved with confidence for their leader had himself served with the

177

Dhofar Force in the past. His name was Said Mistahayl: he followed familiar paths and kept well beyond the reach of the ranging searchlights. Avoiding those wattle *barusti* huts where he knew there were dogs, Mistahayl came to the little house where Naseeb, guide to the Sultan's Army, lived with his parents.

Outside the door, he halted and raised one hand. The others moved into the shadows about and behind the house.

Then he tapped the door with the butt of his rifle. There was a pause for visitors were not expected. The door opened and Naseeb's face appeared in the light of a paraffin lamp. He was delighted to recognise and welcome his brother, Mistahayl.

In the room behind, Naseeb's parents heard no reply from their long absent son, Mistahayl: only the staccato rattle of the Simonoff and the sharp scream of Naseeb.

The shots brought many villagers running. Two tried to stop the killers' escape but they were shot down.

The murder was announced weeks later with pride by Radio Aden on 10th October: no one could dispute that the cause of PFLOAG must be both fine and compelling for a man to kill his own brother in its name.

Salim Amr, the rebel guerrilla, had come back again to the Naheez Valley to meet his leader al Ghassani. When Salim Amr arrived, he found a small elderly man tied to the central wooden support of the village's largest hut. His hands were taut above him and he stood on tiptoe, a position he appeared to find intensely uncomfortable. As Salim Amr entered the prisoner dropped his head. An aide inserted his fingers into the man's nostrils and lifted his head as Salim approached: one glance was enough. It was bin Shamou, a member of the *adoo* militia who had been seen selling goats to the Army and was thus not to be trusted.

Salim Amr and al Ghassani sat in council with various other guerrillas and two Chinese who were seated upon large black boxes. Whilst they talked bin Shamou's throat was cut and the air was split by a scream which tapered away to a wheezing gasp. No one took any notice: all listened intently to their leader and his news. For al Ghassani told them how he had witnessed the fall of Rakhyut, the major town of western Dhofar. Now PFLOAG were masters of two-thirds of Dhofar and overall victory was within their grasp.

Salim Amr was asked for his news from the eastern part of the province. He produced lists of those individuals and sub-tribes whose loyalties were suspect and explained that he was having trouble with Musallim Ali who was using his influence as a political commissar to protect his own tribe and also the Bait Howeirat tribe. The reason for this was that he had fallen out with his wife and now frequently visited a woman of the Bait Howeirat. This tribe was a snake's nest of dissidents any-way and Salim Amr could do nothing until he had his own local *Idaara* to counteract Musallim Ali.

Al Ghassani then told Salim Amr to bide his time until an *Idaara* squad was assigned to him and then he could add Musallim Ali's name to the list of those to be executed.

That night they left the huts and the forest and climbed to the winding army track, already almost dry but for a few puddles. Certainly hard enough for vehicles. The Chinese moved in the middle of the file. Heading north they came at length to the rim of the mountains. The lush foliage ended abruptly. Below them lay the desert.

Under the directions of the Chinese, the men worked furiously with picks and hands tunnelling the earth beneath the long wooden ramp that joined the Midway Road to its mountain extension.

When all was ready the Chinese opened their black boxes. Three Arabs worked with them, learning the ropes. The faint smell of almonds came to Salim: in an hour the work was complete and hidden. Eight men stayed behind.

Far to the south ten other bands moved into position about the mountain road and, not long before dawn on the 15th, the Qara shook briefly as muffled explosions rolled back and forth in the valleys.

On 17th September when the mountains lay clear of mist, all available army units were mustered at either end of the Midway Road. This road was the crucial link across the Qara mountains between the northern desert plains along which lorries and Land Rovers could bring supplies from Muscat and Oman and the coastal plain and sea at Salalah. The Sultan had no air trans-port facilities and no navy so the only way supplies could reach Salalah was by the Midway Road. Major 'Taweel', the Marine with the so-called *djinn*, led his Company from Deefa to the wooden ramp at the northern extreme of the mountain road. He found it destroyed by the most modern Soviet explosive packs, some of which he recovered undetonated.

From the Salalah Plain side of the mountain came two Companies, under Richard John and David Bayley. By midday it was hoped that all nine miles of this mountain road would be covered by the Companies so that the vital fuel and ammunition convoys coming from the north could get safely over the mountains.

During the monsoon mud had made mountain travel impossible, but now the track was dry and hard enough to take transport and the supplies were urgently needed.

We moved ahead of the company lorries. At 08.30 we came to three enormous craters in the road. And beyond, as far as I could see, huge boulders littered the route, rolled on to it from above. Soldiers worked furiously at the craters using their hands and shovels. They cast anxious glances at the thick flowering jungle either side of the track but nothing stirred. Men moved ahead with mine detectors and levered the boulders to one side.

Mike Muldoon, the ex-Katanga mercenary, stood in the middle of the road in white slacks and faded khaki shirt. He wore the brown baseball hat much favoured by Zambian terrorists, one of whom had been its original owner when Mike had joined the Rhodesian Army for a spell.

Taking cover behind a rock in my green and brown streaked clothes, I wondered how Mike had survived for so long. His flagrant disregard for danger seemed to me almost flamboyant. As though he were lifting two fingers at the unseen *adoo* and saying: "Here I am. A Grade One target; a white officer. Shoot me if you can!"

Colonel 'Mad Mitch' Mitchell of the Argylls has summed up this philosophy in his book *Having Been a Soldier*. ". . . he was calmly strolling about at a most dangerous moment exposing himself to enemy fire. But there was method in such madness. Such an ostentatious display of confidence and calm puts as much heart into one's own soldiers as it disturbs the enemy. There is of course a risk but it is one worth taking."

I agreed with this but never got down to emulating it myself mostly, I suppose, because of the sudden sense of prudence which gripped me whenever I found myself being shot at.

Later Mike was blown up by a mine so that now he is partially deaf. And he fell off a bar stool at Umm al Ghawarif which gave him a permanent limp.

Our vehicles managed at length to by-pass the craters and crept by a slalom trail of boulders. We were to reach the southern rim of the deep pass called Ambush Corner and wait until Major 'Taweel's' men reached the northern side. Only then would men move down into the dangerous ravine itself.

The trouble which followed came partly because we arrived too late at the valley. But, afterwards, the mutinous men of 'Taweel's' Company blamed everything on him and his jinx.

On earlier finding their route barred by the sabotaged ramp 'Taweel' and his men had followed another route, via Haloof, on to the mountain. At 09.30 they were shot at but only one man was wounded so they continued quickly dropping off soldiers at strategic points along the road. After four miles, approaching Ambush Corner, 'Taweel' had shed all but a single platoon and a 25-pounder artillery gun.

There was a new officer with 'Taweel' who had just arrived from England. He had seen action only at Aldershot on the Ministry of Defence training ground and now he was going for his first outing to see the interesting Qara mountains.

'Taweel' was also sometimes called *Jalut* by many Arabs, which means Goliath. As he walked over the incline leading to the main slope a rip of machine gun fire burst from the trees two hundred yards ahead and from scrub further to the left.

'Taweel' was caught in the open as were most of his available men.

The 25-pounder crew swung their big gun round without using its platform and, treating it like a kingsize rifle, pumped a single round into the scrub. Before they could re-load, the crew were mown down by another *adoo* machine gun close behind them.

'Taweel' tried to crawl back to the radio in his Land Rover to call for the jets but the merest movement brought a hail of fire from three directions and he had to lie motionless with mounting frustration as he watched the men picked off all about him. He noticed to his alarm that the strike of certain bullets was far from normal. Instead of a quick splatt engulfed by the hard soil, these new projectiles exploded on contact scattering dirt, rock and shrapnel.

One such bullet set the artillery lorry on fire and a stiff breeze fanned the flames towards the closely packed shells. A Baluchi leaped on to the lorry to put out the flames. For moments 'Taweel' watched the inevitable helplessly as the hammer of bullets hummed above him. The Baluchi tore frantically at burning debris as more and more of the *adoo* adjusted their sights on to him. Then, as in slow-motion, he arched backwards with a bullet through the head and toppled to the ground. Someone dragged him behind a wheel but he died not long afterwards.

The new officer, lying by 'Taweel's' Land Rover, crawled to the rear as bullets passed through the chassis above him and buried themselves in the Dunlop tyres. Somehow he managed to get hold of the radio and signalled for the jets. When they came the *adoo* disappeared unseen.

Mike Muldoon came later to the smouldering lorry when the flames had been doused. There were few weapons in the world manufactured by West or East that he did not know intimately. In the main chassis of the Bedford, that joined the cab to the rear section he found a clean bullet hole, half an inch in diameter, which passed through two complete sections of the metal framework. Each section was five inches thick and of high density metal.

Mike whistled softly.

"Jees, man, they've got Shpagins. Now we'll be seeing some fireworks. Bloody great 12·7 bullets; some with high explosive heads, others just the armour piercing type that would go through Sydney bridge and out the other side." He said the Shpagin was also an effective anti-aircraft gun.

Putting his eye to the bullet exit hole, he peered through. In this way he located the exact latitudinal position of the Shpagin when it fired. Since a deep valley separated the road from the only slope where the big machine gun might have been, it could only have been fired from well over a thousand yards and using telescopic sights.

Lorry after lorry rolled past, screaming in low gear down the precipitous pass.

The convoys would take three days to complete the vital

resupply. That evening we dug in amongst the jasmine clumps on a hillock. The pass of Ambush Corner fell away close by. At dusk the forest to the west down in the Wadi Naheez crackled suddenly with hundreds of red fireflies. Instinctively we flung ourselves down. No one was hurt. After five minutes the firing stopped, and darkness settled quietly.

With Fred Wahid, a guide, nine of us crept from the hillock in a great half circle through scrub and forest within the Naheez valley. We moved very quietly following Fred. Before we left he had cautioned me.

"So soon after the monsoon the long wet grass will betray us so we must move through trees, never through meadows. Otherwise the goatherds will see our trail. Then they will know how few we are and where we go. And they will tell the *adoo*."

After four long hours we took cover inside a thick clump of trees and waited. Towards midnight Mubarreq the Zanzibari began to snore. I tickled his nose and he stopped. There were no monsoon tics and few mosquitoes. I took my turn at watch from three in the morning. It was cold and damp with a heavy dew. There seemed no patch of the whole wide sky above our rocks that was not filled with stars. They really twinkled; like wing-lights of aeroplanes but as the new day inched west the twinkling grew less. The galaxies faded one by one as their backcloth diffused with soft pink light that slowly turned to gold.

Flowers grew among the rocks and wide pink petals festooned the lianas which covered the scrub. Their scent was at first elusive. Then it spread until the coming of the sun sucked out every perfume filling the thicket with fragrance.

The clover bees began to work and their buzzing sounded pleasant as I dozed.

Fat Hamid, the pirate faced Browning gunner, successor to Hamid Sultan, looked down at me, his merry rounded face creased with anxiety. It was very hot. I must have slept a long while for the sun was east of its southern zenith.

My head was muzzy, my mouth and eyes dry.

Fred Wahid, our guide, beckoned and I crawled over to his rock.

"There are six men of the *adoo* in the big hut, Sahb. I saw their rifles and packs."

I took his binoculars; there were three huts on the valley floor below us in a clearing among huge fig and tamarind trees. Women played with children close to the huts, one of which was a solidly built rondaaval of baked mud with a roof of hay sheaves.

A man came out and walked into the trees. He had no pack but his rifle was sufficient justification for us to open fire. However some six hundred yards of lush meadow separated us from the huts. The likelihood of hitting someone at that distance was remote. I must call up the jets or artillery.

Four more men came out of the largest hut; one wore a small backpack. The sound of harsh laughter carried up to our hide: they were very confident.

Something held me back from the radio set. Sura rockets or 25-pounders would make short work of anyone in the huts but death and mutilation would not be selective. Women and children who were in no way to blame for the war would be hurt. Here was my chance to avenge 'Taweel's' dead soldiers and, in an indirect way, the death of Hamid Sultan which I still felt keenly.

I grabbed the hand mike but could not bring myself to speak. The men lay watching; tense and eager like cats observing a mouse. Fred the guide glanced at me curiously as though he could sense my inner turmoil.

"We will wait until we are sure there are no more *adoo* to come to the huts, Fred, then I will call the big guns."

He raised his eyebrows with a wealth of meaning. It was his way of shrugging and saying, "A bird in the hand . . ."

I knew he was right but did nothing.

For forty minutes we watched motionless. Women moved between the huts. Then at 3.30 p.m., one tall fellow came out of the big hut and fastened a pack to his shoulders. He carried his gun at the ready position in both hands and looked about him. For a moment he seemed to stare at our rocks. Stared but did not see. Fred whistled softly as fourteen men emerged behind the first. They wore dark brown uniform and floppy khaki hats: all were armed.

I flicked the switch on the BCC 30. "Hallo 57 this is 5. Target over."

The artillery Captain replied immediately and quietly, having noted my own whisper. I was uncertain of the exact location of the huts and so asked for a 'shot' on to a tall hillock across the valley. I gave him the map co-ordinates where I thought the hill was. In seconds a shell burst on its forward crest and from this I orientated the exact position of the huts.

The *adoo* had already left the clearing as the first shell exploded in the trees behind them. They scattered in all directions. Nineteen more shells crashed into the forest but my chance of a sure killing was gone. I had blundered inexcusably. No innocents had been hurt but that was no consolation at the time.

Fred Wahid was sullen for a while but soon forgot my stupidity. It was, after all, the will of Allah that guided even white men's minds.

Later the last convoy passed over the mountains and the Companies were peeled back. At Umm al Ghawarif I visited the men and sat on Ali Nasser's bed; he was ill with a wracking cough. Corporal Salim Khaleefa and Mohamed Rashid of the Beard were there. Until I came they had been talking excitedly.

Scenting gossip, I sat beside them and waited. The news was not long in coming. Corporal Salim had heard it from a Sergeant of B Company flown in for leave.

"Last night there was great trouble in their camp. The men said they could no longer bear 'Taweel' as their Major for his evil *djinn* would soon kill them all. They said it was this *djinn* that caused so many men to be killed at the Pass of the Jasmine."

Salim seemed to have more to say but was embarrassed to continue. I cajoled him successfully. It was said that 'Taweel' had been forced to leave his camp and the men had threatened to shoot him if he returned, and the Colonel himself had had to fly to B Company with Patrick Brook. Patrick was apparently to stay with them and 'Taweel' was coming back to Umm al Ghawarif.

B Company's morale recovered slowly over the ensuing weeks. The main troublemakers were removed quietly to other Companies and watched. Word of the mutiny was hushed. After all it had been directed against an intangible *djinn*. It was unfortunate that 'Taweel' of the Royal Marines had appeared to behave in a manner so readily open to *djinn*-ridden accusations, but then luck had treated him badly.

"Do we have any *djinns* in Recce?" I asked, joking.

But the others found the matter serious. Ali Nasser squirmed under his blanket: such a thing should not be discussed on his bed.

"*Yimkin*," said Mohamed of the Beard, "it is always possible. They come and they go as they please. So far we have been spared, *Al Handu lillah*."

Intelligence indicated that ten Russian Shpagins and a like number of heavy mortars had reached Dhofar during the monsoon. This changed the whole concept of the struggle and the Colonel reacted quickly, deciding to blockade the centre and east of Dhofar with a system of camps and patrols stretching from the desert to the sea. Richard John's men would guard the coast to the mountains whilst David Bayley's were to establish a camp at Raydah, which the Army had christened Idlewild – the ridge where the foliated Qara are at their narrowest and so least favourable to the guerrillas.

North of Idlewild all vegetation stops and a crazy land of ravines and crumbling cliffs called the *nejd* descends in layers to the desert beyond. There were many secret camel trails through this broken wilderness which the local bedu had long used; bedu known to help the *adoo* in return for good pay. This region was to be our responsibility; a hundred miles and more from the cliffs north of Idlewild to the fringe of the Rubh al Khali. There were no other army units in this region and only a few hundred nomads perpetually moving their camels or goats between the scattered water holes.

To reach the *nejd* meant another crossing of the Midway Road. David Bayley's men came across at the same time. The soldiers were on edge for the Shpagin was a new and unseen terror: the word had spread of bullets the size of batons that explode inside the body.

We drove out of the gates of Umm al Ghawarif for the last time, shaking hands with many friends we would not see again. As we approached the foothills of the Qara, we came under heavy fire from the hillocks ahead. Corporal Salim and Ali Nasser took their men very quickly forward. Sergeant Mohamed and I followed. Leapfrogging in this manner, the platoon closed the gap quickly, supported by the guns of David's Company.

Fat Hamid slammed a belt into his Browning and shouted above the hammer of Said Salim's machine gun.

"They're out of range of your peashooter, Said." Two figures were running up the ravine above us. Fat Hamid muttered cheerfully as he fired, adjusting his aim by the fall of the glowing tracer rounds. But a hail of bullets spat close about us and Hamid stopped his muttering. Then David Bayley's mortars opened up and the *adoo* fire eased off.

Intelligence reports later confirmed that six guerrillas were killed that morning.

There was further trouble before we reached the northern desert and three soldiers were wounded. The Russian Shpagin fired with great accuracy and its hiding place was still impossible to locate.

A week later Tom Greening's spies corroborated information given by a captured *adoo* of the exact position of the Shpagin and its ten-man group.

We were to infiltrate by night into the valley east of Ambush Corner. One of the Companies would then sweep down into the Arbat valley from the north and towards us, hopefully catching the Shpagin men in the middle.

But things turned out very differently for at least sixty guerrillas were guarding the Russian gun with a well-sited ring of automatic weapons. The Company was forced to withdraw with its dead and by midday we were alone in the bottom of the Arbat valley. There were twenty of us split into four sections.

In the afternoon two young girls came into the knot of scrub where we lay. I saw Said Salim slip his stiletto from its sheath. Mubarreq the negro tensed beside me gathering his haunches quietly beneath him. But the girls saw us and their eyes widened in fear. I smiled at them and beckoned through the foliage. They stood still, their little almost triangular faces taking on an expression of curiosity.

Behind the bush I sensed Said Salim stirring, creeping around the side.

"*Ish kish, Ish kish,*" I whispered through the leaves: the Dhofari assurance that all is well.

They held hands: one had a semi-shaven scalp and a silver pendant about her neck.

A twig cracked and the girls glanced nervously beside them.

Perhaps they sensed Said's presence behind the curtain of leaves. With a flick of their grubby little cloaks they were off scurrying through the undergrowth to their village.

Said was after them like a flash but I whistled and beckoned him back.

It was possible that the girls thought we were only a group of *adoo* from another region. After all they must have seen many strange faces of late: guerrillas with yellow faces and slit eyes and others, Arabs from the Mediterranean, with paler skin than mine. And they could have seen very little else through the foliage. With luck they would find something to distract them, and ignore their parents' probable instructions to report all strangers at once.

But my confidence wained when excited voices came from further along the *wadi* floor. We sweated in the dappled heat. We were twenty men in the epicentre of the mountains, in the heart of guerrilla territory.

Said Salim pressed his head to the ground. "They are coming here, Sahb. We must move."

We raked over the earth where we had lain and then brushed it carefully with our *shemaghs*. Said led us away from the village and Mubarreq obliterated our latrine area behind us so there would be no sign of our presence save perhaps for our smell. For half an hour we crept through low undergrowth. Then there were no more voices.

My signaller tuned in his set when a series of muffled explosions sounded to the north.

"The Company have been ambushed on their way back off the mountain. They called in the planes one of which has been hit."

I prayed we had not been compromised by the two girls. If we had there would be a warm reception awaiting us on our own withdrawal through the ravine of Ambush Corner and beyond.

The words of a soldier of the 22nd Special Air Service Regiment came to me as we waited for dusk. He had been surrounded by tribesmen in the Radfan mountains of Eastern Aden in 1967.

"The bastards got our officer and one other bloke, but the rest of us got away by night. We heard later that they cut their heads off, stuck them on poles and paraded them around Sanaa. But, you know, if our officer had behaved by the book, we'd never have been caught in the first place. An old shepherd saw us. We all said, 'Cut his throat' but the officer said,' No.' So, once our backs were turned, the old boy upped and told the Radfanis who didn't take long to find us. He'd still be alive today, that officer, if he'd not let his emotions run away with him."

Night came at last and we moved into the open meadows to the wood appointed as rendezvous. Corporal Salim and Ali were already there. They shook my hand in greeting. Men smiled up from the dark rim of the wood and our retreat began. We kept away from the Midway Road itself and the open fields that flank it.

Each section commander held a white phosphorus grenade in one hand and so did the rear man—the enormous *moolah*.

We moved without a rest for nine hours through defiles strewn with loose boulders, crossing endless minor valleys, skirting clusters of thorn huts. On my map there were three villages all marked with official question marks, as though their existence was unconfirmed: names from the imagination of Edgar Allan Poe—Gurthnod, Erikob and Habdoomer. But in practice there were many other unnamed hamlets to avoid. Fortunately there were no dogs in the mountains and we climbed to the safe heights of Haloof soon after dawn.

The Arab newspaper, *Al Sharara*, later commented on our attempt to capture the Shpagin. The description was even more exaggerated than the normal biased reports of the Arab press and is worth noting.

... On that day our People's Liberation Army had several fierce battles against the forces of British Colonisation in Dhofar and ambushed them in many places.

The enemy used Hawker planes and many other heavy arms but 115 of them were killed and wounded and one Hawker Hunter was shot down. Our People's Liberation Army lost one martyr.

The Midway Road was used only once again that year, for the *adoo* grip tightened about its length; their growing strength and heavier weapons meant the use of at least four Companies to open the road safely to transport—and four Companies were not available without moving the vital arms block.

I never saw the road again and when I returned to Dhofar late in 1973, there were only three officers there who had ever motored over the Qara.

The *adoo* held the mountains from the Yemeni border to the Arbat valley and immediately began to press eastwards. Only the lands of the Eastern Mahra and the Samhan Range were now to any degree independent of the guerrillas. Once they were subjugated, the Plain of Salalah would be totally cut off with its back to the sea.

13

THE nights grew colder and desert winds scoured the vast volcanic plateau that forms the *nejd*. Each man was given an extra blanket. At midday the heat was scorching and the dusty gravel wastes shimmered in dancing mirage. I was assigned a lorry to carry water and firewood which we collected from desert *wadis*. Also a breakdown lorry and twelve live goats a week. These I received from the headman of the old oil camp at Midway.

In this way we were self-contained for life in the desert for we were back again in North Dhofar where we had been before. The goats were supplemented when possible by gazelle and ibex meat. Water came from scattered springs that only the bedu knew. Fred Wahid the guide came with us for these arid wastes had once been his home.

When we saw the prints of a lone camel, we would stop to let Fred kneel beside them. No detail escaped him: sometimes he knew the name of the camel's owner by the shape of the beast's hoof, where and when it had last drunk by the amount and frequency of the droppings and, by the texture, in which *wadis* it had last eaten.

We wandered, shuffling under the weight of the heat, to strange dead places which Fred knew. To Thint where, he said, the *adoo* had once lived, drinking from the water hole there. There were no signs of life and very little water since there had been no rain for fifteen years.

We filled our *chaguls* and bottles and clambered wearily along boulder-strewn valleys, climbed crumbling slopes and came to an airstrip.

Only a fool in distress would land here, I thought. Only an aerial nutcase would even recognise it as an airstrip. On the otherwise blank map it was labelled 'Pasadena (Position Approximate.)'

It was no more than a ridge a hundred yards across and 350 yards long. At either end of the so-called runway cliffs fell away sheer for hundreds of feet.

The minimal airstrip length a Beaver plane requires is four hundred yards when taking off from sea level at a fairly cool temperature and without much of a load. I hoped I would never need evacuating from that precipitous runway.

Fred did not tire but the rest of us were thirsty and exhausted. With little water, we could not afford to move further by day. After resting until evening we followed him north along craggy ridges to a little plateau, almost an amphitheatre, surrounded by gravel hillocks.

This was to be our base for many months. From it we made long journeys, saw strange places and killed people about to kill other people. I remember it as the only home we had in those months of wandering.

Through the centre of the plateau a white trail curved. Fred pointed, his flattened fingers following the course of the track through the moonshadows of many hillocks.

"From the Qara at Idlewild to this place there is no route that a camel might follow moving west to east." As we saw at Pasadena, all the great *wadis* cut north and south. Fred placed a finger delicately on one nostril and blew hard, thus clearing his nose by way of the other nostril. This also served to emphasise his point.

"Only here, by this Dehedoba trail can the *adoo*'s camels come from the Yemen. Or else much further north where the *nejd* is ended and the sands begin."

And so we stayed by the little plateau and observed it constantly by day and night for many months. When there was work elsewhere we left only a section, well concealed among the sweltering hillocks.

The *nejd* looked both lifeless and harmless. In reality it was neither: every crack in the crumbling surface concealed something that crawled or slithered.

We ate twice a day; always boiled goat and rice with tea.

A Kathiri from the
Darbat area

A plains bedu wearing
traditional mahfoof

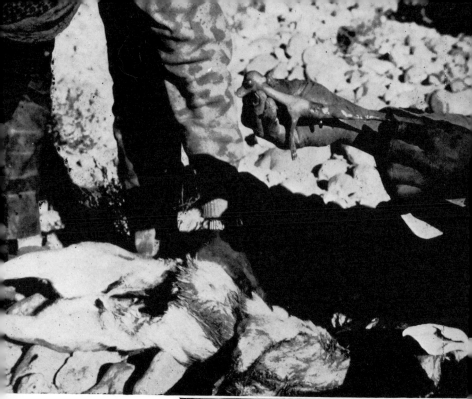

Inside the dead gazelle
we found an embryo

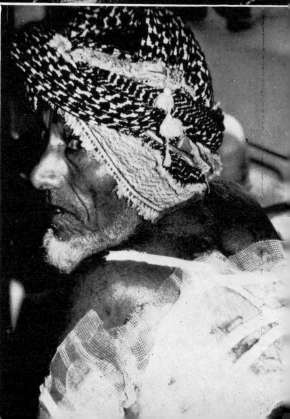

Tortured on hot coals
for praying

With Fred the guide and Sergeant Mohamed, I travelled far along the labyrinth of ravines all about our plateau. Sometimes there were only the trails of long dead camels littered with hyrax droppings.

We would squat beside Fred as he inspected the camel dung and told us the animal's history.

Once, blowing softly at a misshapen hoofprint, Fred declared with wonder.

"These are like the marks of Barak herself, the camel of the Prophet." He looked up with a smile. "She had the feet of a mule but she took Him to heaven and back in one night for she moved with the speed of the desert wind."

When we rose to go Fred whistled through his teeth.

"Allah is good to you, Sahb. Look here."

With his camel stick he picked up the crushed sand-coloured body of a six-inch scorpion which I had trodden on. I normally wore no shoes once the soles of my feet had hardened for it was so much cooler without them. But that day I had and was certainly grateful for their protection.

There were many scorpions. Green and black and white ones. Some were more virulent than others but their bite was never deadly to a healthy man who kept motionless whilst the poison was drawn out or slowly assimilated into the bloodstream.

I collected many snakeskins in the desert; most of the reptiles were small and all had venom sacs. In the smaller *wadi*-beds, cracked and white with saline nitre where pools of rain had long since evaporated, were thickets of *ghaf* acacia and threadbare *marakh* bushes. In such places there were many snakes. Sleeping on the ground it was possible to hear the dry crackle of the serpents squirming through the thorny *chicka* brush.

Our most frequent visitors were the African puff-adder and horned viper both of which have dust-coloured camouflage. "If they bite," Fred Wahid advised me, "kill an oryx and soak the wound with its blood then maybe you will live."

Less common were the camel spiders: these jump from rock to rock and are most difficult to crush for their abdomens are squat and robust. They have large eyes and a beak but, according to Sergeant Mohamed, "They are thoughtful and do not wish to cause pain when they eat your flesh at night. For this reason they give you first an injection, then they start to eat and you cannot feel discomfort. The next morning when you awake you are startled to find much blood and a patch of flesh missing."

After six months in the *nejd*, sleeping on the ground, none of us had been chewed at by spiders, though I twice awoke to find them under my blanket. Perhaps they came in for warmth but the touch of their great furry legs was loathsome and, both times, I jumped up shuddering and could not sleep again for a while.

The spiders provided food for the desert monitors and countless smaller lizards that lived in the *nejd*.

Even in the depths of the *nejd* and the still emptier Sands to the north there were flies; countless thousands of them. And in addition to the flies of any particular area there were also our own flies that accompanied us everywhere travelling on our backs and headcloths or, when we drove, clinging to the metal of the vehicles.

Little scratches on my hands and legs became infected by these flies, grew larger and refused to heal.

Two hours east of our plateau the Wadi Ayun wound north to the desert, floored with huge white boulders too bright to look on when the sun was high. A spring bubbled up from under the boulders with pure sweet water forming three pools in between soaring cliffs. Reeds and flowering lianas rimmed this lagoon and the diving screech of swallows echoed sharply from cavernous galleries in the upper cliffs.

We filled the water barrels forming a human chain from the lorries on the clifftops and when the work was over the men bathed in the nearest of the three pools. None would go near the deeper lagoon that lay around a bend in the ravine for the word had spread of a serpent *djinn* that lived in its depths.

Crawling along a ledge in the cliff wall, I reached this pool. Unobserved by the men I stripped off and swam, floating luxuriously in this strange primaeval place so utterly out of keeping with the land about.

News and fresh goats came to us by a Beaver plane which landed on the tiny airstrip in the centre of our plateau. We heard of ambush successes further south along the blocking line. Several *adoo* had been killed and their camels captured with stores and money on board. Tom Greening predicted that soon the guerrillas would be forced to strike north of the Qara to bring supplies through the *nejd* or the Sands. So we waited and watched.

Leaving Sergeant Mohamed and Ali Nasser to block the *nejd*, I went into the Sands to the north, with the sections of Corporal Salim and Mohamed of the Beard. We took money from Tom Greening to give to local bedu. If they saw or heard of *adoo* caravans they were to inform us; then there would be a further reward.

To the north-west of Thamarit we came to an abandoned fortress at the well of Shisr. The water ran deep below the sand at the base of a limestone cliff. Fred the guide showed us where a meteor had struck the desert and revealed the water to the Bait Kathir who owned the place.

There were no bedu at Shisr nor yet at Fasad, an old oil camp along the edge of the sand sea, so we motored for two hours through soft sand alongside huge white dunes to an airstrip within the Sands. It had no mapped name but Murad assured me the long departed oil prospectors had called it '455'. Now there was only a rash of metal bric-à-brac and broken shacks.

The place was totally quiet as the men slept beneath the vehicles. The plunk-plunk of cooling metal cut across the soft sound of moving sand; tiny particles falling continually in the perpetual motion of the dunes.

Otherwise the silence of the grave ruled the senses as it had since all life in the land was smothered by sand; sucked dry by the sun. Petrified ostrich eggs have been found in the sands, but little else for billions of tons of shifting granules flow annually with the slightest breeze and the great summer storms.

Mountains of sand are formed only to be battered and engulfed by greater mountains. Huge ranges alter their geography over the years and if fabulous cities ever existed in these parts they will be uncovered by the winds that hid them not by the flimsy shovels of archaeologists.

The bedu tell of such places around their camp fires but none can point accurately to the ancient sites. Their ancestors passed on tales of sand 'yetis' that moved with great speed and grace but were hideous to behold, having only a single leg and an arm attached to their chest. Their home was the epicentre of the Sands, that mysterious place where no bedu had ever been and where the lost city of Ubar was to be found. The ancient princes of Ad lived at Ubar but their orgies became so imaginative that Allah drowned the place in sand and turned the survivors into one-legged monkeys.

We drove in the early mornings while it was still cool and the sand was firmer but there were still long stints of pushing the vehicles in four-wheel drive over *ghadaf* palm tree leaves that we cut and lay criss-cross in lanes. Murad lowered the tyre pressure on the vehicles, but this did little good. By the third day in the Sands we had used both Murad's spare half-shafts and another was parachuted to us from a circling Beaver.

Gazelle bounded by, a flash of white in the distance, and we gave chase. The men screamed with delight, bounding high on the food sacks.

Said Salim wounded a female. We stopped by the terrified creature and Ali Nasser quickly cut her throat. They skinned her at once and showed me the twin embryos from her belly: the animal had been pregnant though she had run as fast as her mate. We buried the unborn babies and ate the tender meat with relish.

There was no need for silence by night in the Sands. No armed *adoo* would come this far north where a single jet could kill a hundred guerrillas at leisure. For there was no cover, no shade, nowhere to run. Their food convoys, if indeed they traversed the Sands, would be accompanied by innocent looking youths not armed guerrillas.

So the men talked into the small hours, lying in the sand about the glowing embers of our fire. The men never spoke derisively, trying to score over their neighbour in conversation, as is the way of British soldiers. All had their say and the Baluchis sat at peace among the Arabs. They were happy talking for the sake of communicating, needing no alcoholic stimulus. They could express themselves without the need to swear. I thought of other army nights by other fires: of the Jocks in Germany; the clatter of empty beer cans, the filthy language punctuating every sentence, the crude laughter as someone rose to urinate into the fire.

I felt happy and at one with these Muslim soldiers in a way I had never experienced with my own kind. There was no ever-present barrier of self-consciousness, no superficial officer-soldier gap designed and perpetuated to prevent familiarity gnawing at discipline.

Such a gap was not necesary with the Arabs since they accepted an inch without coveting a mile. Their morals and their manners were built-in as was their respect for authority. In time their traditions would doubtless be eroded by contact with an outside world in which both society and individual standards had degenerated but, till then, they would remain the best companions any man could want.

Sergeant Mohamed often impressed upon me that I was a Nazrani, one of the unbelievers. Therefore I was ranked socially lower than the poorest Muslim. Then his little eyes would twinkle with humour and he would add, "But you are an officer so there are many who rank even lower, thanks be to God."

As with many small men, Mohamed was a supreme egoist, rivalled only in powers of self-glorification by five-foot Ali Nasser. Both had mini-beard tufts which they would stroke lovingly when making an emphatic point or tug with frustration when an argument was not going their way.

There was much of interest in the Sands, even the most desolate stretches for those who knew what to look for. Fred the guide showed me fragile butterflies, pink and blue fritillaries, that hopped about the *kfeeter* plants, tiny bobbles growing just above the ground with knotty roots curled protectively about their seeds.

Fred carefully extracted some of the seeds and sniffed them.

"When a baby child is gripped by a *djinn* spirit, then we put these seeds in a piece of rag, tie it up, and hang it round the baby's neck. The *shaitan* hates the *kfeeter* so he flees to another baby."

He showed me other plants, the gnarled *gha'ader* that provides stomach medicine for the bedu and the *gai'sh* hedgehog bush with its sharp and deadly thorns. Many stretches of sand are littered with strings of tiny Sodom apples which, applied halved and hot to an abscess, draw out poison as efficiently as a poultice. Heated in boiling water Fred had seen bedu use them to cauterise and draw jigger worms out of their toes.

"Melons too have their use," he added. "I have watched men of the Qara heal a broken arm with a melon when one of their number fell from his camel and splinters of arm bone pierced

197

through his skin. The men of his tribe held him down and pulled the arm out straight. Then they burnt a hole in a long melon from end to end and forced it over the arm. After six months the arm was mended though it would never bend again."

Fred took me to an evergreen tamarisk with a fine pink flower. In the cool sand beneath the bush were tiny greenish flakes: He gave me one to eat. It was sweet and moist; quite possibly the *manna* of the children of Israel. Gazelle and the rare oryx can live for months without water drinking only from the tamarisk and other juicy shrubs.

One night, in the wilderness of the *nejd*, I heard the high pure song of a lark but by day we saw only hawks and massive vultures, the funeral directors of the desert.

Very few bedu came our way. A scrawny goatherd of the Bait Ghawwas tribe sold us two scraggy animals at an exorbitant rate and accepted bribe money. His only information was that our movements were being watched. By whom and from where he would not say.

His cryptic warning was corroborated by an unexpected source on the *jebel*.

We moved by night from the pools of Ayun to the Pass of Qismeem. This pass, at the northern rim of the vegetated Qara, is the bottleneck of many paths used by the guerrillas and we used to set snap ambushes along it from time to time. On the morning in question I saw two *jebalis*, both unarmed, hurrying along a track beneath our hideout. Something about the smaller of the two men struck a chord in my memory and I sent Said Salim to collect both of them.

He did so with great expertise and minimal commotion. They were very frightened and it was difficult to quieten their babble once in the hide.

Both were of the Bait Tabawq and came from the Wadi Arbat beside the Midway Road. They were immediately suspect, and knew it, for why should simple goatherds be so far from their tribal area unless they were acting as couriers for the *adoo*? If on the other hand they were not working for the *adoo*, they were in still deeper water since the guerrillas forbade the unauthorised movement of all *jebalis* from one part of the *jebel* to another. This cut down the activities of Tom Greening's spies.

But I did not press the two men for an explanation for one was an old friend of ours—Ahmed Sehail, a goatman. Ahmed Sehail had sold us goats many months ago on the *jebel* and we had given him flour and Aspirins for his family. He shook hands with the five of us and seemed to forget the need for silence. Several times Said Salim placed a hand over the mouth of the exuberant Ahmed Sehail as his greetings grew too noisy. His fear was gone but his companion squatted nervously behind him as though we were diseased. And in a way we were: to be seen with the Army was damning, smacking of collaboration. It would mean immediate arrest by the guerrillas.

Ahmed Sehail was bolder than most *jebalis*; we had laughed long and loud at his antics, imitating the cocky young guerrillas and their political ravings which, he said, they understood even less than their bewildered *jebali* audiences.

But the humour of Ahmed Sehail was hidden by lines of fear. Fat Hamid gave him a scoop of sugar which he took and placed in the leather bag about his neck.

"I must go. If we are seen we will be killed. And there are many watchers. I must tell you to be careful. There are twelve men with guns and binoculars whose work is to watch the movements of your men. It is known that you guard the Dehedoba track but your other movements confuse them as yet. When they know your routine they have mines and they will wait for you."

He looked at the man behind him quickly, then, leaning close to me, he added. "They know you go to Thamarit for food by way of the Ayun crossing. Now that the other Army soldiers have gone from Haloof, the *adoo* will wait for you below the old army camp. You must be careful."

I noticed that he constantly twitched his neck from side to side as though in pain. I asked him if he wanted medicine.

Throwing back his dirty cloak he revealed a jigsaw of dark purple weals over his back and chest. One crossed his right nipple which was broken, swollen and suppurating. Accepting a packet of penicillin tablets, he refused a dressing of any sort saying that it would be noticed and someone would tell the guerrillas he had received army aid.

"But why did they do this to you?"

"I sold some goats to the soldiers at the Aqbat Hamrir and someone told the *adoo*. They tied me to a tree and beat me with a strand of wire. No one dared cut me free afterwards for many hours and the flies were bad."

We thanked the men and they went, keeping amongst the bushes. Five months later I heard that the guerrillas arrested Ahmed and another of his tribe, as spies. They were deported to Hauf and never heard of again.

Thereafter we passed through the ravines below Haloof with the utmost caution and, however bad the terrain, kept off the meandering tracks for fear of mines.

Ali Nasser took his men a mile ahead of the rest and, soon after our meeting with Ahmed Sehail, disturbed two men with automatic rifles at the bottom of some cliffs. Both groups saw each other simultaneously and the *adoo* disappeared into a gully before Ali's men could open fire. He did not follow them, suspecting a larger group in the vicinity. But their very presence in the ravine was evidence that unwelcome surprises were being prepared for us.

We determined not to risk our necks in that suicidal *wadi* again. We would find another route from the lofty *nejd* to the Sands as soon as possible.

At this time the stranglehold of the Leopard Line, the code name for the chain of blocking positions, was beginning to affect the guerrillas' supply line. Several had already been killed in ambushes by day and night and retaliation was expected before long.

At Idlewild David Bayley's men were under permanent observation by the *adoo* who seized every opportunity presented to them. The Company left Idlewild on an operation for two days during which time a light guard from another unit took over their outposts. The guerrillas were quick to take advantage, infiltrating a group of forty specialists with Chinese advisers and arms around the thinly held positions. To cover this move, fourteen men under one Bakhait Ahmad attacked and killed two soldiers from only ten yards away, seizing their weapons before retaliation was possible. It would be only a matter of time before we too suffered such a lightning attack. It would come when least expected, by day or night.

So Recce split into three groups. One to find a safe route to the desert, one to ambush the Dehedoba trail and the third to patrol the Sands. I warned each to be erratic in their actions, setting no daily pattern of movement and never relaxing their guard.

14

I WENT with Mohamed of the Beard and our ten men into the great gravel deserts which skirt the Empty Quarter. We lived permanently on the move, travelling to no set routine between the desert waterholes. For weeks on end we saw no one. At other times, through binoculars, we watched caravans of heavy laden camels plod tirelessly east along the wide storm valleys. Often we searched their loads and, finding nothing, gave the bedu water. One of our jobs was to find a new route between Thamarit and Habarut that would avoid the roundabout track which the Army usually used. Instead this new route would go from waterhole to waterhole, covering many of the springs at which caravans must call.

To help us we had as our guide a true bedu of the *nejd*—Nashran bin Sultan, adopted son of the paramount sheikh of the Bait Shaasha tribe. A thick-set Arab with the hawk-nose of the pure bred bedu, his powers of vision were exceptional.

We pushed through the shimmering heat holes of the *wadis* until we came to the spring at Maashadid. Nashran told me that the same water also fed the well of Ayun. Could I not taste that it was the same?

I shrugged. I could never see how a bedu would know even if the Ayun water did travel underground many miles to this spring. But Fred, our other bedu guide, had often boasted his ability to tell the spring from which any *nejd* water came simply through a sniff and a taste. A true taster of desert wines.

Wilfred Thesiger had called at Maashadid in 1946. Bedu told him that the spring was forty-five feet deep and I was curious to see how the water was reached. None of the men wished to go down with me though I had a torch. It was hot inside and dirty. To help their weary work of filling endless bags the bedu had fixed bits of metal and lengths of hemp at intervals along the corkscrew descent.

As I clambered lower the heat grew slightly less but the air was stale and daylight no longer visible above.

I soon lost count of the twisting turns and came to a narrowing funnel. The torchbeam picked up a dark hole at its base but no light was reflected on water. Nor was there any sound.

I scrambled down the funnel and thrust my arm into its apex. The cold cling of running water came almost as a shock but it was there. I scooped some up and drank: it was but slightly brackish. What a place to work in, filling enough bags for perhaps a dozen or more thirsty camels. Already I streamed with sweat and the air was bad. The impulse to get out grew suddenly strong and I struggled upright in the funnel. The torch struck a rock and it was dark. I bashed the thing with my fist and shook it cursing but the bulb had gone.

Straddling the tube of the shaft with my legs I felt above my head and panic gripped me. For there was space on either side of the rock over my head—there must be two or more shafts leading upwards. I fought back the desire to shout for the men. They would never hear and the vibrations might cause a slide.

I decided to take pot luck for I could feel no rope nor guiding line. My feet were bare and toes found crannies in the shaft walls.

A great flurry set up about me then, so unexpected that I screamed and beat the air about my head.

Hundreds of tiny squealing creatures flew about like flies risen from garbage. Little leathery bodies brushed against me and, as I clawed the air, so the commotion increased. Shaking my head wildly, I climbed upwards only to find the shaft was in reality a mere hollow in the roof above the water funnel: the home of a colony of midget bats. Slithering downwards, I lost all sense of direction, knowing only vaguely where was up and where down.

A foul stench from the streams of bat guana, which my antics had disturbed, added to my desperation.

Then the compact feel of metal touched my hand and I knew

I was in the main shaft. At once I felt calmer: the nightmare receded for that little piece of piping was reality.

Carefully I felt my way up from hold to hold. The blackness softened and grew quickly to an intense brightness as the opening appeared.

I breathed in the desert air till my lungs burned but it was fresh and good.

Mohamed's nut-brown eyes twinkled above the bushy crescent of his beard.

"You sweat like a guilty *moolah* and you smell of the dead, Sahb. Did you see *djinns* down there?"

"Yes, I saw many little *djinns* and I shall die of thirst rather than descend another Arab well."

Mohamed grinned like a bearded Cheshire cat and went off to make tea.

West of Maashadid we had trouble finding a way through a region of broken hills and wide sand *wadis*, but after two days we broke through to a flat gravel plain stretching as far as the eye could see.

A fine white dust plumed behind the vehicles and Murad accelerated. For hours we sped over black plains, wheels puncturing the thin veneer of gypsum. The dry air cracked my lips despite the protection of my *shemagh*. All of us were powder grey as dusk came so that Zanzibari, Baluch, Arab and Englishman took on the same ghostly hue when the desert sunset, black and orange, closed about the *nejd*.

We stopped in a bowl of sand where hunks of dead wood lay half-smothered, like corpses after a flood. Soon a fire crackled under our battered cauldron and the men washed with sand for we were short of water. When their hands and feet and faces were 'clean', they cleared little spaces for their prayer mats and turned to face Mecca.

Wolves howled over to the east and it grew cold. The baleful eye of Sirius pulsed low in the night sky; Dogstar of sacrifice to the ancient Arabs.

A shooting star burnt its brilliant way through the heavens. I saw the Arab on guard silhouetted on a hillock close by, his deep cut features also lifted to the stars. The nine of us lay in the still warm sand, huddled together about the fire for we knew the night would be cold with a heavy dew.

Mubarreq the Zanzibari touched my shoulder. "Do you know why those flaming tails cross the night, Bakheit?"

"No, Mubarreq."

"It is when the angels catch the devils spying at the gates of heaven, trying to find out information about the future. The angels on heaven's ramparts throw burning lamps at them to scare them away. The Prophet saw them do it when he went there by camel."

We spent many days in this region following the trails of bedu and camping with them, gleaning scraps of information here and there, eliminating waterholes one by one as possible *adoo* halts.

The guide Nashran's knowledge of the area was uncanny. One evening, not long before dusk, we drove fast through a featureless waste. Nashran pointed suddenly to the north and Murad swung the wheel. For a quarter of an hour we sped over undulating gypsum flats until a single dark mound appeared amidst a sea of yellow folds—like the mole on the chin of Chairman Mao.

Reaching the mound we found a family of Bait Shaasha camped in its lee.

They were poor folk with one mangy camel and a ragged flock of goats.

The man of the family was overjoyed to see his kinsman Nashran. They seized each other by the shoulders and kissed, nose to nose; on the right side, then the left, then again the right. Greetings spattered to and fro and when these died out, they continued to grasp one another with occasional murmurings of pleasure. There was a time when I would have felt embarrassed. But I too warmed with the sincerity of their happiness. We were all introduced and the goats chased away from the fire to make room for us.

The headman screamed at the beak-veiled crone who was his wife. She skittered off to find a tin. He seized it from her and milked the camel into it.

The milk was warm and frothy, too salty to be pleasant. We were greatly honoured for the bedu produced a filthy grey bag made from the nineteen-inch skin of a *dhub* lizard. Unwrapping it, he revealed some withered strips of pinkish meat like chopped-off thumbs: salted shark guts.

The smell from the bag was disgusting. It was passed around

the circle. Fighting back revulsion I took the smallest piece and tried to swallow it whole whilst holding my breath. But it was too tough and needed chewing first. The taste was not as bad as the stench suggested: fishy and a bit rotten. Mohamed of the Beard chuckled as he watched my expression.

These bedu owned nothing but their camel, the goats and a few leather bags. The crone seemed to be at least fifty years of age and I watched fascinated as she searched among the goats. There were four young children sleeping squashed between the black and white billies.

The bedu's close dependence on the elements – for they die easily at the whim of Allah, at the drying up of a well or the death of a camel – makes them deeply religious. They have no education but the Koran and the harsh tutorage of the desert. Nashran spoke to me of Moses whom he called *Kalamu 'illah* – 'the man who spoke to God'.

"He too was an Arab and like all bedu he was of Allah's chosen people."

I understood little of the old bedu's chatter for he had teeth missing and spoke mostly in a low monotone. Occasionally he would grow angry, fling his arms about and prod the chest of a speaker who annoyed him. A gaunt wild haired figure in the flickering light, his ginglymus gestures duplicated puppet-like and enormous on the sloping sand behind him.

When we left he would be the poorer for the milk and the meat he had spared us would have lasted his family many days. He was not to know we would give him sacks of flour. He might never see us again but the rules of the desert are generosity and open dealing. The bedu are open even in their dishonesty, and their cruelty. Despising petty theft, they frequently raid one another's camels in the Sands and murder men of other tribes – though much less now that blood feuds have been out-lawed and, in the Sands, Saudi police patrols comb deep into the northern desert.

No bedu eats or drinks, though dry with thirst, until his companions have all reached the well that is their goal. When they eat they share their food and their last cup of water with any strangers who care to join them. Perhaps this explains the bedu saying: 'Visit seldom and you will be popular.'

We went south of the massive valley called Aydim and over

plains sprinkled with marine fossils. Then west to Habarut. These were the barren steppes of the various tribes which formed the Bait Kathir, which means 'the many'.[1] They invaded Dhofar from their home in the Hadhramaut in the sixteenth century and have lived there ever since. Many of the Bait Kathir have two deep vertical cuts an inch long below each eye. Nashran explained that anxious mothers perform this operation to ensure that their children develop strong vision.

He pointed west and north from Habarut.

"Many years ago my father rode from Salalah to the Hadhramaut with Mubarreq bin Miriam whom you call Thesiger. In those days we of the Bait Shaasha joined with the Mahra to fight the raiding parties from the Hadhramaut. Once we fought two hundred camel raiders of the Karab, the Dahm, and the Saar. When I was very young my father rode with the first Englishman to travel the Sands. Him they called Thomas. As you can see I am an old man now: I have seen many things in my time."

I remonstrated that Nashran was still a chicken and a very able one at that. This pleased him and that evening he gave me his silk shirt as a present.

Many of his relatives lived in the huts nestling under the cliff and behind the date-palms of Habarut. He stayed with them for two days and on the second night, remembering the assassination of our friend Naseeb, we lay in wait in the bushes about Nashran's house. The palm fronds whispered subtly and over the *wadi*, where the Yemenis manned their whitewashed fort, the ululating dirge of a death chant ascended to the stars which did not reply.

No one came to kill Nashran and a Yemeni died in the fort squirming from the venom of a snakebite. When he died the chanting stopped. He was buried in the cliffside and forgotten.

At Habarut we paid a leper for information, gave food to his family, and Aspirins to a little girl whose once appealing face was ravaged by smallpox scars.

[1] The Bait Kathir sections include the Masahala with the subtribes being the Bait Mohsin, al Tair, Samhan, Raba'at, and Amreet. Also the ShaiShai, the Bait Gidad, the Bait al Ahmar, the Bait Ghuwas, and the Bait Musan. Other Kathir tribes are the Al Kathir who include the Bait Ali bin Badr, the Bait Hamed bin Ahmed, the Shanafir of al Hafa, and the Maraheen and Baith Ruwas of Salalah. All these are of the Hinawi faction.

The atmosphere was heavy with hostility for the inhabitants disliked the Army. Habarut, they felt, belonged to the Yemeni Republic not to the Sultan. Not because of a love for the NLF government in far away Aden but because their historical home lay west in the land of Seiyan.

Later we drove north and slept by the waterhole of Tudho.

A sweet sound awoke me as the dawn turned to burnished gold and the high cliffs above the spring glowed with soft warm colour. It was a sound of liberation, of sheer joy to be alive and free. The notes high and low at once, warbling with melody unlike any tune I had ever heard. I lay back in the sand and listened mesmerised, willing the musician to continue.

I woke Fat Hamid who slept with an arm over his big ·30 Browning and we wandered down to the waterhole.

A family of bedu had arrived in the night with many camels. Pan was a young boy with a cockscomb of hair down the centre of his scalp: the rest was shaven. His little face was of the mischievous Huckleberry Finn sort with a nose that puckered when he grinned. A horn hung about his neck on a thong. This was his flute; the delicately curved horn of an Arabian oryx.[1]

They were Mahra from the steppes beyond Qara to the north. Once, they told us, there had been great pools here at Tudho; enough for a hundred camels to drink from. But now there was only a spring which grew ever lower and more inaccessible as the months and the years passed without rain. It was backbreaking work to raise the water in skin bags for its level was eight feet down in a narrow sand-rimmed hole.

I made a mental note to bring a bucket and rope next time we came to these parts.

The men awoke and came to help the bedu. The sun had climbed above the *wadi* cliffs and sweat poured from the workers at the well. They chanted to the rhythm of the ropes as they lowered and heaved.

"Hey bi, yey-hey bi!" Half the workers crooned a treble chant whilst others intoned the rhythmic chorus deep from their chests.

---

[1] The horns of an oryx suffer frequent mutations. Often only a single horn grows and this brought about the legend of the Unicorn following the travels of Marco Polo and others.

An Intelligence Land Rover in Salalah

Habrut

Captured Russian weapons

A newly built Dhofari school

Green bilge scummed the lips of the waiting camels. They roared their frustration and anger as little Pan kept them from the water with a stick and a great show of strength.

He let three at a time through to drink which they did with deep draughts, grunting and slurping their pleasure.

All Ibadhi Muslims suppress singing as a frivolity but the Arabs have a love of music and a natural rhythm that bubbles over when they feel content.

Mubarreq the Zanzibari sat beside me in the cool shadow of a giant plantain.

"It is good to be away from the mountain eh, Bakheit?" he smiled. "Here we can enjoy the good things of God. You know, it is easy to see that He must be great. You have only to look at the perfection that is a camel."

He shook a fat black finger at me and rolled his eyes skyward as always when waxing biblical.

"The Prophet rightly said that the day of the world's end will be that day when a pregnant camel is neglected by her owner for God's greatest gift to man is surely the camel."

His eyeballs came back to earth and he smiled. "Come, Bakheit. Let us ride."

The Mahra allowed us to borrow two of their camels. The ugly beasts were docile having just watered and we rode them along the *wadi* steering with a touch of a thin bamboo to either side of the neck – for there is only one rein to the Omani bridle.

These Mahra were awaiting a relative who owned a bull camel. They had heard of his impending arrival, and, having only female camels themselves, wanted the free services of this male. They planned to meet their relative as though by chance and ask for the use of his travelling sperm-bank, a nomadic Errol Flynn of the *nejd*, in return for milk or food.

The camel is designed with care: never sweating until her body heat reaches 104° Fahrenheit. Thus, although she doesn't actually store water as many believe, she does conserve it for a long while and, crossing vast hot deserts, her owner will depend on her as his mobile milk bar long after his water has run out.

From the plains we returned to Ayun through a sandstorm. The vehicles were buffeted violently and fine particles of driven sand stung our skin despite the blankets we wrapped around us. We lost sight of the other Land Rovers and stopped to huddle together on the ground. The noise was all about us in the blurred pink gloom: an unbelievable roar as of a coming tidal wave. But the storm went as suddenly as it came and the sun shone again as though nothing had happened.

At Ayun our carefully hidden food cache had been dug up by hyenas. Mangled tins of tomato puree and torn sacking lay over a wide area. The deep pit where the offal and goat bones had been buried over the weeks was crawling with flies and wasps; a sheen of writhing wings. They buzzed furiously over the blood-soaked soil but every scrap of rotten meat was gone.

Sergeant Mohamed met us at the pools. His news was bad: he had driven hundreds of miles searching for a route north to the steppes but sheer cliffs had always blocked his way sooner or later.

Then, east of the pools of Ayun, Murad found a camel trail climbing to the high plateau.

Holding our breath we roared up the side of the mountain, gravel flying as the tyres skidded and screamed. There were three long rocky ramps and the last was the worst. I had long moments of doubt as the vehicle seemed almost to stand on its end, but we made it.

The four other Land Rovers, crammed with cheering men, bounced up one by one.

For a week, we ranged north into a wild new land. Gazelle and ibex were in abundance. We saw two wolves, great shaggy beasts much larger than their Alaskan relatives, and gave chase. But they descended a steep ravine and we lost them. Said Salim found the prints of a big cat—twice the size of the wildcat spoor of the Qara, possibly a leopard, since the mountain lion is now thought to be extinct in Dhofar. Both beasts had been seen from time to time in the remoter reaches of the *nejd*. Every day took us deeper into a country of huge mesa—a jumbled up jigsaw puzzle with narrow corridors of rock joining up many but not all of the fragments.

There were many false trails that led us to crumbling dead-end pinnacles with breath-taking views of the *nejd* and the shimmering unattainable sandsea beyond.

Once the narrow bridge of rock between two ridgeback

features crumbled beneath Ali's Land Rover. His men had got out beforehand but Ali and the driver sweated silently as the vehicle slithered sideways, teetering over a sheer abyss.

We could do nothing but watch. Boulders and earth fell away hundreds of feet to the dark *wadi* below and the Land Rover swayed with half its bulk in the air. Murad grabbed his metal tow rope.

"Fix it quickly," he yelled and reversed slowly to the edge of the chasm.

The tow rope would not span the gap. Two more drivers brought their ropes from behind and linked up the three. Carefully they attached the far end to the gently swaying vehicle: little Ali's beard dripped sweat, his fists clenching the dashboard.

Murad took the strain. Ten of us climbed on to his vehicle to give the tyres grip at the edge of the cliff.

Slowly we advanced and slowly Ali's Land Rover swung inwards away from the void. Its near front wheel came back to terra firma and at that instant Ali leapt as though scalded on to the ground.

"*Wallahi, Wallahi,*" he muttered wiping the sweat from his forehead, "*Al hamdu Lillah.*"

That evening about the fire Ali was quite silent and did not even respond to the jibes of Sergeant Mohamed who made the most of his fellow midget's discomfort. But the death of Hamid Sultan was fresh in all our minds.

Some days later a rope lashing some petrol drums, 450 lbs each, frayed as our supply lorry ascended the new-found ramp. The drums rolled about for a second before the driver could stop and all our meat rations, eight goats, were crushed to death.

The soldiers refused to eat the goats for they had not died by *hellal*, the Koranic cutting of the throat.

Word came from Corporal Salim that his men had arrested a Mahra at the pool of Ayun. The fellow had an unusually large amount of money with him concealed in his *dishdash* and, suspecting that he was the scout for a larger group we laid a careful ambush close to the pools.

There was a full moon. The mosquitoes drank our blood as we lay in the reeds close to the camel track. Towards midnight I heard three soft clicks on my National. It was Corporal Salim.

He spoke with a soft whisper but there was horror in his tone.

"Come quickly, Sahb. It is Salim Mayoof. He will kill us all."

Leaving four men in the reeds, I crept away with Said Salim and Fat Hamid, whose inseparable Browning balanced on his shoulder, its belt of 250 golden bullets snaking into the pouch of his shirt front.

Quickly we climbed the track to the clifftop where Corporal Salim's men were positioned.

A high keening scream cut the moonlit silence. Fat Hamid stopped abruptly behind me. I turned to find him lying on the ground behind his gun: he was tense, his eyes wide with fear.

"Come on, Salim," I whispered, and heaved him up with Said's help.

But he clamped his hand on my shoulder. His teeth, I now noticed, were chattering. "No, Sahb, there is something *zift* up there, something evil."

There was no sound at all from the cliff and I pulled him along by his gun. Grudgingly he came, keeping well behind Said.

We followed the very rim of the cliffs to be sure not to go too far.

I stopped as the ground ahead levelled out for light clouds were passing quickly by the moon and shadows played tricks among the rocks.

Said and Fat Hamid came abreast of me. I sensed Said's body stiffen then he raised his SLR, cocked it and moved ahead with slow deliberation; a mongoose stalking a python. His jaw was set with determination. But there was fear too about him . . . I had not seen Said frightened before. I followed him and as I advanced, noticed a low hissing as of cats from the rocks. The moon came clear at that moment outlining a scene from a voodoo ritual.

Five of the soldiers huddled together, wedged between two boulders. All were holding rifles aimed at a large black figure squatting above them on a boulder. The whites of its eyeballs and its teeth glinted as the head shook with a low sibilant hiss.

Moonlight traced the outline of the man on the rock making him appear more than life size.

Behind me Fat Hamid dropped to the ground, loaded the

Browning on its squat tripod and took aim at the ape-like figure.

For a moment I lost the power to act. Then I kicked sand at his face, blinding him and tore the honeycomb barrel from him.

"Don't be a fool; it's only Salim Mayoof. He must be drugged."

But as I spoke, Mayoof, a big Zanzibari, rose up on his boulder and, clawing the air as though he would tear the moon to pieces, he began to scream.

It was a horrid sound, more animal than human, that rose on a single frantic note till the echoes came back from the pools below and I felt myself shiver.

"Get his gun, Said. Make sure he is unarmed." I knew Said would not let me down. But he did; he cowered behind his rifle and made no move.

My mind raced. I felt the atmosphere of the place take an uncanny hold on me. Soon it would be too late to fight the mounting fear. I went up to Mayoof's rock. His rifle was nowhere in sight.

"Shut up, you fool, you'll have all the *adoo* in Dhofar here in no time."

He stopped screaming abruptly and looked down at me. I saw there was foam and slobber about his mouth. He began to giggle then uncontrollably, holding his ribs as though they hurt, and slowly lowering himself till his head was near to mine. The great protruding eyeballs were hypnotic and I shrank back involuntarily.

Someone tugged at my shirt from behind. It was Said. He whispered with urgency.

"Come away, Sahb. You do not understand. He is Malik the leader of the *Taghut* and the Keeper of hell. He is inside the soul of Mayoof. Come away. You can do nothing."

But the giggling ceased then and Mayoof crumpled sobbing.

A wild yell from behind came as a physical shock for my senses were already bewildered. The terror of the Arabs had crept under my skin.

Fat Hamid lay spreadeagled among the rocks, his limbs vibrating as though in the final convulsions of Tabun nerve poisoning. His jaw clamped, his eyeballs rolled, and every fibre quickened.

Said's grip tightened on my arm, "Look, the *djinn* has flown to Hamid. An Arab soul is better than a Sambo's."

I did not know what to think. Part of me protested that this was all play acting. There were no evil spirits. At worst this was a hallucination brought about by the eerie nature of the place, the white cliffs and the great pools below. The superstitious upbringing of the Arabs was deeply ingrained in them. Islam has never uprooted the Semitic beliefs of animism, fetishism, and blood sacrifice. Their monotheistic beliefs are largely a skin-deep veneer, a showy coat of paint through which the scabrous rust of ancient idolatry bubbles easily.

But I knew Fat Hamid well; a quiet cheerful man, no play actor. And his transformation into a raving lunatic had been instantaneous at the very second Mayoof calmed down.

An unquestionable coldness played about those rocks, an atmosphere so pregnant with unpleasantness that the flesh puckered along my back and I felt my scalp tighten with fear.

I have no claims to extrasensory perception, no belief in ghosts, and am not unduly sensitive to the 'feel' of a place. But nothing would have induced me to approach Fat Hamid.

I lay watching with the others as spellbound as they, as aware of the evil 'electricity' manifest before us. Looking back I feel ashamed because I like to think my own beliefs are more than skin deep.

At length, I cannot say after how long, Hamid was quiet and lay still. Only the muffled sobs of Mayoof disturbed the absolute silence of the white cliffs above the pools and we lay where we were until dawn.

Hamid remembered nothing at all. He was as cheery as ever. Mayoof on the other hand was inconsolable and given to frequent bouts of misery. He wailed over and over again that his soul had been stolen from him. By whom he did not know. His behaviour was bad for the morale of the others and, when a Beaver plane with goats came to our home-made airstrip above Ayun, we sent the sad Zanzibari away to Salalah.

A week later an agitated signal reached us from Patrick Brook, then the Adjutant at Umm al Ghawarif. It read: 'Salim Mayoof says your driver has stolen his soul. It is to be returned at once.'

I asked Murad if he had taken anything at all from the Zanzibari before he left. He had not. I replied accordingly and weeks later heard that Mayoof had been sent to the north for medical attention since his strange conviction was tearing his mind apart.

Days later at Ayun, Said Salim came to me. He said he was sorry he had disobeyed me that night.

"In the past when I have felt evil, I said aloud the name of Allah; then I was strong to withstand the fear. But there is a very great amount of evil in the place of the rocks." Said looked at me shyly. "You must know, Sahb, that the *shaitan* devil is powerful whereas we mortals are weak for God created us only from congealed blood and from the water poured out between the loins of man and the breast bone of woman."

I confessed that I had not known this.

He took me from the airstrip above Ayun to the place of the rocks and showed me a strange phenomenon which I had seen nowhere else in Oman. The ground opened up in a narrow fissure from which a foul but unidentifiable smell issued. I shone my torch down into the crack and saw that it was very deep but the walls of the main shaft corkscrewed so that no bottom was visible.

"What is it, Said?" I asked. "An old well of the bedu."

"No, there is no water here and never has been. We are hundreds of feet above the pools and if the ancients had come here to drink, their trails would still be seen."

Months later at a remote valley in Eastern Dhofar, I experienced a similar though very fleeting sensation that all was not well. We had driven for two days through poorly charted wastes south of the Sands and came to an oasis of great beauty and many date-palms. This was Andhur, site of the ancient frankincense collecting-centre once visited by Wilfred Thesiger.

I climbed a hillock above the palms to the remains of a temple and fortress. The place overlooked the water and the frankincense trails running north to the Sands which came from the coastal city of Mirbat.

Under my feet were two stone slabs about three feet long and basined in the middle, relics of primitive Dhofari worship that appeased the moon and stars by human sacrifice. Young girls were buried alive in the sand, captives were forcibly circumcised, disputes were settled before the Gods with trial by ordeal, and incestuous wedlock was encouraged.

The guardians of Anhur were long dead but it was not a happy place.

Meanwhile, as we patrolled the desert sands, the festering sores on my hands and feet grew worse and the swarms of flies which were our constant companions, smelling the poison, found me more attractive than the others. Life became more and more unpleasant despite the well-meaning attempts of our medical corporal. I began to feel feverish and, leaving Sergeant Mohamed in charge, flew back to Salalah the next time our 'goat' Beaver came.

The Indian doctor advised two weeks' rest and a course of penicillin.

For a week I pottered about Salalah with my camera, lost money to Patrick Brook and David Bayley at poker, and cooled down in the bay at Rayzut.

I remember one evening in the Officers' Mess conversation turned to the Sultan, and his failure to introduce a policy of hearts-and-minds to win over the confidence of Dhofaris.

"The old boy's past it anyway," a visiting pilot remarked. "He ought to step down and let his son take over. He'd be far happier at his age taking a suite at a London hotel and staying there for good."

There was laughter all round. Only Tom Greening, reading a paper in one corner, refrained from nodding his agreement. His face remained impassive; he might never have heard the remark.

At that time all empty beer and Coca-Cola cans in the Mess were carefully preserved and fashioned into deadly weapons. Each became a lethal mine fully capable of blowing a man's leg off and worse. They were Mike Muldoon's ingenious answer to the growing number of Mark 6 British anti-personnel mines being sown by the guerrillas in places where the Army were likely to patrol. The mines had been abandoned in Aden by the British withdrawal but, like poisoning waterholes, a.p. mine-laying had been avoided till now by both sides by unspoken agreement. Now that *they* had started this particularly dirty form of war, we were replying in kind.

Mike formed a production line in his office using tiny torch batteries, electric wire, detonators and plastic explosive. All available empty Coca-Cola and beer tins were requisitioned by Mike's men.

His first products were sent to Richard John's Company and laid along suspected infiltration routes. An innocent camel wandered on to one and was killed. Seeing the carcass, a vulture flapped down, and landed beside it. The big bird also blew up and died featherless.

Deducing the cause of these unhappy incidents, the *adoo* located and lifted fifteen of the mines and replaced them elsewhere. Despite this setback all the Leopard Line officers, including me, laid the mines along their local infiltration trails. I surrounded mine with barbed wire so that although the barriers were obvious to innocent bedu, the narrow trails were effectively sealed.

Over the next five months the 'Muldoons', as the tins became known, claimed only two victims. One was an armed *adoo* and the other a soldier who went to urinate where he had expressly been told not to go. His officer, a friend of mine named Eddie Viturakis, entered the minefield and dragged the poor man clear fortunately without detonating further mines. (Some weeks later Eddie was himself shot at point-blank range by one of his own soldiers, a drug addict, who entered Eddie's tent at night with his rifle and, after the murder, fled to the *adoo*.)

After two weeks resting about the camp my sores were a great deal better and I flew back to join Recce, landing on a gravel plateau above the pools of Ayun. The men looked weathered and hard as teak after the people of Salalah. I had the feeling I was back home. Sergeant Mohamed had shot a gazelle, in honour of my return or so he said, and the men crowded around inspecting my bandages; pulling at the plasters to see if the sores had healed.

"How was my brother Ahmad?"

"Is Hillal still alive?"

"Has Mayoof found his soul?"

"Did you bring my bananas?"

At first they would not admit to there being any news. Then over the embers of a veritable feast of gazelle, rice and dates, Ali Nasser broke the news, for it was his to tell.

Sergeant Mohamed tugged at his beard tuft with frustration

as little Ali took the limelight. Not much taller than the squatting negro Mubarreq, Ali stood by the fire addressing us all—his voice oratorical enough for even the outer sentries to hear—though everyone but I knew well enough what he had to say.

"After five days of hard travel and the building of many ramps to cross deep *wadis* we came to a country where *no* bedu has been before and *no* man has seen."

Ali took a deep breath and picked his enormous nose with care. A sidelong glance at the glowering Sergeant Mohamed assured him that the latter was not missing his moment of drama.

"Allah was good to us to show us the way and *I* was always correct in choosing the right route. So then, on the evening of the fifth day, we came to the top of the world and cornered two big ibex which Saif Musabe of the Ragged Hair killed."

Ali stroked his beard lovingly with one hand—leaving the other free for an alarming sequence of gestures that added panache to his tale.

"After eating I moved apart to pray behind the rocks and, below me, many hundreds of feet down, I saw a great white *wadi* running north. At once I ran down without delay—after my prayers were ended—and found a ledge of rock which led down to the *wadi*. This ledge, Sahb", he glanced down at me, "is, *Imshaalah*, big enough for the vehicles of Recce."

Ali sat down quite dazed by the brilliance of his performance and on the following morning all but the guards of the Dehedoba trail followed the white dustcloud of Ali's Land Rover to the north.

The way was circuitous, following no lie of the land and skirting dizzy ramparts where the slightest skid would spell disaster. At length we climbed a narrow ridge to the highest rampart and looked down to see the wide white floor of a curling *wadi*.

Ali's ramp which he proudly showed me was a precarious ledge down which only a madman would drive in a mini car. And he would never get back up. Quite where the *wadi* led was impossible to tell but here at last was a possible route to the gravel desert and so to the camp at Thamarit.

For several days we worked in chains rolling boulders down to widen the natural ledge and in a week Murad proudly skidded his Land Rover down to the *wadi* below. Since it might well be a cul-de-sac valley, no more vehicles were allowed to descend until, after three more days, we had perfected the ramp. Then, to much wild cheering, Murad urged his vehicle slowly back up the precarious ledge to the summit.

Next day we all descended and, after five hours' journey, came to a fork in the unknown *wadi*. This we followed until the hills fell away behind us and, in open steppe land, we sped north-east until we recognised the Wadi Yistah which led to Thamarit.

We signalled Salalah of the new safe route from the mountains, and not long afterwards, David Bayley's Company from Idlewild withdrew their artillery by way of our ramp to avoid the dangerous Valley of Haloof.

From then on our movements went undetected by the guerrillas; a factor that proved vital in the events to come.

By 10th October the nights had grown colder than was bearable without three blankets. Perhaps the men were not as alert as they might otherwise have been that night for they heard nothing but the wolves of the *nejd*.

15

AHMAD DEBLAAN's friend Kamees told me a great deal about
Musallim Ali's wife Noor, how beautiful she was and how
much he adored her. It was not surprising therefore that
Musallim Ali felt that Allah had deserted him when after all those
years of faithful marriage, Noor finally left him and became pregnant by another man. Now everyone knew and laughed at
him whilst the beautiful Noor desported herself with another.

Sorrow gnawed deep into Musallim Ali's soul. He could
have slit Noor's throat and the tribe would have approved, but
he loved her too much. Instead he had lain every night with a
young orphan girl of a Bait Howeirat village near Qum.

This placed him in an invidious position, for the Bait Howeirat's
leader, the elderly Sheikh Musallim, was a leading voice against
the Marxist leaders of the Front, as were most of his family.
Yet Musallim Ali was meant to be helping Salim Amr to root
out such dissidents so that the *Idaara* squad could eventually
liquidate them. Musallim Ali therefore found his political work
more and more uncongenial to him. He hated Salim Amr for
his sadistic bullying nature and feared him because of his power
from which he knew that he, Musallim Ali, was not immune.
He also feared that Salim Amr would move against the Bait
Howeirat at any moment. His fears increased when he heard
that the long awaited *Idaara* squad had finally arrived and that
Salim Amr's first move was to deal with the Bait Howeirat with
the hopes of capturing and crushing the rebellious sheikh and
his family. The cunning Salim Amr bade Musallim Ali accompany
him on this mission.

They walked all night over rolling downs, and came to the village soon after dawn. It was not necessary to move with caution for no Army patrols had ever bothered the guerrillas of Bait Fiah. The region was ringed with strong guerrilla patrols in radio contact with one another so individual *adoo* could move about freely without fear of ambush.

Moving down an open shoulder into the village they were challenged. Salim replied correctly and soon they were among the round mud huts being greeted by the *Idaara*.

The squad were twelve in number, small wiry men in dark brown uniform. Each had an SKS with folding bayonet. There was that dedicated look of efficiency about them; the stamp of the HVA terror schools whether at home in Pankow, East Germany, or merely one of the international branches such as that in Aden.

On their arrival the preceding evening the squad had confined all the Bait Howeirat to their huts which they then searched one by one. Two men, they said, had made trouble. These they had beaten and tied up to a tree.

Salim Amr inspected the prisoners. One was Sahayl the second son of the village sheikh. The other was a thick-set bedu from a nearby Mahra tribe.

The orphan girl who was Musallim Ali's mistress told him that the two prisoners had been trying to prevent the women from being raped. The *Idaara* had come at dusk and three of them had taken their turn with her through the night. Also one of Sahayl's little girls was badly injured and losing blood.

The mention of Sahayl renewed Mussalim Ali's fears but he could do little. Salim Amr had no more use for him now that the *Idaara* had arrived. At a distance he followed the path the execution squad had taken down into the ravine with their two prisoners.

Soon he heard shouts from ahead. They were in a clearing deep in the scrub. He edged among bushes until he could see. Salim Amr and the squad were clustered about the Mahra bedu shouting abuse whilst they stabbed his arms and legs with their bayonets. Of Sahayl or his body there was no sign at all. He could hardly have escaped since then Musallim would surely have heard shots.

Fascinated despite himself, Musallim watched as the prisoner, hands and legs bound, writhed about in his own blood. One of the *Idaara* had lit a cigarette. Salim and the others were watching, silent now, as the man puffed away. Then he bent over the body. Two of the others held the struggling limbs and Musallim flinched behind his bush at the first scream.

Musallim could not see what they did to the Mahra for they were all grouped tight about their handiwork now. Then they straightened up and, laughing together, moved off into the bush.

When he was sure they had gone, Musallim emerged and went up to the limp body. The throat was slit but Musallim noticed the round black burn marks all over the face, on the lips and the mess where the eyeballs had been. They had burnt the Mahra's eyes out before killing him.

Musallim turned from the corpse and ran back to the village to the orphan girl.

Next day Musallim had to leave for Qum; there was much overdue work to be done. The girl begged him before he left to get word to her sheikh and his sons, the two brothers of Sahayl, not to return to the village.

On 17th October the leader at Qum gave Musallim several letters of importance to take to the militia at Bait Fiah and to the *Idaara*. Some were instructions from Hauf and he left without delay, reaching the Bait Howeirat village by dusk. Salim Amr, it appeared from the villagers, had been there most days with his cronies for camel's milk and fornication. But he had not appeared that day and he was working with a strong *adoo* group not far to the south.

Musallim found the *Idaara* less than half a mile away chatting to some sixty guerrillas. The men were spread about amongst the bushes preparing low *sangars* of stones. Even to Musallim's amateur eyes, an ambush of considerable importance was being prepared.

Obviously an impending Army patrol was anticipated. But why here where no soldiers had ever been before? And if indeed they were coming, who or what had warned the *Idaara*?

When the new orders came through we were at Habarut many long miles from the hills of Qum.

"Why don't you shave under your arms, Bakhait?"

222

Murad eyed me quizzically from under his floppy hat. He was teaching me the game of *hawaalees*, played with fourteen balls of dried dung and double that number of holes scooped in the sand.

"I've often wondered why you do. Does the Koran say it is necessary in order to achieve a heavenly state?"

Murad chuckled. "You are a blasphemer." He held up a single dung-ball and squinted at it. "But perhaps so am I. We Ibadhi Muslims should not play these games for the Prophet said such statues as these are the abomination of Satan's work."

Said Salim whistled from the shade of a withered heliotrope.

"They are coming, Sahb." He pointed through the dancing heat shimmer to the Yemeni fort across the *wadi* at Habarut. Four or five hundred camels roared and shuffled by the pools and three men picked their way towards us. Like us they were unarmed.

The ramparts of the Yemeni fort floated mirage-like five hundred metres from the three of us, doubtless the same distance as the range set upon the sights of the fort's six machine guns.

Behind us the *askars* of the Sultan's fort grew alert as they too saw the movement among the camels. It was midday so the blinding glare favoured the riflemen of neither fort.

We stood up in the very centre of the *wadi* and waited listening to the crunch of white pebbles as the men approached us. Two were tall soldiers of the Hadhraumi Bedouin Legion— now the Aden Federal Army.

They walked on either side of a little man with yellow skin and a khaki baseball cap.

We shook hands and sat in a ring on the hot pebbles.

After the greetings, there was silence. Then Murad produced 200 Rothmans cigarettes from his *shemagh* roll. I prodded him and he found 200 more. These I offered to the little yellow man who took them without the customary feigned refusals with which Arabs precede the acceptance of a gift.

He spoke classical Arabic slowly.

"Men of your Sultan's village have caused trouble. One of our villagers was wounded and his friends wish to avenge themselves. They say we must protect them against the Sultan. Soon I will not be able to hold my men back. You understand?"

His name was Said Allowi bin Ali, Commander of the

easternmost garrison of the People's Republic of Southern Yemen.

"*Na'am Ya Ra'ees*," I said politely. "But His Majesty the Sultan wants only peace. I have come to see you to apologise for the shooting and to make sure that you realise it was the work of local troublemakers unknown to the Sultan." I paused and the wizened little head nodded almost imperceptibly.

I continued: "Any attack by your men on the Sultan's fort or the people on his side of this *wadi* must be considered an act of war and will be met with strong retaliation. But we hope you agree that such a course need never arise."

"Your apology is accepted. You must deal with your trouble-makers; we with ours." His features softened slightly. "We have no luxuries such as Western cigarettes now in the Republic. Times are hard. I have nothing to give you in exchange save the wish for peace".

He arose and the six of us withdrew from the unmarked border.

Soon afterwards the Yemeni garrison filled with guerrillas who bombarded the Sultan's fort and razed it to the ground.[1] Such was the 'wish for peace'.

Back at the Sultan's fortress my signaller was waiting with an Operations Immediate message from Tom Greening. We were to move at once to Thamarit. He would fly there to meet us the following day. There were no further details.

Murad drove hard along the plains of shining black rubble. A high cloud spumed behind us for powdery gypsum lay beneath the black veneer. We raced east to Ayun without delay. There we joined Sergeant Mohamed and the others leaving only a threadbare guard along the Dehedoba trail.

The five Land Rovers bounced *up* the Mugshit Ramp on to the plateau — under the eyes of the *adoo* watchers at Qismeem Pass, men whom, we hoped, were unaware of our escape route to the north. To them we were safetly bottled up on the plateau and accounted for until seen again to descend the Mugshit Ramp.

In three hours we reached Thamarit and the men slept, know-ing that such sudden summonses might mean action and little

[1] In retaliation the Sultan's Airforce bombed the guerrilla camp at Hauf in the Yemen. A war was avoided only through diplomatic moves in the Arab League.

rest. Already a tight and familiar feeling churned my stomach as I thought of the Qara Jebel.

Tom Greening flew into Thamarit late in the afternoon with his head Arab intelligence aide and a small dark-skinned Mahra. I found the latter's handshake soft and weak.

We went to an empty shack with a table where Tom placed his map.

"This man comes from a village south of Qum. Some five miles into the heart of the *jebel*." This, of course, was an area where the Army had not been before, and a centre of guerrilla activity.

Tom's finger traced a line from the desert where it met the *jebel* Qara at O'bet waterhole. Then south over a bewildering complex of spidery black lines denoting deep *wadis* and into the foliated upper valleys of the Wadi Sahilnawt.

"Two nights ago this chap who calls himself Sahayl, a son of Sheikh Musallim of the Bait Howeirat, walked forty miles from his homeland solely to ask us to kill three guerrillas to whom he's taken a dislike. These three arrive every morning, regular as clockwork, to get milk and a quick bump with the womenfolk of Sahayl's village." Tom looked at me quickly to see how I was taking his proposal. "As soon as the *adoo* discover that Sahayl's gone, this village will be crawling with them—which is why I want you to be there by dawn tomorrow. Leave here as soon as you can. There is reason to think two of the three guerrillas are of considerable importance. We want those two alive."

"But how the hell do we know this bloke can be trusted?" I blustered. "Who can vouch for his allegiance?"

I thought of occasions when Companies had walked into carefully prepared ambushes and suffered many dead though their guide, out front, had survived. And dawn cordons that found their target villages empty although *adoo* groups were known to live there. Only the guides had had prior knowledge of such cordons and the opportunity to tip off the villagers.

By such acts some of the guides hoped to gain favour with the Liberation Front; or at least mitigation against torture and execution should they ever fall into *adoo* hands.

So it was only after a period of probation under the surveillance of the older more trusted guides such as Fred Wahid that newly recruited Dhofaris were allowed to lead soldiers into the *adoo*-held areas of the mountains.

Sahayl, however, had persuaded Tom to make an exception to the custom for his story appeared as genuine as his apparent hatred for the *adoo*. The information he brought was fresh from an area about which nothing was known. Tom took him to Colonel Peter and suggested an immediate patrol to capture the three guerrillas of whom Sahayl spoke.

No large Army group could hope to penetrate the area undetected, Sahayl had said, since it lay within a network of *adoo* camps.

When asked to point out the exact location of his village on the map, Sahayl was not helpful. His bony finger hovered around the wall map in Tom's office and finally alighted at random on to a barren part of the Empty Quarter.

"This, Sahb, is our *bayt*. And here," indicating some sand dunes, "are the *adoo* positions."

Since it was clear that he could not understand a map, it might be imprudent to attack Sahayl's intended target by air using him as the observer since, quite apart from his unpredictable reaction to 5 'Gs' pressure during a bombing dive, he was as likely to direct a bombing attack on to a harmless village as against the guerrillas.

The only Company available on the *jebel* was surrounded and under daily attack from *adoo* mortars and machine guns and was anyway many miles from Sahayl's area. However it had been decided that Sahayl was a gift from heaven and his information should be followed up immediately whilst it was still oven hot. So the signal was sent to Recce. For once the firm ruling – of a minimum of half a Company (sixty men) on the *jebel* at one time – would be broken.

Since we had been a desert patrol with independent command for many months no one back in Salalah was too sure quite how many active men constituted the Recce Platoon. But as two troops of Oman Gendarmerie had recently been sent from Muscat to strengthen our desert ambush points, the Colonel was under the impression that we were some fifty in number.

Unfortunately, this wasn't so. I had left fourteen men watching the Dehedoba trail and, as soon as word spread in the platoon of an impending 'deep' patrol, an epidemic of headaches, stomach aches, dysentry and even lumbago began. Some of the men began coughing raucously when they passed Sergeant Mohamed or myself, knowing that coughers were never taken on night patrols. However, Mohamed had dealt firmly with the malingerers explaining to them that, *Imshaalah*, a nice long march would soothe their aches and ease their bowels, that the jolting weight of a machine gun on their shoulders during the coming night move would soon take their minds from lumbago pains.

Tom Greening impressed upon me how important my mission was. The rebels were rapidly gaining the upper hand. Now they had most of the west, they controlled the road into the interior, they had cut us off from our northern outposts and were rapidly closing in on the Plain of Salalah. Already they held sway right round the perimeter of the plain. What was needed was reliable information from a high powered rebel source. It was also vital at this particular juncture that we have a concrete and visible success to give fresh heart to those still resisting. If only we could show those on our side that we were still powerful, that we could and would protect them, then maybe more people like Sahayl would defect to our side and provide information.

He made it abundantly clear that this moment in time was of particular importance although he did not tell me exactly why. He flew off leaving me with the feeling that I must succeed, that much depended on me and that much was at stake. Now.

Tom flew away from Thamarit leaving Sahayl with me. He spoke Mahra which I found totally unintelligible and *jebali* which sometimes made sense to Sergeant Mohamed after several repetitions.

Only Sahayl knew exactly where our objective lay, what route we must take, and how long was the journey.

But all knew that we were bound for O'bet waterhole and that the *jebel* to its south was infested with *adoo*. Any movement by day in that area would be suicidal. Wherever our goal might be, we must reach it before the next dawn. Through Mohamed I tried to impress this upon Sahayl.

As soon as the five Land Rovers were ready, the battle rations and the ammunition given out, I called the men together to explain the mission. They sat around in the dust, their faces grim.

As I spoke they stared balefully at Sahayl.

Many of them had had friends whose deaths in ambushes had been attributed to double-dealing guides. To trust an unknown *jebali* in *adoo*-held territory, a *jebali* whose only credentials were his own words, seemed to them, and increasingly to myself, a fine madness. I determined that, should anything go wrong, Sahayl himself would be the first to die.

We drove south-east from Thamarit over parched plateaux where scattered triliths, the graves of long forgotten bedu, were the only notable features in a dead landscape as we crunched over beds of fossilised oysters.

We stopped for prayer five miles from the mountains. Like many Christians, they prayed more fervently when their immediate future seems insecure, going rigorously through the age-old obeisance set by the Prophet, but washing their bodies only with sand for they knew their water was limited and every drop would be sorely needed in the hours to come.

With engines revving as quietly as possible in the soft sand, the five vehicles left us in the moon shadow of a great gravel hummock and drove back to the north. At such moments many privates pray to Allah that, next month, they too may pass their driving tests and become drivers.

The wind blew from the south that night; an omen for success perhaps.

On the high peaks of the Qara the *adoo* scouts would be settling for the night, their keen ears waiting for the wind-borne whine of motors. Tonight they would have no such warning of our coming for engine noise, along with muffled coughs and the rattling of displaced pebbles would fly north where only lizards, wolves and scorpions might hear.

Sahayl nudged my elbow, pointing south where the Qara loomed darkly; he seemed very keen to be going.

He began to chatter excitedly.

"*Uskoot*, you fool. Shut up." I squeezed his arm.

The Mahra word for whisper, "*Eleuchid*" was not then known to me.

This was unfortunate since Sahayl seemed unaware of the need for silence.

The platoon were quiet to a man, stifling coughs however uncomfortable for they had learnt the hard way the cost of advertising their presence to the *adoo*.

I tapped Sahayl on the windpipe and pressed his lips together. There was no point in his saying anything at all since no one could understand his meaning. All he need do was walk in the correct direction.

The men faded into the gloom behind; each soldier some fifteen yards from the next. This would render an ambush less effective since there were never more than two men visible at any one time or place. The sign came quickly up the line that all were ready and safety catches applied; bolt actions had been cocked and grenades primed before leaving Thamarit as was the custom. All clothes were heavily camouflaged, watches in pockets, shining metal covered by *shemaghs* and no face but my own needed blacking.

I prodded Sahayl and moved my rifle to the south. The Mahra grinned with a flash of teeth, perfectly white from a lifelong diet of camel's milk.

Tom had said the journey would take eight hours "*imshee iebali*" — at the pace of a *jebali*. If Sahayl's pace was typical, we were in trouble for he moved off far too fast. The men would never keep up such a pace. I ran to him and gestured for him to slow down.

Childishly sullen, he carried on at a ridiculously slow pace.

I cursed him silently wishing I had an inanimate and predictable compass bearing to follow instead of this mercurial *jebali* whom I could see disliked any form of authority.

The climb from *nejd* to *jebel* was treacherous and steep to the point where handholds were necessary to keep from falling away from the cliff face.

I paused breathing heavily on reaching the summit after an hour's climb.

Scurrying thermals moaned weirdly between the boulders below muting the occasional scrabble of boots and the sharp thwack of rifle butts on rocks. Ahead the limestone yielded to powdery humus brushed with monsoon grass that soughed in the breeze and, to the overwrought ear, rendered an elusive suggestion of murmuring voices.

The ever swaying blades caught the moonlight to produce

patterns of lilting shadow. The place seemed to move with lurking life.

Ali Nasser ran up from behind. I bent down and he whispered softly in my ear.

"Look back over the *nejd*, Bakhait."

At first there was nothing. Only the song of a million crickets, the twinkle of a billion stars. And the wide gloom of the *nejd*.

As suddenly as summer lightning, a green signal flare shot up soundlessly. Then another and a third in quick succession. There was no telling from how far away.

"That is the second time," Ali whispered. "Altogether six flares now. Either the *adoo* have heard us and signal to others ahead of us. Or it is Murad. Perhaps he is in trouble."

Certainly there was no other answer since there was no Army presence in all the *nejd*.

Time was short but the flares could not be ignored. Leaving half the platoon on the *jebel* with the heavier weapons, I retraced our journey to the place where Murad had left us. No one there and no further tracks so—none the wiser—back up the bloody mountain.

Nearly three hours had been wasted, the men left on the *jebel* were shivering from the cold winds along the clifftop and those who had made the ascent twice were already tired; except for Sahayl.

We pressed on, the men jittery now for they were sure we were walking into a trap. Had not the *adoo* signalled our presence from the *nejd* behind us? Everyone already knew the Mahra were the most treacherous tribe in Arabia. Why prove it by risking death?

All knew the gamble we ran. Each step from the open *nejd* took us further from safety. There were less than thirty of us and already we were south of Qum where over two hundred guerrillas were known to live. Once they knew of our presence they would move in behind cutting off our retreat.

Even one wounded man would cause problems for we had no stretcher, no animal transport and no possible reinforcements to help extricate us. There were no helicopters for the Sultan did not approve of them. The nearest surgical facilities were at Bahrein; two thousand miles away. All this did nothing to boost our morale as we penetrated mile after mile of *adoo* territory.

My signaller, a fine looking Hawasena from the Batinah, came panting up and clutched my shoulder. He waved his rifle at Sahayl and exhorted me, in a hoarse whisper, to turn back.

"We are going to our death, Sahb. This evil man is of the *adoo*. Is he not strong and well fed? Proof that he feeds with the thugs. Can you not smell his perfume? It comes from the Yemen with his *adoo* accomplices. We must go before it is too late." His manner was edged with panic.

I shut him up with promises of demotion.

Time was flying and I began to feel the whole affair was going dangerously badly.

For three hours we stole through thickening scrubland punctured by valleys where Sahayl came into his own. No compass could have shown me the confusing route along the camel paths which led up and down these deep *wadis* where no white man had hitherto been fool enough to wander.

Once within the thick screen of thornbush and creeper that crammed these defiles, there was no room to manœuvre off the narrow camel paths, and the men closed up for fear of taking a wrong turning.

The mosquitoes attacked in humming clouds and a sticky heat emanated from the dark foliage.

Fatigue was setting in as we climbed out of the fourth of these divides.

Sahayl had successfully avoided caves, thorn houses, and even the temporary bedu camps which scatter the Downs; a point very much in his favour.

But dawn would break in only three hours; we must press on faster.

Sergeant Mohamed came forward. He was carrying two rifles.

"Some of the men are badly tired, Sahb, two are even now being helped along by others."

I snapped back at him.

"Too bad. We're all tired but if we go any slower we'll be on the move after dawn, and then we'll be dead. Tell them that."

I regretted my temper as soon as Mohamed fell back. I was on edge.

At any moment I expected the sudden hell of an ambush for

the flares from the *nejd* were fresh in my mind. And the uncertainty of not knowing the country or the distance to our target, further detracted from my self-confidence.

The valleys were growing more frequent, falling away steeply to either side and visible only as dark shadows of indeterminate size and depth. We skirted above them keeping to the high grassy shoulders but just below the skyline.

Skull-size stones lay higgledy-piggledy in the grass. I was amazed at Sahayl's ability to see and avoid them with his bare feet. To me they were invisible and I cursed silently whilst stumbling from one to another, attempting to find even ground. Judging from the occasional scrape and muffled clatter from behind I was not alone in my ungainly progress. Towards three o'clock we cleared the broken ground and, remembering the lie of the map, I felt we must be nearing the target area.

Dark amorphous shapes blobbed the upper slopes, wild fig trees and cattle kraals of thorn. Twice we passed the acrid tang of burning dung which hangs about *jebali* villages.

It was as well there were no dogs on the *jebel* but hyenas and wolves.

To the south-east a patch of spreading grey, as from a large and well-lit town, crept into the blue-black sky.

Sahayl stopped and knelt without warning, looking about him. Again I smelled a whiff of burning camel dung and, straining my ears with mouth half open, picked up a faint birdlike prattle of subdued voices; *jebali* women. Sahayl's hands closed about my shoulders, thrusting his face close to mine. His features contorted in a wide smile, demoniac in the half light. He said nothing but turned and pointed. Further along the grassy shoulder were six dark hummocks: a Mahra village.

Sahayl nodded his head vigorously.

As I turned to signal for the section leaders, a pinpoint of light pulsed from the high ground to the east. It lasted only a second or two: I might have imagined it.

The village was badly placed for a cordon since wooded hills rose sharply on both sides. Were we to remain on the open shoulder surrounding the huts, we might be picked off helplessly from the hills above as soon as dawn came.

With little time left I took Sergeant Mohamed up the right-hand hill to an outcrop of boulders near its summit from where he could cover the huts and also the land to the immediate west.

Within ten minutes we returned to the shoulder and found Sergeant Mohamed's five men fast asleep in the long grass.

To awake them without startling them Mohamed squeezed and twisted the lobes of their ears as was the custom. Taking also Mohamed of the Beard and his men, the little Sergeant left silently for his position. There was nothing to discuss; every ambush is much the same in theory.

Ali Nasser's section found a clump of thorn with scattered rock at its base some three hundred yards from the huts and along the shoulder down which we had come.

With Corporal Salim Khaleefa's men and my own section I climbed the hill to the east of the huts as an orange rash speckled the gathering dawn.

The men were exhausted but, realising the imminent danger, moved fast from cover to cover. Corporal Salim's four men scattered in a low defile where flowering shrubs hid the snouts of their machine guns.

I would have stayed close by him but noticed a higher more dominating thicket above and remembered the light signal I had glimpsed earlier.

Said Salim went ahead with his stiletto. He left his gun with me and moved like a ghost. He entered the thicket from the far side and a scuffle ensued as of many small birds taking flight.

Then silence.

Cautiously we followed and found that the thicket was hollow, containing a ruined thorn hut inside its shell and a floor of stones.

Said held a tall *jebali* by his hair, his stiletto pressed to the man's throat so that blood dribbled darkly onto his indigo cloak.

A Martini Henry rifle and full cartridge belt lay by the *jebali*'s feet.

Fat Hamid had been carrying the ·30 Browning all night and collapsed exhausted among the rocks.

He picked up a tiny wallet from under him and swore softly.

"We are in trouble." He removed a flint and tinder from the leather pouch. "It is still warm, Bakhait; he must have used it to signal when he saw us. Let Said slit his black throat for he is undoubtedly of the *adoo*."

233

Sahayl was pushed into the thicket by Sadeeq the Baluchi. He saw the *jebali* and, ignoring the latter's awkward position, rubbed cheeks with him and shook his hand, muttering delightedly.

Said Salim whispered quietly, "They are brothers in the same family."

My heart sank. This confirmed that we had been led into a trap.

Fat Hamid snarled and would willingly have slit the throats of both the Mahra. But that might have been noisy. Using rifle slings we bound both men together back to back and, as quietly as possible, began to form a protective *sangar* of rocks within the confines of the thicket.

Said Salim remained awake glaring at Sahayl; the rest of us slept at once. There was much I did not understand but we would need rest before the heat of the day made sleep impossible.

The sun was well up when I woke. It took some minutes to clear my head and realise where I was. The realisation was not pleasant.

Said Salim still sat like a sphinx. I told him to sleep and stirred the others.

Humming-birds hovered and darted in the chintz ceiling of our hide. Warm sunlight came dappled through the thorn to play over the delicate black features of Sahayl. I noticed then that his brother had but a single good eye: the other was glazed over and opaquely pink.

Through a break in the thorns I looked to the south; at the scattered huts below and the rolling green wonderland all about us. Beyond the rim of the mountains the Plain of Salalah stretched white as linen fringed by the Indian Ocean.

Four armed men in dark brown uniforms moved quickly from the huts below, into nearby scrub and out of sight. Fat Hamid and the other three were immediately alert easing their safety catches forward. In two years of ambushes none had seen so tantalising a target; but they knew the penalty of firing a shot. Our only safety lay in concealment. Our three guerrillas, if they appeared, must be captured soundlessly or there was little hope of escape.

Jebalis were at work all about us; women cutting grass and taking herds of goats to graze. Children playing in the long grass whilst cows munched in contentment after the months of drought.

Two young men approached our thicket carrying long flint-lock guns; they were Bait Kathir and soon they would spot us. One cry of alarm would give us away.

I moved half out of the bush, gently, and beckoned to them whilst Mubarreq let them see the black snout of his bren.

Surprise showed briefly on their proud pointed faces but they came quietly and Said took their rifles.

During the next two hours, as the heat mounted steadily, seven more *jebalis* including a woman and two children came by the thicket, saw us, and wisely joined our somewhat cramped quarters.

All this time the men had watched and wondered and I could sense their anxiety.

Three uniformed *adoo* had come into the village from the south and sat talking for a while by the furthest hut from our vantage point. From time to time they glanced in our direction and then left by the way they had come.

I followed their movements through binoculars until they disappeared and then carefully scanned the hills beyond to which they were headed.

I felt my blood run thin. Some sixty or seventy figures moved about along the high ground to the south of the huts. It was not possible to tell whether all were in uniform but the intermittent glint of metal suggested that many were armed. Some appeared to be sitting around in groups whilst others moved about busily.

All were positioned as though expecting some form of attack from the south.

To our north the hill rose slightly behind the thicket making observation in that direction impossible but the likelihood that we were already cut off from the *nejd* weighed heavily on my mind.

Since waking I had felt sick with stomach pains. This was nothing new for they had come frequently in the desert. Perhaps the water or the goat caused it.

But usually I could find a bush or rock to squat behind to relieve myself and wait for the pain to slacken: then the sickness would go, leaving me weak and sweating. Now there was nowhere but outside the thicket walls but to emerge even momentarily would put everything at risk.

The pains got worse, extending agonisingly to my rectum. I stifled a groan and knew I could wait no longer.

The space within the hide was overcrowded. The two last bedu to arrive were standing for there was no room for them to sit.

I built a layer of small rocks around my backside between me and the others, and lowered my trousers as my insides seemed to give way in a flood. For minutes it was agony. At once the flies swarmed into the thicket.

I used the rocks instead of paper and collapsed the little 'cubicle' on to the results of my personal crisis.

Not a moment too soon.

As I wiped the sweat from my eyes I sensed movement outside the hide. My rifle was beneath Mubarreq: quietly I slid it towards me releasing the safety catch.

A narrow goat trail ran between our thicket and the top of a steep grassy slope. Two tall men were approaching fast along it.

I noticed their dark clothes and glint of guns in their hands. Also the polished red badge on the cap of the second man. Not the tiny Mao button badge worn by many of the *adoo* but the hexagonal red star of a political commissar.

These were our men. I was sure of it. There was no time to think. They were fifteen yards away; soon they would see us.

The first man stopped abruptly seeming to sniff the air. His face was scarred, his hair close shaven. I watched fascinated as the Kalachnikov, its ugly round magazine cradled in his elbow, swung around slowly as the man turned to face us. A Kalachnikov is an unpleasant weapon; a touch of its trigger will squeeze off a long rip of hollow-nosed 7·62 bullets that rip bone apart and pass through a man's guts like papiermâché.

Inch by inch I lifted my rifle. The sun was in the east behind the man, outlining him. Only his shadow falling upon the thicket shielded my eyes, stinging with sweat, from direct glare.

He peered directly at me now. I remember thinking 'He has seen us. He is weighing his chances.'

My voice seemed to come of its own volition. "Drop your weapons or we kill you."

.The big man began to move with incredible speed, twisting at the knee and bringing the Kalachnikov to bear in a single fluid movement.

I squeezed the trigger automatically. The guerrilla was slammed back as though caught in the chest by a sledgehammer. His limbs spread like a puppet and he cartwheeled out of sight down the grassy slope.

Behind him the other man paused for a minute unsure what to do.

I noticed his face beneath the jungle cap. He looked sad and faintly surprised.

His rifle, a Mark 4 ·303, was already pointed at my stomach when a flurry of shots rang out. Mubarreq and Said Salim, forcing themselves over the bedu, fired simultaneously.

The man's face crumpled into red horror; the nose and eyes smashed back into the brains. Bullets tore through the ribs and a pretty flowering thorn bush caught his body at the top of the grassy slope.

Said Salim crawled on his belly from the thicket. There might be other *adoo* behind these two.

Expertly he searched the corpse, bringing back rifle, ammunition and a leather satchel stuffed with documents.

He handed these to me and began to crawl back with a ·36 grenade in one hand. He would jam this beneath the body with the pin removed.

I hissed at him without knowing why, "Forget it, Said. Come back . . ."

My signaller was calling Salalah repeatedly for fighter support. Sahayl gazed at the corpse on the thorn bush. He did not look happy.

I glanced south; the bush was glinting with movement, dark forms scurrying towards us through the scrub. There was little time for making decisions; the other sections would be awaiting orders.

I flicked the National switch, no longer bothering to whisper. "All stations 5. Withdraw now . . . over."

Fatigue forgotten, the men needed no encouragement and broke from their hides to fan out in a long straggling line. Speed was the only hope and the men moved with the wings of fear.

Shots sounded from behind passing overhead like vengeful hornets. But my fears of a cut-off group never materialised.

For four hours we fled, keeping Sahayl, his one-eyed brother and four other hostages ahead of us. Somehow I was still not really certain who Sahayl was working for; where his allegiance lay. We reached the cliffs by midday.

As we climbed down to the safety of the *nejd* the two little Provost fighters strafed the hills to our immediate rear and the *adoo* never quite caught up with us.

Back in Thamarit the soldiers slept like dead men but I found sleep elusive. I had often shot at people hundreds of yards away; vague shapes behind rocks who were busy firing back; but never before had I seen a man's soul in his eyes, sensed his vitality as a fellow human, and then watched his body ripped apart at the pressure of my finger.

I tried to force away the image of his destruction but his scarred face stayed watching me from my subconscious and a part of me that was still young and uncynical died with him and his comrade the commissar, spreadeagled on a thorn bush with his red badge glinting in the hot Qara sun.

16

TOM GREENING flew into Thamarit to collect the commissar's papers. He was sad that we had not managed to bring back the two guerrilla leaders alive but more than delighted with the papers. From these we learnt that the commissar was Musallim Ali and his fellow guerrilla was Salim Amr. We also learned a great deal of information about the other side which I have already given in this book. We learnt of the unexpected degree of organisation amongst the guerrillas. Many names and ranks of *adoo* leaders were revealed along with their intended policy in the West.

The green flares, Tom explained, had been put up by a low-flying Beaver sent out from Salalah to recall us from the mission when the Colonel had discovered that I had left a number of my men behind to guard the Dehedoba. As it was luck had been with us: the *adoo* had indeed been expecting the Army (had Sahayl hedged his bets? We would never know) – but from the other direction, from the plain, not the way we had come, in from the *nejd*.

The death of the two communists in the centre of their stronghold had far-reaching effects, as Tom had hoped. Some of these effects were not immediately apparent but cumulative. Other *jebalis* in the east took heart from the rebellious example of Sahayl. They too rose up against the aggressive behaviour and tactics of the *adoo*, they came over to our side, gave us information, took up arms against the communists and generally worked to assert themselves as Muslims. It did indeed show many in Eastern Dhofar, in Muscat and Oman that, if they resisted the communists, the Sultan's Forces would support and help them where possible.

Unfortunately many of those who came over to our side, including Sahayl, his brother and his father, Sheikh Musallim, were later murdered. But the *adoo* were so busy fighting this defection in their own camps, trying to suppress revolt and reorganise that they were caught on the wrong foot at the crucial moment a few months later when the Sultan was overthrown and his son Qaboos placed in his stead. It was during the vital months prior to the coup, when both Oman and Dhofar were ripe for revolution, that PFLOAG could have struck with force and sparked off a general uprising. That they did not seize this obvious opportunity was largely due to their uncertainty as to the *jebalis'* loyalty; an uncertainty promoted originally by the actions of Sahayl and his family.

Remembering what Tom Greening had told me previously about Qaboos and his plans, it looked as if, at long last, better times were coming for the people of Oman. I was also able to feel that in some small way I had been able to contribute towards a change in the situation: the months of ambushes and killing had not been in vain.

Later I learnt how the Sultan had been deposed. How in July 1970 high ranking officials, oil and banking directors, whose jobs took them frequently from Muscat to London and back — and almost as frequently down to Salalah — suddenly found themselves involved in a spate of travelling. The key commanders of the Sultan's Forces were contacted and clandestine meetings took place in Salalah itself between the Wali's son Bareik and the Sultan's young intelligence officer Captain Tom Greening.

During the afternoon of 23rd July, whilst the Sultan rested, a group of ten Omani *askars* led by Bareik entered the palace compound, unopposed at first by the Sultan's bodyguard of slaves.

Winding their way through a labyrinth of dark passages they came at length to the Sultan's private quarters. A sudden challenge by the royal bodyguard was quickly followed by shots ricocheting off the stone walls. Bareik was shot in the stomach. Prince Qaboos had meanwhile informed the Army of his intentions. Tom Greening materialised with Omani soldiers and all but two of the slaves surrendered.

The Sultan himself was wounded and eventually he too gave up but refused to leave the palace unless accompanied by the local British Colonel. This officer arrived and held the Sultan's hand, comforting him whilst his wounds were dressed and he signed a letter of abdication in favour of his son Qaboos. An RAF plane then took the ex-Sultan, with three of his palace staff, to England and a private suite in the Dorchester Hotel. There he died in October 1972, a sad and very charming old man.

Had Said bin Taimur ruled much longer in Oman, it is difficult to see how revolution in the internationally vital Persian Gulf arena might have been averted. I well remember a letter I received from Tom Greening only two months before the coup. In it he said, "... only the present Sultan's attitude is prolonging the war and a good progressive government under Sandhurst-trained Qaboos (half Dhofari) would change the situation overnight since the inhabitants of Dhofar do not take naturally to Chinese communism in any form ..."[1]

On his accession Qaboos immediately set about nipping in the bud the impending PFLOAG explosion in Dhofar and Northern Oman. He withdrew all troops from the Qara mountains and proclaimed an amnesty to all the guerrillas. This triggered off a trickle of deserters that soon became a flood: one of the first was Musallim bin Nuffl.

Within three years these defectors numbered over a thousand including many who had earlier received training in China or Russia. These men now formed a counter-guerrilla force to combat their erstwhile comrades. Split into regional, tribal groups, they were trained by men of the Special Air Service, fluent in Arabic and experts in counter-guerrilla warfare.

The adoo did not of course let this happen without a struggle. Following the amnesty, the adoo stepped up their campaign of terror outside and within their ranks, hoping in this way to prevent wholesale defection. They immediately executed and arrested over seventy Dhofaris and sent their children to the Lenin School for corrective indoctrination. At the same time some two hundred influential civilians on both sides of the South Yemen border were executed quietly because they were considered too old to be effectively indoctrinated.

[1] Shortly afterwards Chou En Lai's foreign policy became less aggressive and Chinese involvement in Dhofor became minimal.

The groups of 'deserters' trained by the SAS helped the Army to establish mountain-top Government-held bases in the Eastern Qara where *jebalis* could live, graze their cattle, trade at special 'shop' centres and make use of free medical, educational and veterinary facilities.

Slowly the new Sultan's Forces were able to halt the creeping advance of PFLOAG and with the help of Jordan, Saudi Arabia, the Union of Arab Emirates and Iran, who gave weapons, men and money, the tables were turned.

Recognising however that military advances were worth little without concurrent material progress, Qaboos instigated an ambitious industrial programme. At first money appeared to be a problem for over half the oil revenue (fifty million pounds a year) was spent on the war. But Qaboos joined the Arab League and the United Nations and money was soon forthcoming. Then world oil prices were doubled and so, overnight, was Oman's revenue. By 1975 the oil income reached £300 million.

Tarmac roads, harbours, new towns, lighting and piped water arrived in Oman in lightning succession. Hospitals, schools and employment mushroomed. There were cars, newspapers and cafés. In three short years Sultan Qaboos pulled Oman from the Middle Ages into the twentieth century and in so doing he has, for a while at any rate, whipped the carpet from under the revolutionaries. Agricultural and fishery schemes were soon under way. Wells were drilled, and a harbour constructed west of Salalah so that Dhofar is now no longer cut-off in the monsoon months. In the north, in Oman, sixty hospitals were built, a deep-water harbour for a new fishery industry, an international airport for Jumbo jets and by 1973 the number of students at Omani schools had reached 34,000.

Qaboos has only Arab ministers in his Government. His old friend Tom Greening now acts as his personal equerry but his senior officials are Omani, Egyptian or Jordanian. In the Army Omani officers are now being trained to take over but British officers are still necessary to advise on the technical data of the very sophisticated weaponry used. The Baluchis have now been withdrawn into all-Baluchi regiments and a fourth Omani regiment has been recruited.

The war is not over yet for the *adoo* are fighting for ideological reasons and they have a strong safe base within South Yemen, immune from the Sultan's Forces. There is hope that diplomatic lobbying within the Arab League will finally defeat PFLOAG by removing its lifeline. But should the British officers be withdrawn due to left-wing pressure in Britain, or the Iranian soldiers, due to Arab nationalist pressures on Qaboos, the Marxists might yet succeed in Dhofar.

The Sultan's state visit to Iran in early 1974 went a long way to ensuring the freedom of the Gulf region through a combined policing of the Straits of Hormuz by Oman and Iran. This will remain a vital factor for free trade long after pipelines take oil from Suez to the Mediterranean, since the tankers will have to pass through the Straits to take Gulf oil to Suez.

It will remain vital even if further pipelines are laid between the individual Gulf producers and the Mediterranean ports. Such pipelines have proved vulnerable to sabotage and a large number would be required to satisfy even a fraction of current demand.

If by the 1980s the North-West European countries have developed their own alternative sources of power — although they need over five times the amount of oil they can possibly hope to gain from the North Sea — the political importance of the Gulf countries will in no way diminish, since their economic and industrial co-operation will by then be vital to Western trade. They already have sufficient money to play havoc with the Free World's finances.

Meanwhile soaring revenues bring problems as well as solutions to Oman. The years of autocracy have left the country without a professional cadre to staff the growing apparatus of government. Oman is poor yet rich, old yet new. Television and radio pour into bewildered Omani ears a kaleidoscope of information, only adding to the contradictions and the strains.

As yet there are no experiments with elections or unions, but the oil and the coup have set the ball rolling; whether towards democracy, as in the Union of Arab Emirates to the north, or towards the Marxism of South Yemen only time will tell. The outcome will affect the West very deeply.

17

I STAYED with Recce Platoon in Dhofar for a while after our successful ambush and among other activities we helped Sahayl bring his wife back with him to Thamarit. Here I taught him bad, but intelligible, Omani and he told me much about the communists that had haunted his village and soured his life. The hatred was rooted deep in his mind. He had left his children and his goats in the care of their grandmother and he hoped one day to be able to go back to join them but I later learnt that he and his brothers were cornered one evening whilst eating by a well and shot dead.

I had now been in Oman for the full term of my service contract and it was time for me to return to my own regiment. I left the platoon on the little plateau, guarding the Dehedoba trail. I left them with the hope that they would eventually be able to maintain their Arab Muslim way of life in peace with the additional advantages of better medicine and education. There did indeed seem a fair chance that they would not be over-powered by dissident revolutionaries whose methods, beliefs and attitudes they neither liked nor wanted.

I said good-bye to them there on the airstrip, moving from man to man.

Mubarreq bin Obeid the big Zanzibari grasped my hand and pressed it to his forehead. He tried to speak but did not. His face was averted.

"God stay with you, Mubarreq."

His great shoulders slumped, the negro grasped his beloved machine gun as though it were all he possessed.

The Beaver was circling now, its shadow caressing the dusty plateau.

Ali Nasser and Mohamed Rashid of the Beard came down from their hillocks, the giant *moolah* and the Baluchis, smelling faintly of Jungle Petal. Solemn-faced Said Salim and Saif Musabbah of the wild curly hair, Fat Hamid with his Browning and young Kamis Ali the bedu from Suneina — much favoured by *djinns*: I wondered how the future would treat them all in their uncertain world of *Imshaalah*.

"We are your brothers, Bakhait. Do not forget us, where you go to." Corporal Salim came with me to the plane.

Twelve goats were unloaded and I sat beside the pilot. The wispy beard of Sergeant Mohamed scarcely reached the step of the cockpit door. "I will look after the men, Sahb. Perhaps one day you will come back to us."

Dust cocooned the Beaver. It shuddered violently as the engine roared to maximum pitch. Then away up the tiny airstrip banking sharply once airborne to avoid jagged rocks.

The plateau grew smaller below the spiralling plane. The little dark figures on the hillocks blended with the ground and the plateau with the whole wild moonscape of the *nejd*. I felt then a keen sense of loss, an emptiness that mirrored the wastes of the desert below.

Appendix

DHOFAR—AN OUTLINE HISTORY

LITTLE is known of Dhofar's history. The following is taken from the works of the few travellers and historians who have studied Dhofar's history through manuscripts and letters.

The Book of Genesis (Chapter 10 verses 26–32) states that Shem's son Joktan had thirteen children whose families settled between the Yemen and Dhofar (Sephar) and were the forerunners of the first pure Arabs.

Ancient Egyptian records describe Dhofar as a thriving port from which frankincense derived prior to the period in which Joktan's sons were supposed to have lived in Dhofar.

The geographical writers of Greece and Rome (Herodotus, Ptolemy, Pliny, Strabo and Diodorus) mention that Dhofar frankincense was carried by sea to all ports of the world. Sprenger suggests that it was the first commodity to lead to the idea of international trade routes and that the Queen of Sheba from the Yemen, of which Dhofar was a colony, visited King Solomon of Jerusalem solely to agree upon a safe caravan route for the frankincense convoys.

The Roman Emperor Augustus sent an army south to conquer the frankincense countries in 24 BC, but thirst forced the soldiers to retire long before they reached Dhofar. During the first century AD the countries of south-east Arabia were the richest in the world, deriving their wealth from the frankincense trees of the Dhofari colony.

In 536 BC the Persians under Cyrus the Great conquered Oman and Dhofar. They were subsequently ejected from Oman but the wealthy Persian Manjui dynasty continued to rule Dhofar until 1207. The Arab Haboodi dynasty took over until the end of that century when the Yemeni Rashoolids colonised the country.

Dhofar was converted to Islam two years after the Prophet's death by the military expedition under General Ikrima. Of the pre-Islamic monuments and tribes there are few remaining signs.

Only the Shahara tribe survive. There are some 300 Shahara survivors who live as servants to the Qara tribesmen; originally they ruled Dhofar from Robat, the site of which is close to present-day Salalah.

The Shahara were overrun by the Qara and Mahra tribes from the Yemen at about the time of Christ. It is thought that the Mahra may have originated from the Habasha who colonised Ethiopia in 1000 BC.

The Kathiri tribes arrived much later; in the fourteenth century under Sheikh Al Habrali of the Hadhramaut. They retain nominal supremacy over the other Dhofari tribes to the present day.

In 1285 Marco Polo visited Dhofar and reported that the people were not friendly.

The Portuguese sent an expedition from Goa and built forts along the Dhofar coastline in 1528 and seventeen years later the Turks attacked Salalah unsuccessfully.

During the seventeenth and eighteenth centuries, Ovington and Captain Hamilton visited Dhofar and wrote about the Dhofaris, but little is known of this period, except that there was continual strife between the rulers on the coastal plain of Salalah and the mountain tribesmen, and a perpetual state of war between many of the Qara tribes and factions.

Exploration of the area continued in the nineteenth century with Captain S. B. Haines and some of his crew visiting Dhofar in 1835, as part of an Indian Navy survey of the Arabian coast. They wrote extensively about the country and the tribes.

In 1895 Theodor and Mabel Bent of the Royal Geographical Society travelled over the Qara mountains and collected many specimens hitherto unknown to science. They reported that the plain and the foothills were extensively cultivated and a high level of agricultural skill existed among the Plains folk. Later Bertram Thomas crossed the Qara mountains and recorded the peculiarities and customs of the tribes he found there on his way to cross the Empty Quarter by camel.

During this time tribal unrest continued. In 1805 Said Mohamed bin Akil, a pirate from Mocha, ruled Dhofar but was ambushed and killed by the Qara. Hearing this, the Sultan of Muscat sent his army to subdue the Qara at the request of the Salalah Dhofaris.

In 1876 a Moplah priest Seid Fadhl bin Allawi became ruler of Dhofar but his government was so harsh that he was deposed within eighteen months.

Four years later, again harassed by the troublesome Qara raiders the Plains folk sent their sheikh, Awadh bin Abdullah, to Sultan Turki of Muscat to request that Omani authority be extended to Dhofar. The Sultan sent a further consignment of troops to Dhofar and ruled Salalah as a province through a *Wali*. Successive *Walis* have held rule on behalf of the Omani Sultans ever since.

In the 1880s Sultan Turki sent a freed slave called Suleiman bin Suwaylim as *Wali* to Dhofar. He ruled well and was succeeded by his son who was murdered by Bait Kathir tribesmen. An Army slave named Bachit an-Nubi was then appointed; he suffered a serious tribal revolt in 1916 and was replaced by two other *Walis* who proved equally ineffective.

In 1923 Sultan Taimur of Muscat nominated a relative, Said Saud bin Ali, as *Wali*: he took no taxes and forgave the Qara and Bait Kathir their earlier troubles. He was popular and ruled until 1932. He was succeeded by *Wali* Hamid bin Hamed al Ghafiri who was *Wali* until the palace coup in 1970 when Sultan Said bin Taimur was forced to abdicate in favour of his more progressive son Qaboos. Soon after the coup *Wali* Hamid died and was succeeded by his son Bareik, one of the chief protagonists of the coup.

Sultan Said bin Taimur built the Midway Road across the Qara mountains for the Mecom Oil Company in 1953, and drilling for oil in Dhofar began two years later and ceased in 1965 as no oil was found in commercially worthwhile quantities. In 1958 following insurrection and civil war in Northern Oman, the Sultan moved to Salalah where he lived in seclusion for the rest of his rule.

From 1962 until 1967 the Dhofar Liberation Front under Musallim bin Nuffl caused minor troubles in Dhofar. The Sultan's Forces first moved to Dhofar to deal with the rebels in 1965. After 1967 the DLF was taken over by revolutionary elements and became PFLOAG.

In 1966 the Sultan narrowly escaped an attempted assassination plot at the Dhofar Force fort. In 1970 Sultan Qaboos born of a Dhofari mother ousted his father in Salalah. For the first time in their history Dhofaris had a Dhofari ruler.

OMAN—AN OUTLINE HISTORY

FIRST references to Oman, then called Magaa, were in Sumerian times—in 3000 BC—and it is described as an important and wealthy place in the tablets found at Ur in Southern Iraq. It was also one of the first lands to fully embrace the Islamic religion and abandon paganism in Arabia.

Historically, as now, the majority of the Omani tribes lived in the Al Hajar mountains and on the fertile Batinah Plain, and many of the major tribes are still nomadic. There was sporadic inter-tribal strife over the centuries until the 1950s when Sultan Said bin Taimur finally quelled the fighting and the feuds. All tribes historically supported one of two political/ religious factions, the Hinawi or the Ghafiri. This division can be traced back to the original settlement first by many waves of immigrants from south-west Arabia—the Yemini or Hinawi (sometimes called Azdites or Kahtanites) who,. following the destruction of the famous dam and city of Mareb in about AD 130, moved east through Dhofar and north up to Oman. Secondly by the Adnani (also referred to as Ghafiri or Nizzar), a race also originating in Mareb, who finally settled in Oman after wandering through Saudi Arabia.

When Islam was accepted by Oman after the Prophet's death the Hinawi factions followed the Ibadhi (or Kharejites) in a puritanical way of life under a leader, or Imam, who was elected by the tribes as their political and religious director. The Sunni religion, a more relaxed form of Islam—though more akin to the original, was adopted by the Ghafiri tribes.

Because the Ibahdis were secessionists from the main body of

249

Islam, the early Kaliphs tried without lasting success to reduce Oman.

Vicious wars between the two religious factions lasted for two centuries culminating in the battle of Ziki in AD 891. After this the fighting continued on ethnic rather than religious grounds with both sides allying themselves from time to time with successive waves of invaders from various neighbouring empires and with the chief Ameers (Kaliphs) of Islam who still attempted to reclaim the secessionist Omanis. One such was Ameer Mohamed bin Noor who joined the Ghafiri in suppressing the Hinawi at the Battle of Semed in AD 893, and subsequently dealt with the remnants of the Hinawi by executing hundreds and cutting off the hands, feet and ears of many others.

Subsequent invasions of Oman were by the Carmathians from Bahrein, the Turks, the Persians and the Seljuks.

In 1330 Oman was visited by the famous Oriental traveller Ibn Batuta who found the country peaceful under the reign of a Sultan from the town of Nizwa.

In 1507 the Omani coastal villages were plundered by the Conquistadors of Alfonso d'Albuquerque, and throughout the sixteenth and seventeenth centuries the Portuguese harassed the Omani coast until, in 1646, the ruling Imam made a Trading Treaty with the British who subsequently helped the Imam throw out the Portuguese. This assisted in clearing Arabian and Indian trading routes for the British East India Company though from 1686 onwards Arab and European pirate ships marauded the Persian Gulf. By 1720 they were mostly eliminated, largely by the English Navy.

From 1624 the powerful Yareeba dynasty of Omanis ruled all Oman as Imams. In 1723 a civil war to decide succession to the Imamate took place between the Hinawi and Ghafiri which widened the differences more than ever between the two rival groups, and in 1749 the Albu Saeedi dynasty succeeded the Yareebas. Their line still rules in Oman.

The Imamate were at war throughout the late seventeenth century with the piratical Joasmee tribe from Northern Oman. The Omani slaving Empire centred on Zanzibar reached its heyday during the rule of the early Albu Saeedis. It was also they who moved their capital to Muscat from the Interior of Oman. Until 1856 the ruler in Muscat was called Imam. That year however Muscat separated from its Zanzibar Empire, the ruler of each being recognised as Sultan. Since then various tribal leaders in the Interior of Oman gave themselves the title of Imam.

In the 1920s the Imam of the Interior stirred up discontent against the 'coastal' Sultans amongst both the Hinawi and Ghafiri factions. The main irritant was the decree of the Sultan, under British pressure, abolishing slavery in Oman. After a period of strife the Sultan agreed to a certain amount of independence for the Interior at the Treaty of Seeb. This led to a peaceful period until 1954 when the Tameemas, the election council of both factions decided to elect a puppet Imam (Ghalib) and to declare an independent Interior State, separate from the Sultanate. Their immediate aim was to control the Fahud area where American oil men were already at work. The Tameema's aspirations, under Talib the brother of Ghalib, led to civil war between the Interior tribes with Egyptian aid and the Sultan with his Army and British aid. The war lasted from 1957 till 1959, after which date there were no more Imams in Oman.

British Participation

British political relations with the Sultanate began in 1798 when Britain was at war with France and feared that the French might use Muscat as a naval base for attacks on British and Indian shipping, or even as a staging point for an invasion of India. Treaties of Friendship were concluded with the reigning Sultan in 1798 and 1800. As a result of these treaties and the desire of successive Sultans to co-operate with Britain there have been many instances of mutual assistance ever since.

Until the First World War Britain was mainly interested in the security of her trade routes and in the elimination of piracy. Naval support was often given and military expeditions sent to the Sultanate. Since the First World War British interests have been the maintenance of the Sultan's Government against foreign influence and foreign inspired rebels, and also the security of air bases and oil investments in Oman.

Since 1958 the British Government has provided financial and material assistance to train and expand the Sultan's Armed Forces with seconded Army and Air Force officers. Financial aid ceased in 1967 when the oil revenues reached £30 million a year. (By 1975 they were over £300 million.)

Index